Advance Praise

"An impressive collection on an important topic. Crossing design and planning, this engaging volume brings together a number of different approaches to service-learning—theoretically, by field, and in the scale of the activities in space and time. This makes it useful and important reading for both those starting off in the field of community-based education and old hands interested in critically reflecting on their past practice."

—Ann Forsyth, Professor of City and Regional Planning,
Cornell University

"This collection has its roots in the ideas of education theorists such as Dewey, Bruner, and Freire, all of whom advocate for the importance of experiential learning. The authors individually and collectively advance the idea of service-learning to community participation and social action. Consequently, this book not only challenges conventional thinking about education and practice but also illustrates a variety of successful off-the-shelf approaches. Design and planning educators and practitioners will find it to be a valuable companion in support of identifying directions for the future."

—Henry Sanoff, Professor Emeritus of Architecture, ACSA/Alumni
Distinguished Professor, North Carolina State University

"An invaluable new resource for faculty engaged in interdisciplinary action research aimed at building more vibrant, sustainable, and just neighborhoods, communities, and regions through inspired physical design."

—Kenneth M. Reardon, Professor and Director of the Graduate
Program in City and Regional Planning, University of Memphis

"The time is ripe for advancing a solid service-learning pedagogy in architecture, landscape architecture, and planning. Over several decades of innovation, experimentation, and trial and error, each of these design disciplines has spawned new and critical theory, linking professional work and social change. The wisdom of the twenty-nine leaders in service-learning within this volume provides a collective leap forward that benefits us all—students, teachers, designers, and the general public."

—Bryan Bell, Founder, Design Corps; author, *Expanding Architecture: Design as Activism* and *Good Deeds Good Design: Community Service through Architecture*

D1392776

# Service-Learning

## in Design and Planning

# Service-Learning

## in Design and Planning

Education at the Boundaries

EDITORS

*Tom Angotti, Cheryl Doble,*

*and Paula Horrigan*

NEW VILLAGE PRESS • OAKLAND, CA

Published in the United States by
New Village Press
P.O. Box 3049
Oakland, CA 94609
(510) 420-1361
bookorders@newvillagepress.net
www.newvillagepress.net

New Village Press is a public-benefit, not-for-profit publishing venture of Architects/Designers/Planners for Social Responsibility.

In support of the Greenpress Initiative, New Village Press is committed to the preservation of endangered forests globally and advancing best practices within the book and paper industries. The printing paper used in the text of this book is 100% post-consumer recycled, Process Chlorine Free (PCF), and has been certified with both the Forest Stewardship Council (FSC) and the Sustainable Forestry Initiative (SFI). Printed by Malloy Incorporated of Ann Arbor.

ISBN-13 978-1-61332-001-3
Publication Date: December 2011

Library of Congress Cataloging-in-Publication Data

Service-learning in design and planning : educating at the boundaries / editors, Tom Angotti, Cheryl S. Doble, and Paula Horrigan.
    p. cm.
Summary: "Urban planning and architecture educators challenge traditional community-university relationships by modeling meaningful and reciprocal partnerships."—Provided by publisher.
    Includes bibliographical references and index.
    ISBN 978-1-61332-001-3 (pbk.)
    1. Service learning—Case studies. I. Angotti, Thomas, 1941– II. Doble, Cheryl S. III. Horrigan, Paula.
    LC220.5.S4584 2011
    361.3'7—dc                              232011041987

Cover image by Paula Horrigan
Cover design by Lynne Elizabeth
Interior design and composition by Leigh McLellan Design

# Contents

# Preface and Acknowledgments

**I**n 2007 the Pennsylvania and New York Campus Compact Consortium (PACC/NYCC) embarked on a project entitled, "Building on Our Strengths: Transforming Institutions through Service-Learning in the Academic Disciplines." With a Learn and Serve Grant through the Corporation for National and Community Service, the Consortium set out to fund and support, over a three-year subgrant period, sixteen selected programs and projects at institutions of higher education in New York and Pennsylvania. Their question: "How can we build and sustain networks to establish and expand service-learning, and what is the impact of such an effort on the greater community?" Their strategy: activate and enable cross-institutional interactions by creating networks and, in so doing, deepen service-learning within each institution and among network and community partners (Gray, Heffernan, Norton 2010, 1).

One of the cross-institutional networks the Consortium set in motion is the Erasing Boundaries Project. "Erasing Boundaries—Supporting Communities: Interdisciplinary Service-Learning in Architecture, Landscape Architecture and Urban Planning" was envisioned by its four founders—Professors Ethan Cohen, Architecture (City College of New York); Tom Angotti, Planning (Hunter College); Cheryl Doble, Landscape Architecture (State University of New York College of Environmental Science and Forestry); and Paula Horrigan, Landscape Architecture (Cornell University)—as a vehicle for increasing participation by their fields in service-learning activities. They saw it as an conduit for enhancing the quality of their work with communities, achieving better integration of service-learning in design and planning curriculums, and fostering new collaborations with their sister disciplines, institutions, and community partners.

Over three years, the Erasing Boundaries Project's collaborators worked to create an identity, frame the purpose, design and craft projects and actions, communicate the message, and cultivate an ever-increasing network. Now more than four years later, and well beyond the initial grant period, the Erasing Boundaries Project continues developing, and we are grateful to the many individuals and institutions that helped move it forward. As one of a larger group of PACC/NYCC Learn and Serve Consortium Projects, Erasing Boundaries benefitted from the wisdom and guidance of the grant's coprincipal investigators Char Gray, executive director of PACC, and Jim Heffernan, executive director of NYCC, and their project manager, Kate Dantsin. While they were working with fifteen other sub-grantees, this dynamic trio was always available to assist the Erasing Boundaries Project in negotiating federal grant requirements across several universities and connecting the project to valuable resources and networking opportunities.

Thanks go to the Erasing Boundaries partnering institutions and their faculty who have provided both in-kind and financial support since the project's inception. These include City College of New York (CCNY), Hunter College, Cornell University, State University of New York College of Environmental Science and Forestry (SUNY ESF), and Pennsylvania State University. Special thanks are particularly due to Professor Ethan Cohen for helping to oversee the project's critical first year from his base at City College of New York. In years two and three, when the project's administrative home moved to SUNY ESF, Professor Cheryl Doble facilitated its forward momentum. Richard Hawks, chair of the SUNY ESF Department of Landscape Architecture, deserves special thanks for providing the additional resources enabling Doble to undertake two years of federal grant oversight, recording, and documentation. Pennsylvania State University Professors Mallika Bose and Peter Aeschbacher, along with Hunter College Professor Sigmund Shipp, all deserve special thanks for joining the Erasing Boundaries Project leadership in late 2008 and providing the collegial energy and intelligence enabling it to stay the course.

## The Erasing Boundaries Symposium

As an initial step aimed at catalyzing greater dialogue and network building, Paula Horrigan, Cheryl Doble, Tom Angotti, and Achva Stein (stepping in after Cohen's departure from CCNY) organized the first Erasing Boundaries Symposium held in April 2008 at City College of New York. The symposium asked participants to respond to the central question: How can we overcome boundaries created by our own pedagogical strategies, professional education, disciplinary autonomy, and academic curricula in service to community and to academic service-learning? The twenty-four papers presented at the symposium provided ways to frame and extend our thinking, particularly as it is related to boundaries—how they are understood, created, defined, and addressed. The papers challenged our assumptions and pointed us in the direction of compelling new questions and approaches to service-learning in architecture, landscape architecture, and planning. Together, presenters and attendees, sixty people in all, generated a focused and energized learning community over their two days of interactions. Interactive workshops and dialogue sessions helped to steer future activities of the Erasing Boundaries Project while affirming the need and desire to more widely debate, strengthen, and share the important work being done by educators, students, and community partners in the fields of design and planning. We believe that the breadth and vigor of the symposium's dialogue resonates in this collection of fifteen papers that were revised and selected for publication in this volume.

We hope this book will help spread enthusiasm for service-learning among educators in the fields of design and planning. The authors include committed and seasoned faculty members who present some of the leading examples of practice in the nation. They provide us with diverse methods for teaching in partnership with communities and alert us to the problems and issues that invariably emerge, without falling back on simplistic solutions. We hope that this book will inspire greater dialogue across the multiple real and imagined boundaries that we encounter in our work.

Many people and institutions contributed to the success of the symposium and the realization of this book. We would like to express our gratitude to the symposium presenters and to all participants whose contributions and participation helped to set a working agenda for the Erasing Boundaries Project. We are especially grateful to them for sharing their work. Many thanks to the symposium sponsors, the Rockefeller Brothers Fund and the PACC/NYCC Consortium, with funding from Learn and Serve America and the home departments and institutions of the symposium organizers: the School of Architecture, Landscape Architecture, and Urban Design at the City College of New York; the Departments of Landscape Architecture at SUNY ESF and Cornell University; and the Department of Urban Affairs and Planning at Hunter College. Special thanks to the City College Architectural Center and its director, Achva Stein, for providing space and staff support for the two-day symposium event. Additional thanks for assisting with symposium organization goes to SUNY ESF's Assistant Director of the Center for Community Design Research (CCDR) Maren King, and graduate students Alice Brumback and Au Tau. Finally, many thanks to Scott Sears for facilitating the important symposium dialogue that set forth an agenda that continues to shape and inspire the Erasing Boundaries Project.

In preparing this publication, we are grateful to our many readers and reviewers, to Evangeline Ray, and to New Village Press, its editors and staff, for supporting this publication. We are also appreciative of the additional funding and support provided by the SUNY ESF Center for Community Design Research, the Hunter College Center for Community Planning and Development, and the Hurley Family Trust.

The Erasing Boundaries Project continues to work to support and strengthen service-learning in planning and design while encouraging greater visibility, documentation, discourse, and knowledge exchange. The second Erasing Boundaries Symposium, held in New York City in Spring 2011, is a testament to the ongoing relevance and success of the project. Since we first launched the discussion about erasing boundaries we have come to refocus our efforts on the even more complicated and contradictory task of teaching and working at the multiple boundaries outlined in this book. All readers are welcome to join us at erasingboundaries.psu.edu.

# At the Boundaries

*The Shifting Sites of Service-Learning
in Design and Planning*

Tom Angotti, Cheryl Doble, and Paula Horrigan

**s it always** a good thing for students to get involved with communities? Programs that teach architecture, landscape architecture, and urban planning usually engage their students with communities to help prepare them for professional practice. They do this through studios, workshops, charrettes, independent study, internships, and other classes that employ practice outside the classroom. The movement from learning *about* communities to learning *in* communities has been a positive one. It has helped to strengthen the links between service and learning, theory and practice, learning and doing, university and community. But is it necessarily a good thing?

If community-based education mutes the voices of local residents and makes it more difficult for them to gain control over their futures, then maybe it isn't as good as it sounds. If bringing students and professors into neighborhoods reinforces the power and status of the professionals and disempowers residents, might we have more exploitation than education? And if the university leaves no lasting benefits for the community, it may only exacerbate historic town-gown conflicts.

Community-based education can fail to confront the deeply imbedded boundaries separating university and community, professionals and clients, rich and poor, white and non-white, citizens and new immigrants, men and women, and so on through the long list of social and physical divides. If the professionals of the future are learning how to manipulate people and extract short-term gain at the expense of others, are they then reinforcing the widespread perception among communities that the "Ivory Tower" is by definition distant and irrelevant to their needs? Do they not convince people that universities are irrelevant to the pursuit of a better quality of life in the places where their neighbors live and work?

When learning takes place in low-income communities and communities of color these conflicts with future professionals often deepen. Long-standing notions of class and race, intertwined with cultural myths, prejudices, and orthodoxies, can emerge in ways that create more frustration, mistrust, and failures to bridge the multiple divides. Faculty and students may remain distant from and objectify "the other," reinforcing stereotypes and historic boundaries, both material and psychological.

Despite these potential pitfalls, we believe that professionals in the design professions and urban planning can learn with communities in ways that are mutually beneficial, creative, and progressive. They can understand, address, and negotiate the divisions of race and class in ways that enlighten and empower. Many committed educators, including authors in this volume, have begun to develop a pedagogy of progressive design and planning education that is empowering and not exploitative. They have helped students to learn by doing but they have also learned how to fashion new, more equitable and transformative approaches to education through their own practice. They do this, first of all, by moving away from the narrow notion of providing service to communities to the more liberating process that links service and learning—in shorthand, service-learning.

*Service-learning* is a recognized teaching and learning strategy that integrates meaningful community service with instruction and reflection. It can enrich the learning experience, teach civic responsibility, and strengthen communities (www.learnandserve.gov/). It is different, however, from other education-related service activities because it includes the practice of *reflection* and calls for *reciprocity* between academic and community partners. These basic principles of service-learning are essential ingredients of a liberating approach to community-based education. They are discussed below and echoed in the rich narratives included in this volume.

*Service-learning* shifts the site of learning from the classroom or studio to the community but it involves much more than a change in venue. We will argue here that situating academic activities in the community requires the development of committed academic-community partnerships, open communication, shared goals, reciprocity, and continuing reflection. Service-learning can integrate a community's need to address a problem with the academic need to provide critical learning experiences. However, it must also create a new relationship between academic and community partners in which the contributions of *both* partners are understood and valued. When partnerships involve thoughtful negotiation, planning, and communication, they build mutual respect, generate learning by both academic and community partners (i.e., *co-learning*), and bring about dialogue and collaborative problem solving that leads to valuable outcomes for both academic and community partners.

## Transformative Education and Reflection

A key concept in this emerging trend towards service-learning is *transformation*. Education that seeks to transform all who participate is the most difficult but also the most rewarding. Transformative education will change the educational professional, the student, and the community participants and contribute to the transformation of the built environment, institutions, policies, and social practices that shape the communities where we live and work. Community service too often falls short when it neither seeks nor achieves such personal, social, or political transformation.

In this volume we bring to this transformative approach the central concept of meeting *at the boundaries*. The critical question for us is how to deal with the boundaries that separate community and university as well as the boundaries of class, race, gender, age, and all the others. While we may come up with different answers to these questions in different circumstances, it is fundamentally important that the question is constantly asked. This is why *reflection* has become a central element of the transformative approach to community-based education that we advocate here. When all participants, including faculty, students, and community members, deliberately incorporate reflection about what they are doing, they also help transform the way they relate to each other in future encounters at the boundaries.

In the practicing professions emphasis must be placed on "getting things done." This too often leaves little time for reflection about what has occurred and what has been learned. Without reflection we are unlikely to learn from our experiences and integrate this knowledge into future practice. The need for reflection emerges out of the learning experiences that confront all participants with profound social and political contradictions and that challenge fundamental beliefs and assumptions. We need to establish better mechanisms to systematically evaluate projects and learning experiences so that we are not always condemned to reinvent the proverbial wheel.

To meet at the boundaries we first must consciously *acknowledge* them. There are too many rosy narratives of community-university partnerships that blur boundaries and try to build bridges without even acknowledging the depth of the chasms yet to be bridged. As our starting point we need to uncover, articulate, and examine in detail the dimensions of the real and imagined boundaries that separate us, with honesty and realism. If we get this right, we will have a better chance of dealing with the boundaries—whether we attempt to ease, transgress, shift, or transform them. We will also avoid false promises about overcoming those boundaries that have deep, systemic roots and that will not disappear just because a university class wills it so.

Service-learning offers many opportunities for beginning designers and planners to become consciously aware professionals able to reflect on their practice and values. Interaction with "the other" challenges students to gain increased awareness of the diversity, conflicts, and similarities related to cultural values, social relations, world views, and the distribution of economic and political power. However, moving a student into the sphere of "the other" requires preparation, guidance, mentorship, and some careful choreography. There needs to be a conscious balance and coordination between classroom learning and the service experience. Many instructors are not familiar with and do not seek out the literature and research that might help them gain insights on issues of race, social justice, equity, democracy, ethics, and values. This challenging terrain stretches the boundaries of knowledge traditionally established in the design professions. It requires new teaching and learning approaches, and also suggests new approaches for the disciplines and institutions that we share.

The authors in this collection outline for us the boundaries we confront and suggest how to deal with them. They explore the structural constraints of the academy, the importance of pedagogical grounding, and the value of committed working partnerships. By examining the body of experience across the design and planning disciplines, they provide models on which to build. Collectively, they launch us on a much-needed conversation about the problems and prospects of service-learning.

This conversation is important because faculty that engage with communities are already raising the critical questions. They want to know whether their work influences learning, academic institutions, and long-term partnerships with communities and, if so, how. They are asking what theories and methodologies will help them understand whether they truly benefit the communities they work with as well as advance the knowledge and sensitivity of participants. They are concerned with which standards and measures of evaluation can be used to assess the effectiveness of community collaborations.

Service-learning presents challenges to traditional teaching methods within each discipline, which are still, in many instances, grounded in a culture of artistic autonomy, competition, and hegemony of the professional as "expert." Many of the traditional measures of student achievement are rooted in this paradigm; therefore, new criteria are needed to evaluate both student performance and the efficacy of instructors.

Service is a well-established activity in academia: students see it as a way of gaining practical experience and an entrée to the professional world; faculty see it as a way of helping to ground their instruction; administrators see it as a way to share institutional resources with their neighboring communities. However, service alone too often feeds into paternalistic models of charitable giving instead of transformational approaches geared towards social change. Many community leaders in underserved communities seek committed partnerships to help them address issues of environmental quality, social justice, and community development. However, as communities become more diverse and their issues more complex, good intentions are not enough. Intensive dialogues between academics, practitioners, and community residents are increasingly important. Service-learning helps students and faculty go beyond service delivery and towards a better understanding of the changing social, cultural, and economic dimensions of our communities. It helps us to develop the more sophisticated professional skills needed to address complex issues. By redirecting academic research and interests toward engaged public scholarship, design, and planning programs, we can begin to address our most pressing community issues while preparing graduates for transformative professional careers as citizen-designers and -planners.

## Towards Community Engagement in Architecture, Landscape Architecture, and Planning

Service-learning pedagogy at its best integrates teaching, learning, service, scholarship, and research. For architecture, landscape architecture, and planning, it is a pedagogy that addresses many of the core principles of our disciplines. Over several decades of innovation, experimentation, and trial and error each of our disciplines has spawned new and critical theory linking professional work and social change. Together, we have laid the foundation for a pedagogy for the built environment that clearly unites service and learning. The time is ripe for advancing a solid service-learning pedagogy in our disciplines. We must recognize and build on the collective experiences and the lessons from our histories, and legitimate them in the eyes of the academic institutions and professions of architecture, landscape architecture, and planning. Recent responses to the natural disasters in New Orleans and Haiti are instructive: many schools improvised programs to send students and faculty to communities in urgent need of assistance while design educators and professionals scurried to offer needed solutions. For designers and planners, the call to service runs deep and moments like this remind us of the important contributions we can make in addressing major social and environmental problems. Yet, are we fully prepared to responsibly and effectively meet these challenges, and are we being as attentive as we should to the teaching, learning, and research strategies that guide us? Service-learning and engaged scholarship are approaches that can help direct the way.

The practice of learning through service has deep roots in North America's educational history. The founding of land-grant universities and agricultural extension programs in the 1860s forged a direct link between university-based scientific research and developing agricultural communities. Extension's youth branch, the 4-H clubs, adopted the slogan "learn by doing." Twentieth-century thinkers John Dewey and Henry James hearkened the call for progressive education theories and practices in the United States. John Dewey's central philosophical principle of linking learning and doing joined Henry James' pragmatism in calling for a radical move away from Europe's more traditional, theoretically rooted educational approaches and established orthodoxies.

The writings of both Dewey and James laid the groundwork for the experiential studio teaching and learning pedagogy that remains central to architecture, landscape architecture, and planning education. And their impact went even further as the decade of the 1960s beckoned social activism and even deeper integration between learning and doing.

Inspired by the civil rights movement, designers and planners joined with social workers, lawyers, and other professionals to help low-income communities protect their neighborhoods from urban renewal programs. On urban campuses, students and communities pressured their academic institutions to be more responsive to the communities hosting them. In 1968, when Harlem residents forced Columbia University to cancel plans to build a gymnasium in a nearby park, students from the School of Architecture were at their side. African American architects joined to form the Architects Renewal Committee in Harlem (ARCH). In Bedford-Stuyvesant, Brooklyn, Pratt Institute's students and faculty joined community efforts proposing alternatives to plans that displaced residents in the African American neighborhood. This led to the formation of the Center for Community and Environmental Development, one of the most enduring centers based in an architecture and planning school. Programs facing similar struggles around the nation responded by establishing community design centers to provide service to community and neighborhood groups. By the late 1960s, planning and design programs at several schools were at work supporting community-based planning even before nonprofit and other professional groups appeared on the scene. To fight the destructive urban renewal agenda, practicing professional groups like Planners for Equal Opportunity (PEO) and Urban Planning Aid joined in by providing pro bono planning and design services.

The urgency of the 1960s drew community design and planning advocates closer, transcending disciplinary boundaries to promote collaborations that addressed complex community problems. There was little room for academic hairsplitting when the professionals and students shared a common purpose and had to produce results for communities in need.

As Peace Corps, VISTA, and college work-study programs emerged, the term "service-learning" was used for the first time in the description of a project funded by the Tennessee Valley Authority linking Tennessee college students with local tributary development organizations (Titlebaum et al. 2004). By 1969 the Southern Regional Education Board was providing the first definition of service-learning pedagogy as "the integration of the accomplishment of the tasks that meet human needs with conscious educational growth" (Stanton et al. 1999, 2).

A growing number of design and planning programs began to incorporate service into their curricula.[1] By the early 1970s, eighty documented community design centers were providing assistance to underserved community and neighborhood groups (Pearson 2002). However, this trend would not last into the 1980s. Many of the pioneering centers ceased operations, key leaders of advocacy initiatives lost their university positions, and interdisciplinary study programs saw funding and support disappear.

While the federal government was making a hasty retreat from cities, communities began organizing local institutions to fill the gap, including nonprofit associations and community development corporations. Governments willingly passed their responsibilities onto these small groups, but provided little in the way of sufficient resources to fill their growing needs. In search of assistance, these new neighborhood institutions increasingly turned to nongovernmental organizations, foundations, and universities. Academic programs found themselves challenged by the volume of requests. Some faculty integrated service into their studio courses, a move that was popular with students but also often failed to meet community needs.

The early wave of interdisciplinary collaboration diminished as more universities attempted to co-opt the insurgent spirit of community-based efforts. Interdisciplinary study programs lost funding and support. Universities continued to organize knowledge into departmental silos and often erected new barriers to interdisciplinary exchange. Semester-long courses rarely meshed with community timetables. Above all, community problems and projects related to the complex issues of race, poverty, social justice, local politics, and national policy proved to be an increasing and often overwhelming challenge. Even faculty with a deeper understanding of these issues felt they had not been prepared to deal with them in their professional training. In addition, universities often failed to recognize engaged, community-based scholarship when evaluating faculty for promotion and tenure.

While these institutional boundaries remain entrenched, often the deepest and most intractable obstacles to transformative service-learning reside within design and planning educators themselves. Limits include an obsession with "getting things done," inattention to social justice and personal conflict, and the constant drift within our professions towards more technocratic and paternalistic relations with people and communities. We need to meet at the boundaries and remind ourselves of the more liberating theories and practices from our own history.

## Towards a Pedagogy of Community Engagement in the Design Professions

Many committed academic leaders in the United States continue to broaden the concept of service and heighten its importance for teaching and research. In 1985 the presidents of Brown, Georgetown, and Stanford Universities created *Campus Compact,* an organization that continues to support colleges and universities working to engage their students and communities in partnerships of education and service. In 1990 Congress passed the National and Community Service Act, providing funding to schools for social programs involving local citizens. In 1993 Learn and Serve America was created to coordinate a number of education-based service programs under one umbrella organization; it is one of the largest funders of service-learning activities and research.

The work of Ernest Boyer stands out because of the widespread influence it has had on educational policy, especially in the design professions. In 1979 Boyer, former chancellor of the State University of New York, became the president of the Carnegie Foundation for the Advancement of Teaching, an independent research and policy center, with a mission to support needed transformations in American education. In this position, Boyer authored several reports that laid the foundation for a broader understanding of scholarship and sought a new relationship between teaching, research, and service. In his 1990 report, *Scholarship Reconsidered: Priorities of the Professoriate,* Boyer criticized the narrow focus of higher education and proposed a new paradigm in which faculty would assume four interrelated scholarly functions: the scholarship of discovery, integration, teaching, and application. Boyer's redefinition of scholarship gave it a broader and more encompassing meaning that lends legitimacy to the full range of academic activities. In a 1996 article, Boyer described "the scholarship of engagement" as a collaborative partnership that "creates a social climate in which academic and social cultures communicate more continuously and more creatively," and he encouraged academic institutions to become more vigorous partners in this collaboration (Boyer 1996, 21).

In the mid-1990s Boyer joined with Lee Mitang to conduct an independent study of architectural education and practice. Their 1996 report, *Building Community: A New Future for Architecture Education and Practice,* builds on Boyer's earlier work pointing to the societal need for architectural assistance and the lack of response coming from both architecture's educational and professional arenas. Boyer and Mitang challenged architecture to become more engaged in consequential social problems. They concluded that to meet the challenge, professional architectural education must begin by "restructuring the process by which students and faculty are engaged." Further still, they must strive to develop an "enriched mission" of community service that "connects the schools and the profession to changing social contexts" (Boyer and Mitang 1996, 26–28).

Boyer and Mitang's challenge reverberates through all the disciplines concerned with creating better environments for community life. Within the disciplines of architecture, landscape architecture, and urban planning, many professionals and academics have contributed to the emerging pedagogy of community engagement by fostering more powerful relationships between service and learning, community and academy, design and social change. Professional organizations like Architects/Designers/Planners for Social Responsibility (ADPSR) and the Association for Community Design (ACD) support interdisciplinary community design professionals through publications, conferences, and networking (www.communitydesign.org/). Since 1975 Planners Network has brought together professionals, academics, students, and activists through conferences, a newsletter, listserve, and the quarterly *Progressive Planning Magazine* (www.plannersnetwork.org/).

Many new concepts that link service and learning have emerged within our disciplines. *Advocacy planning* grew out of work by professionals and academics during the civil rights era to engage with communities displaced by urban renewal programs. City planner Paul Davidoff saw advocacy planning as a challenge to the official notion that planning represented an overarching "public interest" instead of a plurality of interests. He encouraged planners to be proactive in assuring that those without voices in the decision-making process be heard. He spoke to all the design professions when he criticized *physical determinism* and the misguided assumption that changes in the built environment can, by themselves, bring about social change (Davidoff 1965).

Many others in planning challenged boundaries while developing new concepts. Norman Krumholz, planning director under Cleveland's Carl Stokes, the first African American mayor of a major US city, used the term *equity planning* (Krumholz and Forester 1990). *Communicative planning theory* emerges with Donald Schön's *The Reflective Practitioner* (1983) and John Forester's *Planning in the Face of Power* (1989). Following an alternative path identified with the work of Paulo Freire, Marie Kennedy (2007) proposes *transformative community planning,* while Ann Forsyth (1996), Leonie Sandercock (1998), and many others highlight the powerful contributions of women and feminism to community development and planning. These and other streams including indigenous planning and socialist planning contribute to the contemporary trend known as progressive planning (Angotti 2008, 8-31).

In architecture, many have forged the link between service and learning. Among the early practitioners of community-based architecture, the work of Henry Sanoff, Christopher Alexander, and Ron Shiffman has influenced architects, landscape architects, and planners. Sanoff's methods for community input and review, Alexander's built projects in low-income communities and the architectural theories they spawned, and Shiffman's long-time leadership at the Pratt Institute Center for Community and Environmental Development are widely recognized. Activist architect and educator Roberta Feldman committed herself to democratic design practice and a research agenda focused on high-quality, affordable public housing and the standards needed to guide its creation. Balancing practice, teaching, and research, Michael Pyatok encourages community participation in the revitalization of low-income communities and works with nonprofits to develop decent affordable housing in the face of shrinking public investment. Auburn University architect Samuel Mockbee's Rural Studio Program introduces architecture students to the social responsibilities of practice.

Landscape architecture may owe its service legacy to one of its earliest nineteenth-century practitioners. Frederick Law Olmsted's service mission—to create outdoor environments addressing direct social and psychological needs—lingers deep in the mindset of landscape architectural educators and practitioners (Beveridge 1986). In 1959 more than a hundred years after

Olmsted came on the scene, Karl Linn left private practice and joined the faculty at the University of Pennsylvania to devote his teaching and practice to service. Here he founded a design-and-build program linking students and faculty to low-income households lacking access to affordable design services. Linn believed that "professional designers could democratize the process of architecture and landscape architecture by introducing participatory design processes" (Linn 2007, 10). Other landscape architects have championed similar approaches by teaching, practicing, and researching community-based design processes and approaches. Randy Hester's participatory community design processes and projects provided the concrete examples from which his concepts of *ecological democracy* emerge. His well-documented early projects provided important models for integrating public participation in the design process. Mark Francis's focus on *spatial democracy*, Lynda Schneekloth's theory and practice of *placemaking*, and Daniel Winterbottom and Stanton Jones's adoption of alternative design-build curricula all promote ways of making places that are meaningful to the people and the communities who use them.

With the emergence of the environmental movements and interest in global sustainability after the 1987 United Nations Conference on the Environment, many community-based initiatives began making connections between the built environment and issues of public health and social welfare. In low-income communities of color, environmental justice advocates found themselves fighting not just for a better environment for all but also to correct the dramatic imbalances in the distribution of environmental hazards and benefits among neighborhoods and cities. Architects, landscape architects, and planners increasingly concerned themselves with the broadest environmental issues and those with roots in communities of color engaged the issues of environmental justice (Sze 2006).

*Participatory action research* contributes another innovative strand to the discourse on service-learning and civic engagement. Turning away from rigid social science research that relies heavily on objectives and methodologies developed solely by academics, participatory action research recasts academic and community participants as coresearchers. Together they design the research, collect, and analyze information, and use it for the purpose of taking action. Many of the dialogic participatory theories and practices of community-based design and planning are found to be particularly relevant when integrated with a participatory action research approach. Often design projects include initial research, which both informs the design process and enables academic and community partners to advocate effectively for the implementation of their design recommendations. When students are involved, the collaboration is even broader and is often an example of service-learning (Stringer 1999; Stoecker and Tryon 2009).

Perhaps the most radical influence in current discussions of the pedagogy of engagement is the pioneering work of Brazilian Paulo Freire, whose *Pedagogy of the Oppressed* was first published in English in 1970. Freire, a prominent advocate of liberation theology, was critical of what he called the banking theory of education, in which the instructor "deposited" knowledge in the minds of passive students. Freire believed that people learned by engaging actively in social and political change, and the role of the educator was to engage in dialogues on an equal plane with those who are both learning and doing. In her *Teaching to Transgress* (1994), bell hooks further developed Freire's ideas and brought new insights related to North America, feminism, and multiculturalism.

## Moving Forward

The resurgence and growth of community design centers provides evidence that engaged pedagogy may be on the rise. While there remains only twelve of the eighty original centers documented in the early 1970s, a 1998 survey by the Association of Collegiate Schools of Architecture (ACSA) identifies another seventy community design centers providing assistance to communities. Of these, twenty-four are characterized as independent centers and forty-six are associated with academic architecture programs (Pearson 2002). This number increases when adding centers, not accounted for in the study, that are hosted by planning and landscape architecture programs. The majority of these academic centers were established in the early 1990s and are located in public institutions.

The evidence of service-learning and engaged scholarship is readily apparent in the programs, projects, and efforts of faculty and students currently at work in architecture, landscape architecture, and planning programs. Faculty, like the authors in this book, are pursuing a scholarly approach to community-based work that integrates their teaching, service, and research. While they build on the work of the designers and planners that came before them, they are also expanding their work to include pedagogical theory even as they continue to encounter the multiple boundaries to service and learning. However, today we are also witnessing many new examples of the deeply ingrained tendency to undertake service without addressing issues of race, class, and social justice. This requires a constant interrogation of our own practice through reflection and honest criticism.

We hope to help fill some of these many gaps with this volume. The chapters, described in greater detail below, include important stories about service-learning in our fields and reflections on practice. Our purpose is to help build knowledge towards future advances inside and outside the academy. We seek to address service and learning as transformative and deal with reflection and evaluation as essential elements. We would like to invite all readers to meet, and engage, at the boundaries as we all seek to develop a new transformative pedagogy.

## How the Book Is Organized

The book is organized to take the reader through four major challenges we face by embracing service-learning: seeing "the other," reflection and evaluation, crossing borders, and confronting academic boundaries. An introduction precedes each of the book's four parts and synthesizes key ideas and concepts drawn from the chapters that follow. Each introductory section also hints at specific prescriptions for change that can help to strengthen and bolster efforts to more effectively integrate service-learning into design and planning education. The four themes that tie together the chapters arose from the first Erasing Boundaries Symposium (April 2008) and its call for papers asking: "How can we overcome boundaries created by our own pedagogical strategies, professional education, disciplinary autonomy, and academic curricula in service to community and to academic service-learning?"

In Part One: Beginning to See "the Other," five chapters tackle the fundamental problem of encountering, acknowledging, and understanding the boundaries distinguishing self and other. They reverberate with stories of struggling to "see" and expose differences and boundaries that define and characterize relationships, perceptions, and values. In "Uncovering the Human Landscape in North Philadelphia," Sally Harrison tells the story of her studio's nonlinear route into the "open-ended territory of lived space and human relationships" and the dialogic process she adopts to uncover and discover problems, while ultimately finding imaginative ways to address them. In "Reconsidering the Margin: Relationships of Difference and Transformative Education," author Jodi Rios directs us to the meeting ground, the marginal space we share between academy and community, designer and community, self and "the other." Rios asserts that confronting boundary distinctions and differences leads to willing shifts toward greater dialogue, relationship, reconciliation, and transformation. Like Rios, author Jeffrey Hou recognizes that the work begins by acknowledging differences. In "Differences Matter: Learning to Design in Partnership with Others,"

Hou suggests that, while they often pose a challenging barrier, differences remain, more often than not, a meaningful device for transformative learning and discovery.

While differences surface and conspire to dramatically impact and effect the outcomes of service-learning courses and projects—for both academic and community partners alike—what can we do to ensure their contributions are being fully maximized? In "Educating for Multicultural Learning: Revelations from the East St. Louis Design Studio," authors Laura Lawson, Lisa B. Spanierman, V. Paul Poteat, and Amanda M. Beer share their findings related to multicultural learning by students at the University of Illinois. Finally, in "People and Place: Communication and Community Development," authors Keith Bartholomew and Mira Locher describe the techniques and strategies they use to guide students on a journey of relationship building to disclose differences and reduce the gap between future professionals and the communities with whom they collaborate.

In Part Two: Learning to Reflect and Evaluate, design and planning educators share ways they are integrating reflection and evaluation into their service-learning projects and courses. Reflection and evaluation must gain a stronger foothold if service-learning pedagogy is to succeed in providing opportunities for learning and knowledge generation that move beyond professional skills. For educators Susan C. Harris and Clara Irazábal, service-learning has a role to play in encouraging students to become better collaborators, doers, coeducators, and socially responsible professionals. In "Transforming Subjectivities: Service that Expands Learning in Urban Planning," the authors analyze their design for an urban planning service-learning course and methodology for evaluation. In "Operative Sites for Dialogue and Reflection: The Role of Praxis in Service-Learning," Michael Rios argues that it is only with increased reflexivity that professionals gain in their capacity to advocate for "the other." In an increasingly plural society, design education and practice stand to benefit from embracing what is considered service-learning's central pedagogical goal—self-reflection, or greater reflexivity through praxis.

Authors Peter Butler and Susan Erickson, in "Potential and Limits of the PLaCE Program's Design Extension Studio Model," offer a profile of the program's emphasis on using community values, processes, and priorities to guide outreach projects undertaken by design and planning studios. Based on their experience the authors suggest new directions to deepen their program's service and learning dimensions. Finally, author Lynne M. Dearborn draws our attention to the lack of studies examining service-learning's long-term impact on students of design and planning programs. In "Moving from

Service-Learning to Professional Practice: ESLARP's Impact on its Alumni," Dearborn assesses the impact of the East St. Louis Action Research Project's (ESLARP) service-learning experiences on its alumni and reveals findings that underscore the importance of linking service-learning program design, implementation, and evaluation.

In Part Three: Crossing Borders, we learn how boundaries extending across geographic and cultural distance challenge us to be attentive to the complex dynamics of integrating service, learning, and research goals in partnership with community-based problems and needs. Both chapters in this section illuminate approaches that were developed and adjusted over considerable time to achieve the highest level of reciprocity between community and academia. Since 1991 university students from the United States have been among a team of seasoned design educators and local community partners taking part in a place-based research collaboration in Monteverde, Costa Rica. In "Easing Boundaries through Placemaking: Sustainable Futures Study Abroad Program," Lynda Schneekloth and Scott Shannon describe participants' immersion in local worlds using service-learning pedagogy and place-based theories and practices. In Daniel Winterbottom's design/build capstone studio at the University of Washington, described in "Effecting Change through Humanitarian Design," students apply their design learning to a public service project either locally or abroad in Mexico, Guatemala, and, most recently, Bosnia. Building strong relationships and fostering community empowerment are core principles of such design/build studios that aim to confront and address complex social and ecological problems and community needs while exposing participants to alternative "compassionate design" practices aimed at addressing social injustices.

In Part Four: Confronting Academic Boundaries, authors point to the institutional and disciplinary boundaries that shape educational and professional relationships and practices. They ask us to rethink our academic frameworks and consider the catalytic role that service-learning can play in realigning and reintegrating our goals for education, practice, and research. Why is interdisciplinary collaboration in solving community problems so difficult in academia? Institutional and individual transformation will only come by casting off a restrictive "boundaries model" of design and planning education, argue Pat Crawford, Zenia Kotval, and Patricia Machemer in "From Boundaries to Synergies of Knowledge and Expertise: Using Pedagogy as a Driving Force for Change." In "Integrating Disciplines, Practices, and Perspectives in the Commonwealth Avenue Project," authors Paul Kelsch and Joseph Schilling encounter many of the institutional obstacles and disciplinary and pedagogical boundaries that make it difficult to fully achieve holistic, cross-disciplinary approaches to design and problem solving. In contrast, author Jack Sullivan, in "Forging Lasting Community Impacts and Linkages through the Capstone Community Design Studio," shares a capstone studio program at the University of Maryland that reflects his university's widespread institutional support for the scholarship of engagement and service-learning. A synergistic model is at work in the University of New South Wales' FBEOutThere! program, which activates connections between student learning, teaching, research, and community needs. In "Toward a Scholarship of Engagement: A Model from Australia," Linda Corkery and Ann Quinlan describe how this program operates as an institutionalized resource unit heightening the legitimacy of community engagement at both the academic and community level.

# PART ONE

# Beginning to See "the Other"

## Editor's Introduction

**The first challenge** in service-learning experiences is to see "the other." If designers and planners are to interact with "the other" in community settings, they must learn to perceive, engage, and confront issues of identity and difference, including their own. They must penetrate the boundaries between self and "the other" just as they confront the boundaries between academia and community.

The authors in this section show us how they design service-learning experiences that help to see and understand others. They consciously acknowledge differences between cultures, people, and social institutions. These differences may become barriers, but they can also be potent opportunities for knowledge discovery, relationship building, personal transformation, and real collaboration. Each author calls upon us to recognize boundaries and confront them, not as a threat but as a vital starting point.

These authors believe in putting themselves and their students in circumstances that are outside their usual comfort zones. They share the conviction that possibilities for greater transformation arise from working with differences and recognizing, negotiating, and responding to them. Resistance, whether based on personal, community, or cultural difference, can be a point of entry leading to enhanced understanding, relationship building, innovation, and the transgression of disciplinary boundaries.

*Sally Harrison* emphasizes a "problem-seeking and relationship-building approach." *Jodi Rios* aims to cultivate a state of radical openness in students and community partners. *Laura Lawson* and coauthors are concerned about increasing multicultural learning competency. *Jeffrey Hou* and *Keith Bartholomew* and *Mira Locher* attempt to integrate awareness of the causes of societal injustice with self-recognition of values and beliefs. To address these learning outcomes, these educators adapt, expand, and reinvent conventional curricular design, content, and methods. This deepens the impact of service-learning on all participants—students, community partners, and faculty.

How do we build relationships and raise consciousness related to "the other"? The authors put forth a variety of approaches that enable "hearing and seeing" our own and others' core needs, values, and concerns.

Relationships with others grow through what *Sally Harrison* calls "collaborative problem-seeking." Problem seeking is a shared experience and attitudinal "space" that co-locates all partners, including the designer, planner, community member, and academic. To this space all partners are drawn to collectively investigate, understand, and define the problem at hand. All partners make use of their respective knowledge—professional, local, and experiential—to reveal root causes, issues, and challenges. Harrison's story of her studio's nonlinear route into the "open-ended territory of lived space and human relationships" reveals how students, faculty, and community partners create a dialogic process for digging deeper into the human landscape of a neighborhood to collectively uncover problems and find paths for change. Harrison beckons her students to step outside their boundaries and "see the neighborhood" by using a problem-seeking and relationship-building approach where designer and "the other" occupy a shared ground.

*Jodi Rios* carefully moves her students from a classroom-directed immersion seminar to a community-embedded service-learning interaction. This aims to sensitize students and cultivate a foundation of awareness and knowledge. It is a prelude to slowly opening her students to community understanding and relationships, including dynamics of race and class. She uses walking tours, volunteering, and one-on-one personal meetings along with readings and discussions on broader cultural and urban history, current events, and issues of race and class. These experiences are the basis for written and visual reflections. Dialogues that include students, faculty, and community members encourage honesty, openness, and transparency about feelings, fears, and assumptions. From the immersion seminar Rios gradually moves her students to undertake jointly conceived community-based projects.

*Jeffrey Hou* shows how service-learning begins by acknowledging differences. He highlights the role of difference in creating a dynamic community-university partnership where cultural learning and creative design commingle. When predominantly white students from the University of Washington meet first- and second-generation Asian American youth from a Seattle neighborhood, the differences present a challenging barrier but also a meaningful device for transformative learning when cultural differences are voiced and cultural knowledge is discovered.

*Laura Lawson et al.* examine the degree of multicultural learning by predominantly white students at the University of Illinois working in the African American community of East St. Louis. The team of landscape architecture instructors and education psychology researchers learn that even though design competencies increase, learning related to race and racism remains limited. If there is to be multicultural learning, there will need to be changes in curriculum that foster greater consciousness of social injustices. Otherwise, students risk viewing themselves solely as outside professional experts and remain blind to racial and class inequalities.

A problem-seeking approach is advocated by authors *Keith Bartholomew* and *Mira Locher* who encourage their students to use qualitative methods of narrative storytelling. They listen to community concerns and build relationships before presuming to act or intervene as designers. Such reflective, problem-seeking approaches beckon participants to discover and represent one another and the environments in which they find themselves. Values maps and reflection mapping visibly portray and interpret these relationships.

## Prescriptions for Change: Seeing "the Other"

Acknowledging boundaries and difference is a critical first step in designing a service-learning interaction in design and planning. However, we also need better models and a more developed literature. Designers and planners have traditionally used practice- and problem-based learning to teach professional skills and knowledge. Service-learning, however, expands and transforms the pedagogy of the typical studio by incorporating social, political, and ethical issues into the learning objectives. Another essential element is reflection on the personal roles and relationships of students and teachers with their community and "the other." To address "the other" and reflect upon their experiences, design and planning educators need the skills to address complex issues of race, social equity, and environmental justice as well as the social and environmental problems encountered in practice.

Design and planning professionals need to work with other disciplines and communities outside academia, with people from varied social, economic, and cultural backgrounds. Furthermore, the lack of dialogue among the design and planning professions is a major obstacle to realizing the full potential of service-learning pedagogy, which necessarily transgresses boundaries separating disciplines and communities of knowledge. Architects, landscape architects, and planners must begin to acknowledge and wrestle with the boundaries that define and often limit their relationships with one another before they can fully realize the transformative potential of service-learning pedagogy.

## CHAPTER 1

# Uncovering the Human Landscape in North Philadelphia

*Sally Harrison[1]*

Every culture proliferates along its margins . . . Bubbling out of swamps and bogs, a thousand flashes at once scintillate and are extinguished all over the surface of a society. In the official imaginary, they are noted only as exceptions or marginal events . . . In reality, creation is a disseminated proliferation. It swarms and throbs. A polymorphous carnival infiltrates everywhere . . . —*Michel de Certeau*

## Introduction

**ooking north from** the ninth floor studio, my students and I gaze over a gridded landscape that extends for miles until it merges with the horizon. We see a fabric that is regular and monochromatic, dominated by brick row houses and punctuated by the sweep of rail lines, patches of bulky nineteenth century industrial structures and vacant land. In the near middle ground, just beyond the embankment for the trains that connect the university with the center city and suburbs, are two public housing towers. I ask the students to look just to the right of the towers and to the ground. There a spot of brilliant cerulean blue comes into focus.

Tiny in relation to the terrain within our scope of vision, this flash of color—the fragment of a mural—connects us to a specific place that will emerge as the locus of an on-going service-learning project undertaken by Temple University architecture students. The mural is the most visible landmark of the Village of Arts and Humanities, a unique art-based enclave in the Hartranft/Fairhill community only six blocks from the dense and busy urban campus of Temple University.

In spite of being under the gaze of the architecture building, North Philadelphia's neighborhoods have figured little in the mental maps of the students. Mostly the students sustain a generalized concept of the decaying urban context: an undifferentiated, troubling landscape, functioning on the margins of their studio-focused life. But the Village of Arts and Humanities and the community where it is situated has inspired our imagination. A self-built network of parks and gardens woven into the interstices of North Philadelphia's deteriorating residential fabric, the Village asserts that decay and loss open the possibility for beauty and innovation. This particular place and the polymorphous carnival of everyday life that infiltrates it have offered to the students a complex local narrative, and a threshold for learning about design in the contemporary city.

## Walking in the City, Seeing, and Connecting

From the architecture school, students now regularly tread a path north to the Village of Arts and Humanities. With this ritual they craft a continuous spatial bond that connects their experiences of the university and the neighborhood, expanding if not erasing boundaries. Up 12th Street they walk past the newish housing that abuts the campus, and as they approach the city recreation center they see the basketless hoops and cracked concrete pavement. They pass a stretch of row homes that stand in various states of disrepair across the street from an imposing stone railroad embankment. Through the underpass they emerge into the open space of Fotteral Square; the two high-rise housing towers we can see from the studio stand at its south. The students cut diagonally across the square.

Turning onto tiny Warnock Street between a prolific vegetable garden and the local bar, the Village of Arts and Humanities unfolds in the ellipses of the residential fabric. First, they see a field of colorful posts against a mural of angels. Facing it, there is a row of abandoned row houses painted white, waiting. Halfway up Warnock is a sign announcing another Community Garden, but it is densely overgrown with honeysuckle, and we can't see inside. Across from it is a well-tended flower garden bounded by a tiled mural. The students proceed up the street—a continuous wall of brick homes, some abandoned, some with people chatting at their stoops—and they pass between two abandoned houses into a tiny walled park, all hardscape with a floor like a mosque, that connects them mid-block to Alder Street. Like Warnock, Alder is small in scale, though better maintained and active; people walk down the middle of the street or move purposefully from building to building.

At its far end the monumental cerulean blue mural stands, the backdrop of a public park, shady and filled with mosaic sculpture. On a stage at the base of the mural, a group of teenagers are coached in a step-dancing routine. Beyond, the bustle of Germantown Avenue can be seen and felt—sunlight and motion, the music from a passing car, the metallic clatter of security gates opening, the acrid smell of blue exhaust from the Number 23 bus. Around the park side of the building, the students step out to the sidewalk; they have reached the official front door of the Village of Arts and Humanities, a nineteenth-century storefront at a bend on Germantown Avenue. The neighborhood commercial street with its variety stores, clothing shops, take-outs, and check-cashing establishments stretches north, faltering, uneven, but still gathering and focusing community life.

## The Village of Arts and Humanities and Shared Prosperity

The Temple students have joined the scores of neighborhood residents, artists, and activists who have participated in the building of the Village since it started as a single public art project over two decades ago. The Ile Ife Park was built over three summers by the artist Lily Yeh in several vacant lots with the help of neighborhood children, and framed by the monumental mural on the three-story blank party wall of 2544 Germantown Avenue. The Village evolved organically, reaching into and transforming the fragmented physical space of the neighborhood. Seventeen parks and gardens were constructed for public use, and six abandoned buildings on Alder Street and the building on Germantown Avenue were rehabilitated to house after-school arts programs and workshops. Committed to the belief that creative engagement in place can change lives, Yeh engaged neighborhood residents in the land transformation process. Two recovering drug addicts with natural artistic gifts became her chief support. Together, their presence in the neighborhood as productive, skilled craftsmen and mentors tacitly communicated that renewal can be found in even the most degraded conditions.

The Village of Arts and Humanities was thriving, but its near neighbors on the commercial corridor were not. Once essential to a cluster of North Philadelphia neighborhoods, the historic Germantown Avenue shopping corridor now struggled to survive in a world of big box enterprises. The small business owners along the avenue began to recognize the Village as a potentially powerful ally in a shared revitalization effort. No longer an idiosyncratic "marginal event," the Village, almost in spite of itself, had developed an institutional presence in the community. Its work had gained recognition well outside of its immediate sphere, winning national awards for its hands-on approach to rebuilding the physical and social structure of its inner-city neighborhood. Perhaps the place-centered rebuilding process and the unique identity of the Village could be extended to include Germantown Avenue and its neighborhood; perhaps at a larger scale the arts could become a catalyst for change.

The merchants approached Lily Yeh with the proposition of a partnership, and the Village agreed to take on the role of leader and convener of a community planning and design project called "Shared Prosperity." The Village secured major planning grants for the project from the Wachovia Regional Foundation, the Advocacy Institute, and the National Endowment for the Arts. The grants required a large study area: two hundred square blocks that flanked the Germantown Avenue shopping district were identified and the steering committee of multiple stakeholders assembled—residents, pastors, political representatives, community developers, activists, and business owners.

For the Village, Shared Prosperity demanded a thorough redefinition of its established mode of operation and thinking about context. The Village process was fundamentally tactical, concrete, and incremental. Like many of the community-based organizations and businesses it thought locally and acted locally (Hamdi 2004, *xviii*). Now as a leader of a planning and urban design project, the Village and its steering committee would have to contend with both local *and* global concepts of place. They would enter the unfamiliar realm of strategic thinking and projection. As Lily Yeh remarked, it was time to "call in the experts."[2]

## Outside In and Inside Out:
## Two Universities and Two Disciplines at Work

It was at this juncture that our collaboration began. Temple's undergraduate architecture studio, the "Urban Workshop," and the graduate planning studio at another local university were enlisted to provide design support for the project. The planning studio would address the systemic needs for housing, transportation, and social infrastructure of the study area. Ours would focus on the specific conditions of four key blocks of Germantown Avenue that included the Village as its terminus and formed the center of the shopping area.

Shared Prosperity began with a meeting of both of the studios, the Village of Arts and Humanities staff, and the community-based steering committee. In a state of mutual watchfulness, introductions were made and a generic set of community issues put forth, including needs for economic and housing development, supporting youth, combating crime and vandalism, and building neighborhood identity. From this set of problems, each studio was to embark on its semester work.

The planning studio worked from the outside in. For them the generic set of problems presented by the steering committee was a reasonable point of departure for developing a strategic plan for the neighborhood. Operating mostly from their studio across town, their sources were drawn from data in the public record and best practices from similar projects nationwide. Accepting the role of expert consulting team, the planning studio adhered to a professional service model. Work was organized around a formalized set of meetings and client presentations that would structure their participation in the project. Careful of the semester timetable, their progress was steady and focused on the tangible end product. The scale of their work permitted them a comfortable distance from the "swamp of problems" that suffuses direct spatial and human experience (Schön 1985, 17).

While the planning studio moved forward in a relatively linear fashion using methods that simulated a professional consulting role, the trajectory of the architecture studio was labyrinthine. Neither supported nor encumbered by a mantle of expertise, the studio undertook a process of engaged trial and error. Presumptions were challenged, and missteps and course corrections were made in an effort to find and problematize issues from which design might emerge. Our proximity to the neighborhood allowed us to erase certain boundaries: we were drawn into the open-ended territory of lived space and human relationships, a dynamic present that would be the primary source for design speculation.

## "The Craft of Experience": Learning from Missteps, Making Course Corrections

After the first steering committee meeting, the architecture students were still unclear as to what their mission might be, so they began with what they had learned from their site analysis course—mapping context patterns, documenting neighborhood space, researching case studies and neighborhood history. These first weeks yielded a predictable set of documents that were as valuable for their flaws in process and perception as for the information itself. Through a dialogic process with Lily Yeh and a local pastor who came to the studio to review our preliminary work, we were able to find from the two most problematic studies an open door to further inquiry and creative possibility.

One group of students presented a laboriously detailed timeline tracing the history of Germantown Avenue and its environs from its origin as a Lenape Indian trail to its establishment as a cartway connecting Quaker farms and small villages outside the colonial city to its development during the industrial expansion as a cobbled shopping street serving teeming immigrant neighborhoods. Its buildup over time was mirrored by the erosion of manufacturing, redlining for inner-city financing, crime, riots, white flight, and vandalism—to its current depopulated state. As gleaned from the Internet, newspapers, and books, the situation was grim and definitive: the neighborhood was without hope of renewal. But our guests challenged the students. Yes, as *information* this was all true, but they needed to examine *whose* history this timeline really represented, and to find other sources for defining the evolution of a place. What was/had been the lived culture, and how was it manifested? Were there creative improvisations within the official narrative of decline? What memories of the past were held there in its physical space and in the collective consciousness of the community? Who were the local heroes?

A similar response was evoked by a photomontage documenting the façade of the four blocks of Germantown Avenue within our scope. Photographed on a gray Sunday morning, the long image showed an aggregation of storefronts, shuttered at street level, vacant, and boarded up above. Only the signage suggested vitality. To the mortification of our visitors, the students who were accustomed to the unbounded commerce of the mall pronounced it a "ghost town." "Well," said the pastor, "everyone's at church —or they should be!" She suggested they return to the street on a weekday or a Saturday morning to see the place in action. However, she conceded that Sunday on the avenue hadn't always been this quiet, and reminisced about the times when restaurants there did open for social gathering after services, and there were Sunday afternoon shows at a now defunct movie theater. There had also been families living above the shops, providing built-in security in a layered neighborhood that had its own weekly and diurnal rhythms.

Though the montage was a shocking and not fully representative snapshot, it revealed a basic truth about the shopping corridor. Despite being physically intact, the corridor had flattened spatially and temporally: it had lost complex patterns of three-dimensional inhabitation and its overall environmental porosity was contracting, limiting depth of public access and transparency (Franck and Stevens 2006, 24).

These realities notwithstanding, the students were admonished to consider the frame of reference for their study and to dig deeper into the human landscape, to ask why conditions were so, and to see if they could identify emergent patterns that might suggest regrowth. They began to value their own time differently, spending it inside the neighborhood in the company of various members of the steering committee, seeing the place through local eyes. They experienced the vitality of Germantown Avenue at street level, the diversity of its commercial enterprises including a plethora of sidewalk vendors, the density of pedestrians, buses, and cars. They visited the barbershop and nail salon; were introduced to building owners who gave them access to vacant upper floors; interviewed shop owners, elders, and community leaders; measured streets; and observed the intersection of local and city-wide activity at the corner of Germantown and Lehigh.

Through trial and error, and with the support of the community, the students had begun to master what Richard Sennett calls the "craft of experience" as a means of design. The students began to see problems from the problem's point of view; small everyday things rarely admitted to the lexicon of the studio were valorized as design problems, often providing thresholds into more difficult terrain (Sennett 2008, 286-296).

## Drawing Out the Community through Drawings of Place

At the next formal meeting of the steering committee, both studios made presentations of their research and preliminary strategies. By now the polite restraint was let go and work could be undertaken through dialogue around visual representation of place. With a few notable exceptions, the planning research was based on the reformulation of existing data to conform to the site boundaries and the nascent proposals, typological and abstract. The architecture studio work, though less polished, was provocative, imbued with knowledge from direct human exchange and invited controversy.

A new historic timeline in its final iteration had integrated on-site interviews and proffered home photographs and community portraits, placing local practice of everyday life side by side with the events and figures that constituted what is established as historical "fact." Stories of neighborhood heroes had emerged: the neighborhood had been home to abolitionists, civil rights leaders, artists, housing activists, and adults who changed the lives of children.

The architecture students' land use maps were drawn to reflect a nuanced tapestry of commercial enterprises. Section drawings showed the intimacy of Germantown Avenue compared to the excessive width of Lehigh Avenue, the erstwhile trolley corridor for workers to and from a once thriving factory district, and how the spatial divide was reinforced by jurisdictional boundaries (we had learned that for decades rival gangs had patrolled the border crossings). The "ghost town" label stuck, despite our efforts to bury the gaffe, adopted without offense by the community as a way of identifying the Germantown Avenue vacancy issues. One student had made a drawing that showed the shuttered Sunday and evening streetscape transformed in Photoshop with a continuous hip-hop mural. This intrigued the shop owners, though the "graffiti bomb" made them anxious—a creative anxiety that mixed desire for legitimacy and attraction to the energy of the handmade expression.

Then the more complicated problem of the second floor vacancies, first understood as an artifact of an obsolete economy, was examined in a new light. The systemic vacancy was not a market problem: there was plenty of demand for rental housing by young couples or even artists or students not ready or interested in home ownership. It was simply a design problem: how to get independent access to upper floors in buildings originally planned for the exclusive use of a single tenant shop owner and his family was the stumbling block.

Our enthusiasm for the vital street life contributed by the sidewalk vendors was not shared by the merchants. They claimed that the vendors clogged the sidewalk, and their low overhead enterprises, often selling the same merchandise at higher prices, were in direct economic competition with their legitimate struggling businesses. In addition, it became clear that the vendors were appropriating valuable public real estate into which the shop owners themselves wanted to expand. The Merchants Association had mounted a plan to relegate the vendors to an open lot at the end of the shopping area—an action that surely would deal a fatal blow to these fledgling entrepreneurs.

The most controversial discussion emerged from ideas generated jointly by on-the-ground research of the architecture students and macro-scale patterns identified by the planners. The intersection of Germantown and Lehigh was a highly visible crossing of a large traffic and transit corridor with the small neighborhood-scale pedestrian thoroughfare. It had been observed as a vital activity node, with Nino's pizza and two pharmacies, and stops for three bus lines. With considerable enthusiasm the students suggested that Germantown and Lehigh could be further developed as a local arts and entertainment destination, building on the presence of the Village of Arts and Humanities just to the south, giving the neighborhood a strong sense of identity that the community had hoped for. Moreover, it made district-wide sense as the intersection had a location that was central to several community arts organizations, potentially reinforcing a shared identity. It could become a real locus for diverse, high-quality activities, night and day, that would both serve the local constituency and attract people from around the city.

This exciting proposal was followed by a curiously long and awkward silence. Eventually one of the steering committee members spoke up. He asked if we had been there at night. We had not. The intersection already had a very strong identity: Germantown and Lehigh was a major "corner" in the city's drug trade, and Nino's its epicenter. At nightfall Germantown and Lehigh was exceedingly dangerous and dominated by drug dealing and prostitution. The proposal to make it an arts and entertainment destination would "never work." It was simply *unimaginable*.

Thinking as urban designers, we had inadvertently exposed a fundamental neighborhood threat that permeated everyday experience and dictated the neighborhood's health and functionality. In all our interactions with community members, crime had been discussed only as a generic urban "brand"; the highly specific Nino's problem hadn't been mentioned. Although physical manifestation of fear was evident in the battened streetscapes, it was most powerfully conveyed by community resistance to sharing this truth. We realized that we also had avoided the subject in its concrete reality, tacitly neglecting any nighttime investigations of the neighborhood. One night after leaving the studio, several students drove through the intersection. Under the dull orange haze of street lamps, security gate drawn tight, Nino's was the only bright spot, buzzing with commercial activity that was casually and blatantly illegal—a constant coming and going from the restaurant, while outside knots of people gathered, cars idled then sped off.

## Finding Our Agency, or How We Stalked Nino's Restaurant through Design

It was humbling to realize how beyond our scope the problems of crime were. We experienced a very low point in the project, feeling powerless to solve the most critical issue. One student keenly remarked, "If crime and drugs are the big problem, why did they ask designers for help?" Well, why indeed?

So we began to look for our particular agency in this situation. This was an urban design project conducted by architecture students accustomed to designing theoretically in places that did not push back. We would have to delve more deeply into our creative resources and transgress disciplinary limits; we would have to embrace the reality of the place and think like artists, landscape architects, sociologists, community developers as well as architects. Though we could not claim expertise in any of these areas, we had a remarkable knowledge of the place, and we possessed imaginative ability and representational skills that could be used to serve the community. We had the power to visualize transformative opportunity in sites fraught with problems.

After much discussion, we resolved to suspend our own disbelief and to work on the problem at hand. We decided to be bold and to start our design work with the intriguing and problematic node at Germantown and Lehigh, proposing it to the community as a "what if" proposition. What if this intersection could form a threshold to this unique community? What if a vibrant multifaceted place could emerge using the arts as a catalyst for renewal? What would it be made of? How would it look? We had done enough groundwork to believe the idea plausible; now, in growing recognition of its challenges, we had to transform it from the "unimaginable" to the imaginable.

To succeed at this we needed to adjust our thinking, and to adopt a more tactical, incremental approach space to reclaiming the neighborhood's public space. Rather than focusing directly on an overhaul of this toxic locus, we proceeded obliquely, seeking to build up a kind of spatial resistance in the immediately surrounding urban tissue. Our proposals sought to represent alternative patterns of inhabitation that, over time, could subvert the dominance of the drug corner. We took a lesson from the tactics used by the underground economy itself, insinuating into the available rifts, holes, and ellipses in the context. The "ghost town" could not be dismissed as moribund—it was in de Certeau's terms a haunted space, steeped in the past anticipating new life (de Certeau 1984, 108). Perhaps the vacancies and opacities, discontinuities and danger zones represented opportunity and could be reimagined the way the Village had reimagined vacant lots as gardens, and crack houses as learning space.

First, we set about exploring ways to reappropriate the nightscape. In view of the threats posed by the street life at night, our narrative of spatial claim would be indirect, starting at the second story where light and sound emitting from above would be a constant reminder that the street activity was not unobserved. Apartment-living above the stores reestablished the three-dimensionality of the street space, layering the place also in a temporal frame. Once the need for this type of dwelling was identified, the functional problem of creating street access to the upper floors could be resolved though design. A study yielded responses to the handful of different conditions, revealing how minor physical interventions could spark the emergence of a new—or renewed—urban system. Students also addressed the mix of uses in designs for new construction on one of the rare, large open lots on the avenue. Senior housing above a farm market, with a bingo parlor and a big sit-down restaurant were proposed toward the north end of Germantown Avenue, near a cluster of storefront churches where we had observed the only significant activity on Sunday.

Gradually the arts would permeate the commercial corridor as a twenty-four-hour presence. In a new interpretation of "living above the shop," students designed a combined renovation and infill site near the Village as live-work artist studios with a street-level gallery, extending the Village activities farther up Germantown Avenue. Community-led site investigations had brought students to a large vacant music hall on the second floor of a building near the intersection of Germantown and Lehigh. The space was reimagined as a place for performances—or as the movie theater that the community so desired. With existing street access, the public use of this wonderful space could be achieved with strategic design changes. Similarly, across the street above Nino's, there was a highly transparent vacant loft-like space. Closing in on the drug corner, we proposed a dance studio that would project from its prominent corner site the presence of positive local activity, day and night.

A second strategy was street-based. We proposed a plan that would activate and enhance the Germantown and Lehigh Avenue intersection as a binding threshold into the community. A median filled with trees, lighting, and Village-made public artworks would replace the defunct, dedicated trolley lanes, and provide an identifying landmark visible for blocks as cars and pedestrians on Lehigh Avenue approached the intersection. In addition, a stretch of widened sidewalks at the Lehigh Avenue crossing would increase pedestrian safety and offer space for informal public use. Dramatically reducing the street width would slow daytime traffic and at night impede the vehicular "stop-and-go" of the drug trade. Enriched with color, shade, and pro-social activity, the streetscape would also shrink the physical divide on Germantown Avenue created by Lehigh Avenue, so damaging to the internal social coherence of the community.

On the expanded sidewalk in front of the long, deadening, blank Lehigh Avenue sidewall of a corner Rite Aid, the vendors were given a homeland. Here students designed a frame structure for the vendors to occupy and shelter their goods. Located just around the corner from the storefront businesses, the vendors were visible and easily accessible to pedestrian traffic, but not imposing on the merchants' territorial claim. The Rite Aid's franchised market share was unthreatened by the small operation of the vendors, and we speculated that a colorful mural along their ninety-foot stucco wall would be acceptable, and provide evidence of a "good neighbor" policy should they need it. The vendors might catalyze much needed new public activity along Lehigh Avenue.

Our last move was to show Nino's as a café rather than a take-out, with maybe some tables and chairs set out on the more spacious south-facing sidewalk. Perhaps the drug trade, which had recognized the strategic value of the urban site, would be undermined—if only to slink away in search of untapped potential somewhere else.

In a carefully orchestrated final presentation to the steering committee, we shared our narrative for the gradual transformation. Together with the planning students' neighborhood context proposals, the architecture students' more detailed representations of physical changes were a compelling argument for the real possibility of change. The visual representation, both in drawn and model form, was a powerful means of expression—at once real and not real—that allowed creative excitement to develop. This time the committee was willing to suspend disbelief and to enter into our projected narrative.

They saw that the students had engaged their world of competing interests, marginal resources, and contingent operations; they had used what was present in that world to weave a story that could turn the unimaginable into the imaginable. In the end it wasn't simply Nino's corner that ruled the community, but an overall ethos of powerlessness that the drug trade had come to symbolize. The sense of loss and uncontrolled erosion of neighborhood fabric that our "ghost town" metaphor had first brought to the surface had dominated the collective consciousness and impeded the imagination. Stalking Nino's corner was a dramatic tactic that focused our work and generated a new vision from the diverse needs of the place. Like the fable "Stone Soup," the resources for collective well-being were already there, needing only a little magic for them to coalesce.

## How Reviving the "Ghost Town" Became a Springboard for Action

Following the final presentations, anxiety and excitement about how to proceed was palpable. It was a well-understood fact that at the end of the semester, the student energy would vanish, and a slow process of sorting through and implementing aspects of the proposals must begin. The Village was particularly anxious to fulfill its promise to the steering committee not to end with another "shelf-dusted study." New funds were sought, and eventually obtained, to support the Shared Prosperity Working Group, a reformulated steering committee that would drive the project forward. But immediate action that made *visible* change to the community was essential for sustaining commitment.

Though most of the students did leave the scene (the planning students graduated), several Temple undergraduates remained connected to the Village and members of the steering committee. In July 2004, following the studio I received an excited e-mail from one of my students, Ansel Radway.

> I've just spoken to Jamie Moffett, one of the instructors at the Village, and he has informed me that my idea of having a long graffiti bomb/mural down Germantown Ave is presently being executed! Right now they are in the design process . . . He told me that the kids have interviewed store-owners to get feedback as to what they could put on the store fronts [security screens] . . . A number of the fronts have been cleaned and prepared for this project. There are two instructors, a painter (or muralist I believe the term might be), and a graf art designer working on this project for the kids. I'll keep you posted as the project further develops, and I plan to go down within the next week to check out what's going on.

The architecture student's idea of painting murals on the roll down security doors, a response to the contended "ghost town" epithet, had intrigued the shop owners; Lily Yeh saw the art project as a way of rededicating the Village's role as an arts institution and a stakeholder in the ongoing work of community development. She offered to bring together shop owners, local teens, and artists in this streetscape project. Knowing that the merchants were immensely wary of teens, she convinced them that their partnership could yield both immediate aesthetic benefits and long-term social bonds. An ethnographer who observed the process remarked: "The security screens become the merchants' representations of themselves to the community, channeled through the eyes and ears of the teens . . . The screens materialize a dialogue between inside and outside, between self and other, that is foundational to human and community development" (Hufford and Miller n.d., 55).

As the mural work was being done, the Merchants Association also sought to make links between immediate action and future vision. They had the architectural presentation boards—full of imagery and the implicit narrative of renewal—displayed in storefronts along Germantown Avenue. The informal exhibition of speculative ideas in concert with the immediacy of full-scale work being made illustrated how small things can embody the emergent potential of the place. This was what the Village had brilliantly accomplished over its many years of incremental, self-generated reinvention in North Philadelphia.

*Village teens painting the security screens.*
*Photo by The Village of Arts and Humanities*

Muralized screens add life to Germantown Avenue while shops are closed. *Photo by Sally Harrison*

Proposed Streetscape: Hip Hop Graffiti on Store Fronts

Before

After

Photomontage of Germantown Avenue "ghost town" with shuttered storefronts and the student's graffiti art proposal for security screens. *Photo by Ansel Radway*

## Tactical Victories: Keeping the Lights on Upstairs, Closing Nino's, and Celebrating Local History

The studio's architectural design proposals from the Shared Prosperity project, tactical in their approach and underpinned by local knowledge, have seeped into the ongoing work of community-building and community development. While some ideas, like the "graffiti bomb," were immediately taken up, others percolated and emerged later, transformed by discussion and events in the community. In his book *Small Change,* Nabeel Hamdi describes this quiet truth drawn from years of slow and thoughtful work inside communities. He says: "Acting in order to induce others to act, of offering impulses rather than instructions, and of cultivating an environment for change from within, starts on the ground and often with small beginnings which have 'emergent potential'" (Hamdi 2004, *xx*).

Remarkably, a process of stalking Nino's that had been thought out in the studio was adapted by the Shared Prosperity Working Group. The security screen project on Germantown Avenue, together with the students' careful design study of upper floor access, has helped to tip the balance away from the empty ghost town; new apartments are being let above the storefronts. Senior housing is actually being built on the huge empty lot. With lights on upstairs, dwelling claim is quietly being reestablished on the avenue at night. Moreover, a community-wide walking program was organized to get neighbors out and about, day and evening, further asserting the collective ownership of their public spaces. As described in the Shared Prosperity Working Group's report, the walks have been a vehicle for exercising, visiting, and for demonstrating a "dissuasive presence against drug dealing." Building an authoritative challenge to the claims of those who would control the public realm, the working group has collaborated with the police district to shut down Nino's, clearing the way for more auspicious uses at the intersection.

Reclaiming the neighborhood's public history also became a subject of activity in the community, having begun in the studio with the challenge to our students: "*Whose* history are we talking about?" Local human heritage, so often ignored or rewritten in the official record, was what mattered most in the collective imagination of a community. It was as ephemeral as it was powerful and affirmed intrinsic culture, especially for those who had lived in the area for many years. Building on this, an informal ethnographic project was formed by elderly residents who gathered in each other's homes to reminisce, share, and capture the unique stories about life in the neighborhood "back in the day." Inspired by our original historic timeline, they began to articulate the need for celebrating the lives of the men and women from the neighborhood who had touched North Philadelphia's social and cultural history, some who had gained notoriety and some whose deeds had gone unsung. Under the auspices of the Village, a major exhibition called "Evoking Spirit, Embracing Memory" was conceived.

By the time the exhibition was being planned, Temple architecture students had become familiar to the neighborhood, having been engaged in building, design, and service activities with the Village. Trust, and a kind of neighborliness having been gained over the three years since Shared Prosperity was begun, an advanced studio was invited to collaborate, picking up the threads of work begun by students who had gone before them. Sculptures commemorating twelve neighborhood heroes were to be installed on a large open lot near the Village. We were asked to provide an exhibition site design, to assist in the installation of sculptures and to build a threshold into the site. This time the studio literally "started on the ground." Working collaboratively with residents and artists on site, new relationships were made, building an ever-deepening awareness of the complex ecology of the place. And the relationship with this remarkable organization continues to the present, as we design for the second growth of the Village campus itself in a well-funded project called Digging Deeper.

## Finding the Human Landscape

The human landscape is a critical source for design, yet it cannot be fully experienced in the traditional studio setting where most design instruction takes place. This is a hole in our design education that is beginning to be filled. As an alternative way of teaching and learning, direct and sustained engagement with a community can be a powerful force in the intellectual and affective lives of students and faculty, and it presents a challenge to our inherited studio culture.

The community-based design studio opens an expanded field of relations, plunging us into a churning subjective world, rich in information that must be interpreted without our comforting frameworks of authority. It repositions the student in relation to his or her work, the faculty in relation to the student, and the studio "problem" in relation to a web of human and environmental realities. Conducted as a *shared* enterprise among students, faculty members, and community members, the "expert" model that implicitly defines most studio work does not hold. The professor is not the atelier chief, nor is he or she the primary means of knowledge transfer, but rather a framer of questions and experiences, a convener and interpreter. The students are not lone authors of their individual works, nor are they uncritical exponents of received aesthetic values, but rather explorers, synthesizers, activists in creative problem solving. The "design problem" itself is not determined a priori, but constitutes rather a constellation of problems to be found within the social and physical environment, and addressed within an inclusive definition of environmental design. Most importantly, the "user," only an *éminence grise* in most architecture school projects, now becomes multiplied as a polymorphous, dynamic force. A community of would-be users and clients are respondents and creative participants with many voices. Both teachers and learners, they can show the students how to look, listen, and interrogate and fully use their agency as designers.

Years later, reflecting on the Shared Prosperity studio, one student remarked on its intensity: "the project became emotional at times when [we experienced] the passions of the community" (quoted in Nalencz 2006). The presence of the emotions of others—pride, shame, ambition, imagination, stemming from an attachment to their place in the world—was the uncontrolled and vital force that penetrated the opacity of studio practice as usual. Our normative methods of representation and research, our presumptions about the purposes and products of design, and our unseemly role as expert consultants were unmasked as inadequate means for engaging a place. In the presence of emotion, the community also set aside its mantle of resistance to being examined—perhaps judged—by an exogenous elite.

The exchange of alternative imaginations had begun to form a porous membrane for creativity. Bubbling out of the swamps and bogs of North Philadelphia, precious, significant, deeply felt neighborhood problems too long hidden from public view struggled to the surface; sites of creative interest, too nuanced or mundane to be recognized without their local narratives, were revealed, and the aspirations for an empowered community began to emerge and take shape through design.

In reality, creation is a disseminated proliferation.

## CHAPTER 2

# Reconsidering the Margin

*Relationships of Difference and Transformative Education*

Jodi Rios

Architecture's primary task is to create a paradise on earth. —*Alvar Aalto*

The end is reconciliation, the end is redemption, the end is the creation of the beloved community. —*Dr. Martin Luther King, Jr.*

**O**ver the past forty years, community engagement has become a stated objective of many institutions of higher learning in the United States. The scope, definition, and outcome of such engagement, however, can be as varied as the disciplines themselves and are always shaped by the individuals who spearhead this work. In an effort to evaluate engagement between the academy and the community and seek to recognize pedagogical frameworks that support positive outcomes on both sides, it becomes important to reflect on how transformative and reciprocal relationships are defined and fostered. If traditional service-learning models are to be challenged, and I argue that they should, then it is necessary to ask the most basic questions: Who is served? and What is learning?

This chapter considers these questions in the context of architectural education. It also reflects upon the experiences that have impacted my teaching and the curricula that I have developed over a decade. This experience has been shaped by the disparity between the largely privileged students at the private university where I have taught and the marginalized African American communities where I have spent much time. I have also been influenced by my colleague, Bob Hansman, who embarked on this journey ahead of me and whose mentorship and support encourages me to keep pursuing the more difficult path.

What I hope to communicate in this essay is that meaningful and transformative engagement is always messy, often unpredictable, and dependent on sustained human relationships. When true *relationship* is achieved, it is inherently transformative because one cannot remain indifferent to those with whom one is intertwined. This level of engagement changes outcomes in addition to transforming individuals, as the grounds for assessment and decision making must reflect the values and priorities of both parties—and learning will occur in multiple directions.

I will first establish the context for how I found myself in community-based teaching and the initial failures that prompted me to question what it means to engage students with a community in a meaningful way. I then outline a theoretical framework for why engaged pedagogy is important to academia and design by discussing viewpoints that have informed my own theoretical assertions. Finally, I summarize the concepts of transformative education that have influenced my pedagogical approach to community-based teaching and describe the courses that have resulted from them.

## The Context

Architecture has an implicit role to examine and question what it means to build in the urban context and how interventions may challenge, transform, or reinforce meaning, identity, and power embedded within a particular place. Upon joining the architecture faculty at Washington University in St. Louis in 1996, I was struck by the number of design studios that were using areas defined by disinvestment and vacancy in the city as sites for student projects. These sites were presented to students as the equivalent of a blank slate with a few potential *remnants* from which design explorations could emerge. Even as I embraced theoretical inquiry and creative intent within design, the blatant dismissal of the people who lived in these areas and the attitude that "anything is better than what is there" was disconcerting because it reinforced the fact that design reproduces power: for whom will it be "better," and by what set of criteria is "better" defined? While architecture alone is incapable of solving social inequities, I reject the argument that architecture is a benign, apolitical practice that lacks social responsibility or political agency, or that an architect's responsibility is solely to the client. Architecture and urban design certainly operate within structures of power.[1]

Setting out to take a different approach to the urban studio, I chose the same sites of perceived disinvestment and decay but hoped to bring a different perspective from the one I describe above. I demanded that my students spend significant time in the area and meet routinely with different groups of residents. In spite of this effort, the students were quickly overwhelmed by the contrast between the neighborhood and their own experiences and could not go much beyond their personal perceptions, fears, and stereotypes. Good intentions did not suffice, and the students found it difficult to see any significant value or meaning in the neighborhood because they held up the comparative lens of middle-class values and expectations. Concurrent to this viewpoint was the adherence to a disciplinary elitism that fetishizes form and valorizes the artist/architect as creative genius. The students were anxious to show the residents what their neighborhood *could be* if only they embraced the values, expertise, and insight that the students had to offer. Communication between the students and the residents remained polite; however, suspicion and disregard was clearly evident from both sides.

For their part, the residents were distanced, somewhat suspicious, and unwilling to confront the students. While they desired to see change in their community and initially welcomed student input and ideas, subsequent interviews revealed that they resented the implication that the outsiders knew what was good for their neighborhood and that terms like *at risk, marginalized,* and *underprivileged* were used to describe the area. The residents reported that their critique was dismissed as simplistic and nostalgic. They did not, however, confront the students because they stated that they were familiar with these attitudes and did not believe that the students were capable of change; it was simply not worth their time or energy to take the encounters past a superficial and gratuitous level. Ultimately, the residents politely accepted what the students proposed, which was a butterfly garden with shelter and seating, but they did not find much value in the students' vision, nor were they invested in it. It has since fallen into disrepair.

The level of respect and understanding on both sides did not occur as I had hoped, and I learned that spending time in a community and talking with people does not guarantee understanding, nor does it ensure a design response that engenders the values of a community or ownership of it. In retrospect, this should have been obvious and I was guilty of the same naïve idealism and judgment that my students had brought with them. It led me to question whether it is possible to teach design which aspires to the highest standards of excellence while responding to the specificities, strengths, and complex identities of a place quite different from that of the designer. How does meaningful engagement occur that leads to something beyond that which could otherwise have been conceived—a profound creativity that is dependent on the conflict and the interaction itself?

## Conceptualizing a Pedagogy of Engagement

Over the past four decades there have been many advocating for democratic and inclusive design processes that emphasize community building,
and consistent calls for an end to the residual structures of a post-colonial
society and paternalistic altruism. Unfortunately the scenario that I just
described and the "blank slate" approach are still too often the methods
used in both education and practice when professionals bring services to
communities for whom they have little respect. Even when there is a sincere
desire to help communities considered less fortunate—using words such as
*empowerment* and *development*—the neoliberal elitism that can result often
reinforces dominant structures through subversive means. Paulo Freire observed in *Pedagogy of the Oppressed* that as those attached to the dominant
culture attempt to shed oppression and move to the side of the oppressed,
previous prejudices and judgments will subconsciously emerge in the form
of knowledge and control. Even in their attempts to subjugate the power
structure, the privileged lack confidence in those they are trying to empower and dominate the effort to disrupt an unjust order (Freire 1970).
This is the irony and the danger of dominant classes seeking to elevate
marginalized classes without first shifting their own position; the ethicist
can become the imperialist. Author bell hooks speaks of the tendency of
dominant culture to usurp the narrative of the oppressed:

> Often this speech about the "Other" annihilates, erases: "No need to hear
> your voice when I can talk about you better than you can speak about
> yourself. No need to hear your voice. Only tell me about your pain.
> I want to know your story. And then I will tell it back to you in a new way.
> Tell it back to you in such a way that it has become mine, my own."
> (hooks 1990, 151)

The students tried to understand the community on their own terms
and they did not trust the community to know what was good. The community was thus framed through a limited lens of *difference* and the students'
need to define difference relative to what they perceived to be a normative
perspective, both socially and architecturally. They therefore took ownership
of both defining and solving the communities' problems, even though there
was a *listening* component embedded in the class.

Fincher and Iveson (2008) discuss such observations, noting the post-
critical[2] assumption held by many enlightened academics such as my students—that they had overcome closed-mindedness and that the academic
realm itself was outside of any structural oppression that might be in play.

Rather than considering how their own background might influence not only their response to the community but also their own reflexive capacity, the students maintained that they had been conditioned not to see race or class and could therefore achieve an objective viewpoint. Because a seemingly inclusive and communicative process was used, all potential for exclusion was ruled out, thereby neutralizing any criticism of the outcome and denying any responsibility for unintended consequences since good intentions were always assumed and not questioned. This assumption led to the corollary that if the process was inclusive, the product must be inclusive as well. Initial student discussions had consistently centered on what the students perceived to be alarming destitution. Fincher and Iveson (2008) again point out that discourses regarding design that focus on the disadvantage of people and presume that a community lacks an acceptable future without intervention result in further stigmatization and subsequent decline. Indeed, the students found it difficult to speak positively about what they saw, which resulted in further alienation from the community.

As I reflected on this experience and considered how the outcome might have been different, I looked again to bell hooks' writings on cultural theory and transformational pedagogy, particularly her concept regarding a marginal space of resistance brought about by what she calls "radical openness" (hooks 1990). This idea seemed to me the only way to describe what needed to happen in order for there to be any hope of bringing dissimilar people together in a meaningful way, or of envisioning Dr. Martin Luther King Jr.'s concept of the "beloved community." What does it look like to be the beloved community that King imagined? Based on King's words, the beloved community is the aftermath of nonviolence that makes the struggle and resistance truly meaningful and transformative (1960). It is a new relationship between oppressed and oppressor based on reconciliation, redemption, and a love and hope that can transform oppressors into friends (King 1957). According to King, love is inseparable from justice and it is the basis for evaluating that which is transformed and that which is merely cloaked in rhetoric. "Therefore the first hope in our inventory must be the hope that love is going to have the last word" (King 1967, 191). According to King, the beloved community is both the location and the goal of transformative struggle and any hope of creating and entering such a community requires love (Marsh 2005). Love as affect and its role in the practice of relationships has also been discussed throughout philosophical discourse, including the work of Deleuze (1994), Spinoza (1996), Levinas (2006), and Irigaray (2008). More recently, affects such as love and hope relative to the urban condition are explored and valorized in the work of nonrepresentational theorists such as Thrift.

The *margin* is the location of intimacy and perhaps another location of the beloved community and transformative struggle. This requires a different way of thinking about the meeting of disparate groups. Rather than speaking about *bridging gaps* or *erasing boundaries* between defined groups, let us consider a space in which the centrality of all actors is given up or denied—denied by the individuals themselves. All become "other" in the marginal space, which thus erases "the Other" and displaces the subject/object paradigm. This is not the same as the universalistic notion of synthesizing difference into a unified whole because individual identity is understood and indeed necessary to this kind of engagement. Choosing the margin, as bell hooks points out, is much different from being placed in the margin.

While hooks theorizes choosing the margin from the perspective of the marginalized, I would argue that choosing the margin can occur from the direction of the dominant culture as well, although the reasons for and experience of such a choice will be different. Choosing the margin involves struggle regardless of the departure point—any time one acts outside of the norm, some level of resistance will occur. From the standpoint of the marginalized, it is an act of choosing to stay in the margin whereas from the position of dominant culture it is an act of entering the margin. Those who already occupy that margin must be willing to embrace such an entry. From that perspective, power is shifted to the marginalized. This raises the philosophical question, must one be powerless to occupy the margin? Author bell hooks elaborates on this concept:

> Marginality is much more than a site of deprivation . . . it is also the site of radical possibility . . . it is not just found in words but in habits of being and the way one lives. As such [it is not] a marginality one wishes to lose—to give up or surrender as part of moving into the center—but rather a site one stays in, clings to even, because it nourishes one's capacity to resist. It offers to one the possibility of radical perspective from which to see and create, to imagine alternative new worlds. (hooks 1990, 149)

The marginal space of resistance is a space of creativity that resists normative assumptions about the way things are. It is not just a space for the oppressed. As I saw the ensnarement of dominant culture in my own life, I realized that hooks was speaking to all of us. This *positive* marginal space is a space of resistance for both oppressed and oppressor, regardless of how enlightened one views oneself. It is intentionally chosen and entered from any cultural perspective—a third possibility which requires all sides to shift and does not exist otherwise. This marginal space of resistance differs from recognition models[3] in that it requires relational participation and acknowledges each group's need for the other in a truly reciprocal manner. From this standpoint, it is not enough that the marginalized are recognized; what must occur is the recognition that those occupying the center are in need of those at the margin to be, themselves, liberated from walls and boundaries—resulting in a form of mutual care. Discovering oneself to be an oppressor can result in much remorse, but such realization does not always lead to solidarity. More often, a paternalism that holds the marginalized in positions of dependence will result. Only entering into the situation of the marginal will produce freedom on all sides (Freire 1970).

Regardless of how we frame or reframe our understanding of transformative openness and its potential, a radical position is required that takes us outside of clearly defined jurisdictions of practice and into the places of honest relationship with those who expose our own need. It is a dangerous position. The binary of Whiteness/Otherness has maintained the privileges that the middle class in the United States have come to expect (Lipsitz 1998). To assume the radical position is to risk jeopardizing our expectations and finding ourselves in potentially uncomfortable situations. From an academic standpoint, this position destabilizes long-accepted methodologies and traditional modes for the production of knowledge rooted in the social sciences. The *study* of culture, race, and class has neatly packaged theoretical premises for larger disciplinary consumption—leading to convenient conclusions that do little more than valorize discursive formations within the academic realm (Kelley 1997). The choice to pursue the radical position certainly implies consequences.

## Teaching a Pedagogy of Engagement through Relationship

It has been fourteen years since my first attempt to bring students together with communities. In that time I have developed a critical pedagogy intended to encourage opportunities for marginal spaces of engagement and to expand the critical consciousness of my students and the communities with whom they interact. This has meant squarely addressing issues of racial reconciliation and challenging many aspects of dominant culture, including those within architecture and urban theory. These things are not peripheral to the practice of architecture, nor do their considerations devalue other facets of design exploration and process. Rather, if architecture reflects and reproduces the nature and values of a society, then it should grapple with what that society is and ask questions regarding what it should be. More than ever, it is important to understand that the decisions we make have consequences. They are not benign, and how we make them certainly reveals how we view the world. Author bell hooks states: "Spaces can be real and imagined. Spaces can tell stories and unfold histories. Spaces can be interrupted, appropriated, and transformed through artistic and literary practice . . . 'The appropriation and use of space are political acts.'" (hooks 1990, 152). Architecture and the design disciplines indeed have agency and have a critical role to play in moving toward a just society.

In higher education the stakes of pedagogical choices cannot be calculated in the narrow range of best practices or design thinking or even critical thinking, but only on a complete terrain that encompasses the broader implications of what learning might be. By developing curricula that raise questions regarding personal and professional accountability for the status quo within the context of a broader social and cultural encounter, I am utilizing my position as a professor to challenge my students to become designers who understand the agency that they possess. Furthermore, if attitudes and tangible life decisions are going to be transformed, as I suggest must happen in order to destratify our society, then it must occur within higher education and certainly within our most elite institutions.

Noah De Lissovoy (2008) accurately writes about the problems that arise when attempting to reframe difference through the educational process for the purpose of transformation. He offers three principles that support a transformative pedagogy that I have found useful toward linking theory with teaching and in articulating the purpose of taking a transformative approach to education. Although De Lissovoy specifically addresses the classroom setting, his pedagogy of difference argues for something not unlike hooks' radical openness and is useful for furthering a critical pedagogy for academic/community engagement. I have adapted these three principles for this purpose.

First, if assimilation racism erases cultural identity and fails to value difference, then to embrace minority culture and value its communities will inherently challenge the dominant culture and attitudes that deem them deficient, thus achieving a transformative pedagogy (De Lissovoy 2008). This is a simple idea that is difficult to implement among politically correct students who will deny difference at every turn in an effort to not offend or feel uncomfortable. I have found that to overcome politically correct silence, it is effective to ask students to consider the ways that erasure of cultural identity and failure to acknowledge difference oppress rather that equalize. There is a difficult balance to strike between the transformative potential of opening oneself up to different ways of understanding the world and the tendency to essentialize difference in order to define, describe, and ultimately consume it. By looking at specific examples of how power structures are reproduced within the built environment, effectively neutralizing difference, and how consumer culture will essentialize and co-opt difference when difference cannot be denied, helps students to realize that design and the built environment is far from benign.

Second, since dominated voices themselves reflect hegemonic values, all voices need to be interrogated as well as affirmed. Critical reflection and transformative pedagogy assume a complex conversation in which affirmation and interrogation are not opposed but are complimentary to the process of liberating the assumptions of different people groups. When it is possible to get students to accept the first principal—to openly speak about and listen to previously marginalized voices—they often complain that this second principal contradicts the first. It is useful to point out that sociological studies have consistently shown that when marginalized populations in the US are asked if the poor have themselves to blame for their condition, they answer yes, even if they cite other reasons for their own individual situation (Wilson 2009). Thus, minority groups often perpetuate the dominant narrative.

Third, developing a pedagogy that seeks to *hear* all of the voices at the table regardless of viewpoint will reveal that many discourses that proclaim openness within the academic realm end up excluding voices that do not fulfill the accepted narrative, resulting in a paradoxical closure of ideas. Students generally view themselves as independent and enlightened thinkers and they are quite surprised to find that they have participated in the silencing of voices or have, themselves, been silenced. This is generally when a conscious shift occurs and they choose to recognize and resist both a conferred social construct and an assumed academic objectivity. Students begin to practice the freedom of speaking honestly and challenge one another without the fear of judgment.

These three principles are critical to a pedagogy of difference and establish the means by which to also bring about a crisis of thinking in which the subject position of the individual, regardless of location, is inescapably problematized and requires a choice: one must make a choice to adjust their locational position or affirm it; ignorance is no longer an option. This crisis of thinking has become foundational to my teaching and provides the metric for evaluating that which I am doing.

## Developing a Framework over Time

One semester is not sufficient to initiate a crisis of thinking, to engage with a community in a meaningful way, and to carry out a design project. At least two, if not more, semesters are required. Overcoming curricular requirements and structures in order to carry out a two- or three-semester sequence poses many logistical obstacles. I began by establishing relationships between courses, and as I gradually developed a strong pedagogical basis for the time and momentum needed to do this work, I was able to implement a formal engagement curriculum with the help of a sympathetic dean. I was emphatic that a minimum three-year commitment by the university to a community was essential if trust and reciprocity were to be achieved. Bruce Lindsey, who has a notable background in community engagement in his own right, was willing to make such a commitment, and we began to implement such a sequence at the Sam Fox School of Design and Visual Arts.

The Reconsidering the Margin seminar is the first course in the sequence and is an introduction and immersion class intended to problematize prior assumptions and begin to establish relationships within a community. Students are required to get to know individuals from the neighborhood with which they are working, and frameworks are put in place that facilitate such relationships, such as helping seniors in their home and volunteering in an after-school program. Throughout the semester, students are pushed to openly interrogate their own ideas relative to those around them, which include both their peers and the communities. The concept of reconciliation and what that actually means is an underlying theme to the semester, and students are asked to consider the impact of relationships on their understanding of the community throughout the semester by means of reflection and the act of making.

Reflection is a critical component of this type of learning because it helps students connect individual observations with larger aspects of the world around them. Because architecture is a visual discipline, the course requires a weekly visual reflection, usually a form of mapping, which documents their transforming perspective of the neighborhood. Each student develops a methodology for documentation that they then carry through the semester. I have found visual reflection to be very effective on multiple levels. The many decisions that must be made by the students regarding what they are communicating, how they will represent it, the act of making, and the resulting interpretations all inform both the individual and the group, and prompt provocative discussions. Students also present their reflections to the class, ensuring that each student has a voice that is recognized. Sometimes the *voice* is made known through the viewing of the artifact itself, but is heard nonetheless. Often the quietest student will produce the loudest representation and is, therefore, able to express emotion that would otherwise go unnoticed. Such recognition goes a long way in creating a community of learning within the classroom, which is entirely

different from relying on discussion alone. Author bell hooks, when refer-
ring to Freire's work, speaks of this community:

> Rather than focusing on issues of safety, I think that a feeling of community
> creates a sense that there is shared commitment and a common good
> that binds us. What we all ideally share is the desire to learn—to receive
> actively knowledge that enhances our intellectual development and our
> capacity to live more fully in the world. (hooks 1994, 40)

The seminar makes every effort to force discussions about, rather than
step around, the two topics that students have been groomed to avoid—race
and class. In order to create an environment of open dialogue, I have found
that it is essential to expose weaknesses and struggles in my own thinking
to my students if I am going to ask them to enter into risky dialogue and
reflection and thus expose potential "problems" in their thinking. I must
be willing to initiate a self-critical examination of personal attitudes and
decisions in the context of the class discussion. This kind of humility in the
classroom is antithetical to the typical teacher/student dynamic, but it is
critical to creating a space of personal engagement, both in the classroom and
in the community. Developing a tolerance for opinions other than my own
and not attempting to immediately dispel what I might consider "problems
of thinking" is also critical to this kind of teaching.

Residents often find the students' desire to discuss issues of race and class
surprising and initially suspicious; however, discussions that would be impossible to have between relative strangers begin to occur when foundational
friendships precede them. While they are not neighbors, the rapport between
student and resident often goes beyond that of mere recognition in that long-
term personal bonds are established that sometimes include integration into
social networks. The fact that I have established many of my own relationships within the community goes a long way in encouraging residents to
enter into difficult conversations with students. Because a commitment has
been made to their community and they are co-participants, they understand
theirs is a role of power as opposed to being a subject of study.

The outcome of the course differs from semester to semester and is
determined by the degree to which relationships are formed. Students are
asked to produce a collaborative representation that attempts to document
the process of the reflection throughout the semester. Many students have
reported later that they have maintained relationships in the community and
have continued to spend time there in some capacity. In two cases, students
later moved to the neighborhoods where they initially worked. In terms of
an introductory course, it has proven extremely useful to subsequent courses

that work with these neighborhoods as the students have already developed an appreciation and have begun to think more critically regarding their own participation in what they have found.

The second class, the Urban Issues and Development course, is an interdisciplinary, community-based class co-taught with faculty from law, social work, public policy, and business. This graduate-level course solicits Requests for Proposals (RFP's) from neighborhood groups, nonprofits, or government agencies that desire assistance with development projects in under-resourced neighborhoods. Several RFP's are selected by the faculty, one of which always includes a project from the area with which the Reconsidering the Margin seminar has worked. Students are placed on an interdisciplinary team that then responds to the individual RFP with a comprehensive development proposal.

Ideally, many of the architecture students who take the Urban Issues and Development course have taken the Reconsidering the Margin seminar; it is hoped that the critical thinking skills and intimate knowledge acquired in the seminar regarding these neighborhoods will influence the interdisciplinary teams. Many of the students who have not taken the previous seminar, especially those in law and business, sign up thinking that they will simply learn how to make money developing underdeveloped areas. Because the class is not simply "preaching to the choir," discussions frequently elicit vocal and angry responses. Students often ask questions such as, "Where are you trying to steer us, anyway?" which is the same question that Freire observed when working with professionals. Freire states, "The participants begin to realize that if their analysis of the situation goes any deeper they will either have to divest themselves of their myths, or reaffirm them" (Freire 1970, 156).

Although sometimes hostile, I welcome these discussions and it is quite rewarding if, after engaging and problem solving with the community, these students are willing to consider differing viewpoints, even if they do not embrace them. Maintaining an acceptance among students for differing viewpoints and moderating discussion is the primary focus of classroom interaction, and it is always challenging to remain objective. Often, discussions between other faculty members and myself serve as a model for how to debate widely differing ideas while maintaining respect. Like the Reconsidering the Margin seminar, the course utilizes texts from a range of disciplines intended to provide a framework for dialogue,[4] and students are asked to write reflection papers prior to classroom discussion that take a position with regard to the reading. It has been interesting to note that students from different disciplines consistently react to and approach urban problems in very different ways. The reflection papers tend to be broken down along disciplinary lines, which raises the question: Do students with particular belief systems gravitate toward certain disciplines or does each discipline produce such systems of thought? Likely it is both. This supports the argument for transdisciplinarity, which maintains that complex problems are best addressed from multiple points of view—regardless of where they are formed and provided that each informs the other.

It is difficult to recreate the relational aspect of the initial seminar in the interdisciplinary course, which is why it is essential to include students from the earlier seminar in the second course. The relationships built with the community during the first seminar often prove to be the guiding influences for the team responses, as a level of trust has been established between members of the team and members of the community. This trust facilitates a more sincere dialogue and leads to a response that reflects the actual, rather than perceived, desires of the community. The benefit of including team members who truly value the neighborhood and no longer fear it goes without saying. The transformative nature of the trust relationships, developed in the seminar through time and intimacy, provides a better context for reciprocity to emerge because community members understand that theirs is a role of teaching and challenging the students in addition to receiving student input. Service, like learning, occurs from both directions.

Even in the best of circumstances, the possibility for conflict, misunderstanding, and other hindrances always exists and should be understood as part of the learning process. It is important that expectations—those of students, faculty, administration, clients, and community—are realistic and recognize the fluid nature of the process. If problems that arise along the way are seen as obstacles rather than opportunities for learning, then disillusionment will quickly set in. Organizations may be disorganized, residents may not agree, political power and jurisdictional struggles may be in play, project goals may change mid-course, student group dynamics may break down. Any of these scenarios can stifle what is ultimately produced; however, they force the question, *What is learning?* and represent the reality and fragility of the project and of human relationships. They should not be understood as failures to be avoided.

The fact that development interests do not always coincide with resident interests becomes an important issue for many of the projects. For example, we have had instances where students working on an RFP have rejected the policy initiatives proposed by their client because they were deemed unjust and discriminatory. In these cases, the client is not always happy with the outcome of the proposal; however, the students have learned about the issues facing the community and have decided to use their proposal to illuminate and challenge unjust practices. One such example involved a municipality (client) that was using records of trash service and mortgage payment delinquency to target property that it wished to acquire for development. The municipality had taken legal action toward back taxes on these parcels but had not taken action on properties with similar delinquency in more affluent areas. The students were able to shine light on this practice, thus informing residents of their rights, and the municipality backed off. In other cases, in response to overwhelming resident concern, student proposals have supported the use of targeting tax delinquency and code noncompliance for the purpose of ridding blocks of specific drug and crime activity, which illustrates the complexity of ethics and questions with which the students must grapple. Therefore, we do not always base success of the proposal on the satisfaction of the client, but rather on the comprehensive nature of the student response and full consideration of the question, *What is service?* in the context of what they have been asked to do.

The third course in the sequence is a design/build studio. Students from prior semesters are encouraged to sign up and it is hoped that previously established trust relationships with the community are further developed and nurtured. The design problem that was identified in the prior semester is addressed and student teams quickly develop different design solutions, one of which is selected by the community. As an example, one Spring semester the Reconsidering the Margin class discovered that a grassroots art program was taking place every summer on the blacktop of a local playground, which attracted over forty children from the community who attended in spite of lack of shade and temperatures over ninety degrees. The design problem that was defined with the community ended up being a shade and performance pavilion for the art program that was later designed and built by the subsequent Fall design/build studio. During the summer between semesters, two student interns were hired for the purpose of maintaining communication with residents and laying the logistical groundwork for the design/build project, such as coordinating site work and confirming funding sources.

The designs developed for the design/build projects are rigorous and prove that residents can visualize and embrace sophisticated conceptual ideas. Several events are planned during the design development stage, all of which have a component focused on the youth in the area. Usually this component consists of drawing and model-making activities, and, in some cases, we have utilized a photo-voice element in which children document important aspects of their environment. I have found that the creative capacity of the children and their openness to working with students is the most effective way of ultimately engaging the adult residents who are eventually drawn in by the children's enthusiasm. Working with the children also allows for alternative design processes to be employed by the students and can often challenge traditional modes of design thinking and problem solving. During the last nine weeks of the semester, the students spend four to seven days a week at a physical site in the community building the project. This aspect of "just being there" (Hansman 2009) leads to a certain degree of ownership on their part and certainly provides many opportunities for getting to know residents.

Tangential to the courses described above but essential to the pedagogy is the synthesis of teaching and research efforts within this academic realm. Linking the efforts of the classes with funded research is important in order to assist these communities with identifying inequities, targeting resources, fostering citizenship, and gaining the attention of policy makers. Recently, my research entailed a Health Impact Assessment funded in part by the Robert Wood Johnson Foundation that focused on a proposed development project in the community in which my students had been working. This interdisciplinary research project required extensive community engagement that would not have been successful had the relationships and trust not been previously established with both residents and leadership. Integrating funded research also provides the means to employ students over the summer to bridge the gap between the Spring and Fall semesters and sustain the momentum. Hiring students involved with the classes during the academic year to work on research projects taking place in the same areas with which they have worked further links curricular objectives and leverages the knowledge built in the classroom.

## Practicing a Pedagogy of Engagement

I know now that I cannot introduce service or design projects to students until they recognize the filters through which they see, understanding that they are in need of the people whom they wish to serve. In the same way, it is necessary for communities to recognize the possibility for attitudes to change and to value the necessity of their own role in that transformation. Author bell hooks reinforces this sentiment when she states that "people of color who truly believe that white people cannot change can only embrace the logic of victimhood [and] anyone who denies that this change *can* happen, is acting in collusion with the existing forces of racial domination" (2003, 53–55). Communities that do not feel that such change has meaning to them will feel used when students enter their neighborhoods; those that do will feel a sense of power. If students seek to serve without understanding the truth of their own accountability and do not embrace what they find, their work will be an exercise of domination. If the residents of these communities see only the truth of a dominant culture, and do not open themselves to relationship and accountability in building bonds of trust through dialogue, then we are left with a false hope.

Transforming people and communities is relevant to architecture and the design disciplines, and design education has a responsibility to make this relevance evident. The design professions are fundamentally human endeavors situated as practices between power and need. The built environment produces and reproduces the values, opportunities, and constraints of a society and, therefore, the designer is either active or complacent in recognizing his or her role. There is no middle ground. Architects and design professionals can argue that as proxies of a client, they are powerless to effect change and that theirs is not a social role to play. This attitude is naïve and shortsighted at best and an excuse to reinforce and profit from oppressive practices at worst. Designers who are acting on the built environment have the power regarding the projects that they take, the places in which they choose to work, the processes that they employ, the voices that they hear, and the design decisions that they influence and control. Let us also reconsider what it means to embrace the margin as a means of practice.

## Conclusion

I have sought out my own community of reconciliation and we have created marginal spaces together. It has required a constant intentionality on my part. The longer I am part of this physical and figurative community, the less sure I am about my opinions regarding the issues at hand. After fourteen years of seeking a worthwhile process for teaching community engagement, I continue to learn and make mistakes. I am constantly reminded that this is extremely hard work: when students resist critical reflection and base their strongly-held opinions on little knowledge; when they voice frustration and discomfort or demand answers to questions; when community members speak out in anger, shun opportunities for interaction, hold on to feelings of hopelessness, or attack my motives; when logistics fall apart and finances evaporate; when I am angered by the ambivalence of those around me, struggle with acting on my professed convictions, am tempted to insulate myself and my family from discomfort, or just lack the energy required for this kind of teaching. When one struggles to enter the marginal space of resistance, however, they are changed and there is no turning back. It is there that I look for and sometimes find the beloved community.

## CHAPTER 3

# Differences Matter

## Learning to Design in Partnership with Others

Jeffrey Hou[1]

**G**ould Hall Room 114 was exceptionally crowded in Autumn 2006. It was occupied by not only the usual cast of landscape architecture students at the University of Washington (UW), but also high school minority students from a neighborhood youth program. In weekly, two-hour sessions, the mixed teams of students sat around large tables to design installations for a "night market," an event foreign to most of the UW students but one that brought fond memories to many of the participating youths. The UW students and the high school youths looked remarkably different. Besides the obvious age difference, the UW students were predominantly white, while the youths were mostly first or second generation Asian Americans. During the weekly sessions, there were moments of active exchanges as well as prolonged silence as the youths and the UW students stared at drawings and notes on the table. As the students worked together, they were confronted with one of the most challenging barriers in a community-university partnership—the sociocultural and institutional differences between community and university partners.

This chapter attempts to explore the instrumentality of such differences in the process of a community design studio. It examines not only how such differences exist but also how they contribute to the learning and design outcomes. Using the Night Market studio at the University of Washington, Seattle, as a case study, this chapter describes how the studio process addresses the multitude of social and cultural differences that face many community-university partners, and how such differences were harnessed to produce a transformative outcome in learning and design. Based on participant observations of the studio process, student feedback,[2] and by the examination of the outcomes of the studio, this chapter reflects on the experience and offers four basic steps to address and incorporate social and cultural differences into the learning and design process of a community service-learning studio.[3]

## Community-University Partnerships and Differences

Community-university partnership has proliferated in recent years as a model for higher education institutions and local community organizations to collaborate and achieve mutual gains (Baum 2000; Reardon 2000; Rubin 1998, 2000). Through service-learning programs, such partnerships provide opportunities for students to learn from and experience different cultures as well as the complexity of real-world design problems (Forsyth, Lu, and McGirr 1999; Lawson 2005; Hou 2007a). The process of learning can also take place in the community and contribute to capacity building and empowerment (Dewar and Isaac 1998). In practical terms, faculty and students can bring expertise and leverage resources to assist the community in need (Bringle and Hatcher 2002).[4] Outside players such as the universities can also have a strong influence in the political arena to assist the disadvantaged inner-city neighborhoods (Hutchinson and Loukaitou-Sideris 2001).

Over the years, community-university partnerships have transformed from a "professional-expert model of community planning" (Reardon 2000) to one that increasingly emphasizes collaboration and reciprocal learning. Unlike the earlier consultant model of service-learning with limited involvement in the community process, recent cases of community-university partnerships often engage a broad range of players (e.g., students, residents, university, community-based organizations, and public agencies) in a collaborative, less hierarchical, and more dynamic pursuit of social and educational goals.[5] However, as the students, faculty, and community stakeholders work more closely together, the engagement also opens the door for conflicts and negotiation of social and cultural differences among the partners. In other words, as boundaries are "erased," differences are revealed, and the active negotiation of such differences becomes paramount.

Discussion on the differences between community and university partners is not new to the service-learning literature in design and planning. In fact, there is a wealth of articles and papers that address this issue (Forsyth, Lu, and McGirr 1999; Lawson 2005; Prins 2005; Dewar and Isaac 1998; Reardon 1998, 2000; Baum 2000; Hutchinson and Loukaitou-Sideris 2001). The differences as addressed in the literature include contrasting priorities, modes of work, expectations, different levels of commitment to social change, and even scheduling (Baum 2000; Prins 2005; Reardon 1998; Dewar and Isaac 1998). There are also communicative barriers including jargons, vocabularies, and graphics (Forsyth, Lu, and McGirr 1999). Furthermore, unequal power relations can also present a stumbling block (Baum 2000; Dewar and Isaac 1998; Lawson 2005; Prins 2005). The diverse needs, perspectives, and culture of organizations among the different partners can often lead to tensions and conflicts (Dewar and Isaac 1998; Prins 2005). Lawson (2005, 158–159) further argues that "without cultural competence the ability to provide useful service to the community might be compromised."

Instead of something to be simply mitigated or avoided, how do the differences between the collaborating partners contribute to the learning process and outcomes? How can the differences become a meaningful device for a critical investigation in community-based design? These are the questions to be explored in this case study.

## The Partners

The Night Market studio that took place at UW in autumn of 2006 involved two partnering organizations, the community-based Wilderness Inner-City Leadership Development (WILD) youth program and the Department of Landscape Architecture at the University of Washington, Seattle, through its Cultural Landscape Studio as taught by the author.

WILD is a youth leadership program based in Seattle's Chinatown International District—the hub of Asian American immigration in the Pacific Northwest (Chin 2001). Established in 1997 as a program under the International District Housing Alliance (IDHA), WILD provides high school students in the broader Asian American community in Seattle with opportunities to participate in community-driven projects in the district that promote social and environmental justice.[6] Specifically, the program emphasizes intergenerational interaction as a method of community building in the context of the Chinatown International District where a significant portion of the populations consists of non-English speaking elderly immigrants. During summer and academic terms, the program involves teams of high school students in projects that provide service to the local community.[7] Supported with grants from various public agencies, the program activities included elderly ESL classes taught by the youths at the local community center, bilingual and intergenerational environmental education that take students and residents to state forests and national parks, and pedestrian safety programs with youths walking with elderly residents. Other activities include career exploration and internship placement.

The Department of Landscape Architecture at the University of Washington, Seattle, is an accredited professional program that offers both Bachelor of Landscape Architecture (BLA) and Master of Landscape Architecture (MLA) degrees. The program emphasizes urban ecological design through four specific focal areas of learning and research—sustainable infrastructure, ecological literacy, culturally based placemaking, and human and environmental health.[8] In recent years, the department has actively engaged in community service-learning activities through its design/build program and partnerships with local schools, public agencies, and community organizations.[9] Like many community-focused programs, it has chosen to work frequently with underprivileged populations such as immigrant communities, squatter communities, and indigenous people. The Cultural Landscape Studio, which worked on the project, is the first design studio in the second year of the BLA program. It is also the first studio where students have a chance to participate in community service-learning. In recent years, the studio has worked with native tribes in Washington and immigrant communities as well as communities in Taiwan through distance collaboration (Hou and Kang 2006). Reflecting the general student and professional population in landscape architecture, the students are primarily Caucasian with a limited number of Asian and Latino minorities.

## The Partnership

The collaboration between WILD and the Department of Landscape Architecture at UW has been ongoing since the Fall of 2005 as they worked together to organize an intergenerational design workshop in the Chinatown International District. The workshop was the first time in the district when residents including youths and adults were directly involved in a design exercise to propose improvements in the district. The successful outcomes of the 2005 workshop led to a series of collaborative studios.[10] Through the studios, WILD youths along with graduate and undergraduate landscape architecture students at UW have engaged the broader community in developing proposals for neighborhood improvements to address issues of safety and the underutilization of the existing parks. The Night Market studio was the first full studio that engaged the WILD youths and the UW students in a quarter-long collaborative exercise. This was followed by another studio that focused on the renovation of the Children's Park in the neighborhood and a community open house on the expansion of another neighborhood park.[11]

The collaboration between the two groups of students in these workshops and studios reflects a shift in the model of service-learning programs from that of an expert-client model to that of a collaborative partnership involving multiple stakeholders. Rather than simply providing a technical service to the local community, the studio was equally concerned with the empowerment of the youths and other stakeholders in the community. The bilingual youths, in turn, provided an important cultural bridge between the non-English speaking residents and the students from UW that has been critical to the success of the workshops and studios.

As expected, the new model opened the door to a variety of creative and community-driven opportunities. At the same time, however, the attempt to develop a collaborative relationship across the institutional and sociocultural barriers also unleashed a host of practical and pedagogical challenges that centered on differences among the partners and between the students and the community. Specifically, the major differences include the cultural backgrounds and skill levels among the student partners, perspectives among the students (who live outside the district) and the local residents, and contrasting goals and priorities between the university-based design program and the community-based youth program.

## The Night Market Studio

From selling food and clothing to public performance and entertainment, night markets have been an important part of the bustling urban life in many Asian cities. In Asian communities in North America such as San Francisco and Vancouver and Richmond, BC, community-organized night markets have emerged not only as a popular form of leisure and commercial activity, but also as a vehicle for community building and revitalization (Hou 2007b). In Seattle's Chinatown International District, the idea of creating a night market to attract visitors and revitalize the neighborhood had been a subject of conversation for some time. The idea finally became a reality in Summer 2006, following the before-mentioned community workshops organized by the UW studio and the WILD program in the Fall of 2005. Among the ideas generated during the workshop was to have food vendors as a way to bring people back to the parks. As in real life in Asia where the gathering of vendors soon becomes a market, the discussion later led to the youth-led initiative to create a pilot night market in the district in the following summer.

The pilot night market took place in Hing Hay Park, located in the center of Chinatown, as part of the community's National Night Out event.[12] The event attracted hundreds of residents and visitors who rarely go to the park and brought much excitement and interest in making the night market a regular event in the district. Following the event, WILD and the Landscape Architecture program at UW decided to undertake more extensive collaboration to further develop the Night Market program and activities. In Fall 2006, a collaborative design studio was organized to explore the design and construction of outdoor installations that would help strengthen the identity and functions of the Night Market.[13] The studio involved the WILD youths and UW students in weekly workshops to collectively design the installations. The installations were constructed by the student teams and presented to an audience of community stakeholders and professionals at the end of the school term.

Altogether, six installations were constructed and designed to adapt to different locations throughout the district where future night markets could be held. As functional objects, they support the activities of the market through seating, signage, lighting, etc. In an event that would attract outside visitors as well as different cultural groups within the district, the installations also function as interpretive elements for understanding the diverse cultural heritage and the everyday life of the neighborhood. As artistic and interpretative elements, the installations would expand beyond the predominantly commercial focus of most night markets. Combining both functional and interpretative elements, they would draw users to examine and understand the multiple layers of meaning and cultural significance behind the night market. Finally, the installations would also add to the visual excitement and provide opportunities for social interactions in the public space.

## Studio Challenges: Differences and Adjustments

Prior to the studio, the studio instructor and the WILD program coordinators worked closely together to develop a work plan for the studio to address potential conflicts between the two bodies of students. Nevertheless, as the studio took place, a number of challenges unfolded. First, the difference in skill level and familiarity with design vocabulary between the UW and WILD students resulted in conversation and discussion dominated mostly by UW students.[14] At first, many WILD youths felt frustrated by their inability to participate in the discussion. According to one WILD student, "The difficulty was trying to understand the UW students because sometimes they used big words or it wasn't visual enough." "The difficulties/barriers that I experienced," said another WILD student, "was that at times maybe not all the UW students listened and accepted your ideas willingly." The limited English ability of some of the WILD youths presented additional difficulties. On the other hand, the UW students also felt frustrated for not being able to get feedback from the WILD youths. They expressed difficulties in communicating with the community and with people of different cultural backgrounds and, specifically, the need to avoid using design jargon.

Secondly, it was clear that there were contrasting goals and priorities between the UW program and the WILD youth program. The UW students generally expect to acquire and practice their design skills through studio projects and are more used to a goal-oriented process with clear instructions on deliverables. On the other hand, the focus of the WILD program was on youth leadership development and empowerment. The focus was more on the process, vis-à-vis the design outcomes. The leadership focus thus required the studio to ensure that the youths participate meaningfully in the process and to adjust its goal-oriented culture.

Despite the differences, most UW and WILD students do have one thing in common. When asked to come up with design concepts for the night market installation, most UW students and even many WILD youths chose objects that reflect the stereotypical image and iconography of Asian culture, such as lanterns, parasols, the zodiac, the Great Wall of China, and so forth. There was little initial attention to the everyday life of the immigrant residents in the community. The reaction calls into question the differences between the external image and perception of the community and the everyday reality that takes place inside the community. It also reflects an important gap between the simplified, iconographic symbolism of the community and the deeper, more nuanced understanding of the everyday cultural practices in the community.

In light of the initial challenges, a number of steps were considered through discussion between the studio instructor and the WILD coordinators. First, to find out how the student collaboration could be improved, a separate session was held with the WILD youths so they could speak freely without the intimidating presence of university students. The results were then conveyed in another meeting to the UW students, who had since become more sensitive to the perspectives of the WILD youths. Second, to equalize the different skill levels, both groups were led through a series of brainstorming exercises together that required everyone to contribute either by speaking, writing, or drawing on sticky notes. All the ideas were then presented, discussed, mapped, and reconstructed to form each group's concept. Third, to address the differences and barriers between the two groups, both the UW and WILD students were challenged to learn about the everyday reality of the community through further observations and interviews. But rather than completely discounting the external, stereotypical representation of the community, the students were asked to create designs that addressed the multiple layers of interpretation and understanding.

Finally, producing the actual deliverables within a tight schedule and in the midst of differences presented yet another challenge. To resolve the challenge of having the installations designed and constructed in time, each installation was deliberately divided into structural and interpretative components. The UW students were asked to design and construct the structural component, given their knowledge and skill of construction. The WILD youths were given the responsibility for creating the interpretative component, using their knowledge and access to the community.[15] The ideas and preliminary design for each component were then presented and discussed within the group and in front of the class. This process took several reiterations so that the structural design was informed by the chosen narrative, and vice versa, through negotiation between the student partners.

## Design Outcomes: Night Market Installations

By the end of the ten-week academic quarter, six installations were created, each by a team of WILD and UW students. The installations ranged from seating structures and lighting fixtures to a game booth and an installation that incorporated video projection. As tangible outcomes, these installations

The Giant Lantern is a projection of everyday life in the neighborhood veiled behind the stereotypical icon. *Photo by Jeffrey Hou*

Storytelling parasols are the highlight of the end-of-term presentation by university and community student partners. *Photo by Jeffrey Hou*

represented the results of students overcoming initial barriers to arrive at design solutions that reflect their creative process. Specifically, the designs reflected how the students worked through and incorporated cultural differences in their design.

In the projects *"Giant Lantern"* and *"Parasol Project,"* the teams of students explored the outside perceptions and everyday realities of the community. Built with plastic pipes and layers of red, screen-like fabric, the Giant Lantern is a ten-foot structure in the shape of a Chinese-style lantern. Inside the structure is a video installation created by the WILD youths, showing footage of everyday life in the neighborhood. The octagonal lantern is open on one side to allow market-goers the opportunity to view the video. The flickering images are also visible in an angle through the translucent screen on the other sides of the lantern. The veiled images and the inside-outside metaphor highlight the distances and barriers between the immigrant community (inside) and larger society (outside).

The Parasol Project consists of three large freestanding structures with arms stretched out from which parasols of various sizes were hung. The topside of the parasols, visible from a distance, was painted in red or gold—two commonly found colors in the community. As one approaches the

The Great Seat Wall re-interprets and transforms a cultural icon into a seating space for gathering and interacting.
*Photo by Jeffrey Hou*

installation, the underside of the parasols is revealed, showing rich illustrations that depict the folktales of different Asian cultures, painted by the WILD youths. At the bottom of the structure are large round bases that function as weight and storage, as well as benches for market-goers to sit and view the rich illustrations. Similar to the Giant Lantern, the Parasol Project mixes stereotypical iconography, inside-outside perceptions, and representation and interpretation of the community's history and cultures.

*"Great Seat Wall"* and *"Silk'en Seattle"* are two projects that integrated seating design with interpretative components. The Great Seat Wall is obviously a playful and practical take on the Great Wall of China. However, rather than building a wall that separates people, the structure is a seat wall that provides opportunities for gathering and social interactions at the market. Consisting of modular and interchangeable parts, the installations can be reconfigured to create different seating and gathering arrangements.

Reflecting the festivity of the market, the interpretative component, in a series of panels hung inside the columns, focuses on the stories and history of folk festivals in China.

Silk'en Seattle is a series of three islands/benches that represent the history and experience of migration in the community. Similar to the Great Seat Wall, the configuration of the benches can change and adapt to different locations of the future night market. The adaptability also reflects the constant flux and instability of an immigrant community. The interpretative element features a display box built into each of the benches, containing artifacts representing different stages of the immigration experience. Representing the past and the present, the first box contains mostly copies of old photos, documents, and articles that represent the past history of the community, followed by a second box that contains artifacts from the present, such as flyers, restaurant menus, and photographs of WILD activities. The third bench is built with an opening for market-goers to write in and provide inputs on the future vision of the community.

*"Cycle of Lights"* and *"One Dollar Project"* are two other projects created by the students. Cycle of Lights is a series of twelve lighting fixtures, each corresponding with a Chinese Zodiac sign. Under the lights is a kiosk with corresponding cards that contain quotes and commentaries from local residents and community members born in the year of the corresponding Zodiac. The lights represent, again, the external image of the community, while the cards convey the actual voices of its residents. Finally, One Dollar Project is a game booth design based on the story of the nearby Danny Woo Community Garden. The garden, serving primarily elderly Asian immigrants, was created in the mid-1970s during a period of intense community activism to revitalize the declining neighborhood. Through the generosity of private landowner Danny Woo the property that became the garden was leased to a community organization for one dollar a year (Santos 2002). The game booth functions as an interpretation device for reading the history of the community. It also provides entertainment as market-goers toss beanbags into the miniaturized garden to win prizes. By collecting a dollar from each customer, it also serves as a fundraising booth for the garden.

Through the interpretative elements, the Cycle of Lights and the One Dollar Project, as well as the other installations, expose the market-goers, especially the outside visitors, to the voices and stories of the community. The play on the stereotypical iconography heightens the awareness of cultural barriers and differences, and invites critical interpretation and understanding. The projects were displayed at a final review in the presence of community members and professionals where the teams of WILD and UW students made joint presentations of each project. One project in particular, the Giant Lantern, was installed in the actual night market event in the following summer.[16]

## Learning Outcomes: Cross-Cultural Understanding

As a community service-learning studio, what do the students take away from the experience? How do the cultural and institutional differences contribute to student learning?

In the course evaluation following the studio, many students commented on how much they learned from working with non-designers including the high school students: "This studio allowed learning from many people, i.e., younger students, the shop manager, etc." "It is good to work with non-designers sometimes to keep things in perspective and ask them for opinions (which often vary a lot from ours)," described another student. "They all have a valuable insight and contribution just waiting to be given a chance," commented another UW student, specifically on interacting with the youths. The positive outcome for the group work was confirmed through a similar survey of the WILD students. One WILD student stated, "My favorite aspects were getting to work with older people and giving my ideas." "My favorite aspects of the studio were working with UW students and getting the sense of college life," said another.

Almost all students found the class to be intellectually stimulating. The exposure to the community through interacting with the WILD students and the field trip to the Richmond Night Market left a strong impression on the students. "Travel and exposure to the real-life International District and Richmond, BC was great," commented one student. The WILD students have helped the UW students learn about the complexity of immigrant and ethnic community in the International District. One student stated, "I learned that the [International District] is actually divided into different cultural subgroups." The exposure to the complexity of working with the immigrant community further allowed the UW students to raise questions concerning immigrant community and design process, such as "How do multiple cultures make a new home?" and "How do outside designers help and not hinder?" Designing with unfamiliar cultures posed a particular challenge to the UW students; as one student commented, "It was really hard trying to come up with something that was culturally appropriate without being too culturally specific." The complexity of these questions demonstrates the level of learning that the students have engaged in through the collaborative studio.

## Strategies in Reflection

What specific strategies and approaches have contributed to both the design and learning outcomes of the studio? What are the lessons learned from the studio in terms of working with social, cultural, and institutional differences in community-university partnerships?

In reflection, a series of four basic strategies and steps have played an important role in producing the outcomes of the Night Market studio.[17]

**Recognize.** Before the cultural and institutional differences between the collaborating partners can contribute to positive outcomes, they need to be first recognized, acknowledged, articulated, and examined. The goals, priorities, and cultural and institutional backgrounds of the community-university partners (including students, faculty, community participants, and others) are inherently different. Articulation and understanding of these differences are not only important to reduce conflicts and barriers to successful collaboration, they are also important to the learning experience of the different partners. In the Night Market studio, listening to the frustrations and voices of "the other" was the first step in recognizing the differences. It provided the basis for subsequent adjustments and the development of critical awareness. By learning about the multitude of differences between the collaborators, students understand more about the community they are serving and communicate better with their partners. By learning about the specific differences in organizational goals, priorities, and expectations, the faculty, students, and community organizers can find ways to work together and achieve multiple objectives.

**Negotiate.** As differences are recognized and acknowledged, they must also be actively negotiated. In the Night Market studio, the negotiation of cultural and institutional differences took place through the adjustments to the studio schedule, structure, and modes of collaboration. Furthermore, in the design process itself, negotiation also took place as WILD and UW students worked through their differences and exchanged ideas, understanding, and interpretations. The "divide-and-conquer" approach, with WILD youths in charge of the interpretative elements and UW students in charge of the structural component, allowed the different students to claim ownership of the project but without having complete control over its development and outcomes. As one part cannot be completed without the other, the process reflects the overall mode of collaboration between the community-university partners. The process of negotiation, in turn, facilitated new understanding as WILD youths learned about design and UW students gained insights into the local communities.

**Improvise.** While differences may present barriers to collaboration, as they are recognized and negotiated, the differences and new awareness also provide the tangible materials and sources of inspiration for learning and design. In the Night Market studio, the initial concepts that consisted of stereotypical iconography, for example, became an important vehicle to discuss the differences and barriers between the community and broader society. In addition, rather than subduing the differences and barriers between the two groups of students, their different skills, backgrounds, and levels of community access were applied to enrich the different aspects of the project. For example, the bilingual WILD students made effective use of their knowledge and access to conduct research and outreach in the community. At the same time, the UW students aptly applied their knowledge of design and construction in the making of the actual installations. Improvisation ensures that conflicts and differences become opportunities for learning both inside and outside the classrooms or studio.

**Transform.** Transformation is one of the important outcomes of community service-learning. The literature has suggested that experience can be transformative as students experience different perspectives and understanding. The outcome of the Night Market studio further shows that just as the studio experience can be transformative for those who are involved, the cultural and institutional differences can also be transformed and instrumentalized in the process. For example, by critically incorporating cultural iconography into the design of the installations, the meanings and significance of the preexisting differences were transformed. Here, the differences are not just barriers but also cues for critical reflections and learning. This unexpected transformation represents the outcome of active negotiation between the studio partners and the recognition and improvisation of their differences. It represents the power and opportunity of collaborative partnerships and the possibility of change in cultural perspectives and understanding.

## Collaborative Differences and Design Pedagogy

In community-university partnerships, the differences between cultures, organizational goals, and priorities are an important reality to be confronted, negotiated, and harnessed. As Prins (2005, 57) argues, "Tensions and conflicts are inherent in community-university partnerships, yet they can also lead to learning and growing." What this chapter attempts to illustrate is the process and outcomes of a service-learning design studio involving direct and extensive collaboration among university students and community partners—an approach distinct from the expert-client model of community service-learning. Furthermore, it reflects on the specific pedagogical and design strategies that can help harness the differences to produce positive outcomes. In the Night Market studio, the strategies of "recognize, negotiate, improvise, and transform" have allowed the students, faculty, and community partners to navigate the complex terrain of social, cultural, and institutional differences. They offer possible ways through which cultural and institutional differences can be actively incorporated into the collaborative process, rather than something to be simply subdued or overcome.

Boundaries are a reality of institutionalized settings as well as a diverse and multicultural society. While the erasure of institutional boundaries can be desirable and necessary to facilitate effective collaboration in the context of community-university partnerships, the underlying differences among different institutional partners in the community design process should not be overlooked or simply overcome without critical reflection. In fact, this study shows that acknowledging and working with the differences can result in a highly productive and culturally rewarding learning and design experience that addresses the complexity and diversity in the contemporary society. Furthermore, as community design is often criticized for producing unexciting and common denominator design, engaging the complex, social and cultural differences can also bring much needed depth, rigor, and richness to the practice and outcomes of community-based design.

## CHAPTER 4

# Educating for Multicultural Learning

*Revelations from the East St. Louis Design Studio*

*Laura Lawson, Lisa B. Spanierman,*
*V. Paul Poteat, and Amanda M. Beer*

## Introduction

**C**ommunity-engaged design studios are often praised for linking the resources of a university and the skills of a design department with the concrete needs of a community.[1] When this work engages students with organizations serving low-income communities of color, it is generally considered a win-win solution because it potentially provides a strategic use of university resources to underserved communities and a multicultural context for student learning. At the same time, there can be uncomfortable associations with "do gooder" charity or with expert, outsider-imposed solutions. Such critics are suspicious of the motives in bringing design students—quite often white and middle-class—to work in low-income communities, especially when the benefit to the community is unclear (Reardon 1998; Thompson 1992).

In response to such criticism, there are opportunities to acknowledge the racial, ethnic, and class differences between community residents and students and to integrate multicultural education with design instruction. Multicultural education—emerging from the civil rights movement of the 1960s—reveals the diversity of experience and tradition in different cultural groups while also addressing the role of oppression and social power in perpetuating inequitable social relations (O'Grady 2000). For environmental design disciplines, multicultural education enhances a deeper understanding of community diversity and how inequalities manifest in communities and cities (Reardon 1994).

With over twenty years of experience in community-engaged teaching and research, the East St. Louis Action Research Project (ESLARP) at the University of Illinois at Urbana-Champaign is in a position to evaluate student learning through engagement in a multicultural context. Since 1987 ESLARP has been a conduit for architecture, landscape architecture, and planning students and students from other disciplines to work with community partners from the city of East St. Louis. Once a busy industrial and railroad city, East St. Louis today has high unemployment and approximately 37 percent of the population live below poverty level (US Census, American Community Survey 2007). Currently, 98 percent of the population is African American.

Students work with residents who have organized to address myriad problems, including environmental degradation due to industrial decline and depopulation, inadequate public services, and lack of economic opportunities. While ESLARP courses have provided important services to community organizations and unique opportunities for students, how students process the experience—both in terms of their academic learning and their personal experience—has varied according to instructors, staff, and community project. While having predominantly white and middle-class students work with low-income African American residents on community concerns suggests opportunities for discussion and learning about race and class, this outcome has been largely assumed but not systematically evaluated.

To better understand multicultural learning through ESLARP, faculty from the Department of Landscape Architecture and the Department of Educational Psychology initiated a research project to study students' personal and professional experiences in the program and their perceptions of race, privilege, and racism.[2] In this chapter, we discuss findings from data collected in the 2005 Landscape Architecture East St. Louis Design Studio, which engaged students with several community groups to develop park and open space designs.

Literature from community-engaged design and multicultural education share many of the same concepts about balanced relationships between parties, communication, and reflection. However the difference lies in how explicit issues of race and class are addressed. In community-engaged design the focus is on the immediate project, while multicultural education includes a broader understanding of race and class, particularly in the context of unequal power. Without conscientious acknowledgment of race, there is a tendency to rely on code words such as "inner city" or "poverty" that provide indirect references to the condition without acknowledging possible racism at play (Kivel 2002). To foster opportunities for students and community to address race and class difference, multicultural learning models examine key structural components—a collaborative structure with the community, preparation for the experience, and opportunities for students to process their thoughts and feelings related to their experiences in the field (King 2004; O'Grady 1998). *Collaboration* refers to the structure of engagement whereby community and students work in partnership and share in decision making about process and outcomes. Instead of structuring engagement as service to a community, multicultural service-learning is based on the premise that community partners have knowledge from which students will benefit and that teaching and learning are reciprocal. *Preparation* for the experience includes didactic training related to constructs such as structural oppression and the formation of stereotypes, as well as reflective exercises to encourage critical thinking and to examine assumptions about self and society. As multicultural psychology scholars have emphasized, awareness of one's self (including one's racial biases and assumptions) is equally important to understanding the sociopolitical realities of other racial groups in the US (Sue and Sue 2008). *Reflection* by students about their own perceptions of self as racial beings is important as they gain awareness of their own assumptions and biases. Advocates stress that students often fail to consider multicultural learning outcomes unless they are explicitly incorporated into the curriculum in concrete ways, such as journal writing, group discussion, role playing, and other exercises that specifically ask students to address feelings and experiences around race, class, and power.

## ESLARP and the East St. Louis Design Studio

The University of Illinois first became involved in East St. Louis in 1987 as a result of a challenge put forward by State Representative Wyvetter Younge, then chairperson for the Illinois House of Representatives Standing Committee on Education Appropriations, to clarify the university's urban service commitment to distressed communities, particularly East St. Louis (Reardon 1998). While this engagement started as technical assistance in the "professional–expert" model, an empowerment model quickly evolved that encouraged participatory action research in close partnership with community organizations. The resulting ESLARP program initially involved the faculty and students from Architecture, Urban and Regional Planning, and Landscape Architecture, but has grown to include many other departments. ESLARP works with community partners—neighborhood groups, nonprofit organizations, local agencies and service providers, and churches—through courses and research as well as outreach weekends that bring in a broader pool of student and faculty volunteers. For over twenty-three years, the project has sustained its commitments to partners by involving classes and extending work over multiple semesters.

For students in the Department of Landscape Architecture, one of the primary means of involvement is the East St. Louis Design Studio, which is offered as one of the Spring studio options. This course engages undergraduate and graduate students in projects identified by community partners and might involve park design, urban design, neighborhood planning, and flood remediation. A version of this studio has been taught for many years.

In 2005 the studio engaged students with three community organizations working on park design projects. The first project involved working with the newly formed Emma Wilson King Foundation to develop a plaza around the historic Jones Park Fountain. The second project was to develop a master plan for Pullman Porter Park, a new community open space proposed by the 41st Street Neighborhood Action Coalition as a way to revitalize a swath of vacant land vulnerable to illegal dumping. The third project continued work with the South End New Development Organization (SENDO), which in a recent neighborhood planning process had

As a first stage of the Jones Park Fountain redesign, students met with residents at the site to discuss some of their initial ideas.

*Photo by Laura Lawson*

identified the 14.2 acre Lincoln Park as the "heart of the community," and wanted some design concepts that addressed concerns about safety, provided recreational opportunities, and conveyed local history.

As typical of studios, the design projects served as the central venue for student learning about community concerns and desires, site conditions, and design opportunities. Students participated in lectures, readings, videos, and class discussions to raise awareness about East St. Louis history, park planning, and multicultural planning. The students and instructor traveled the 175 miles between campus and East St. Louis for three two-day visits. On the initial visit, they participated in a resident-led bus tour to learn about the history and current community development efforts underway in the city. The rest of their time was devoted to conducting fieldwork at their project sites, meeting with residents, attending community meetings, and participating in service projects.

Evaluating the capacity for multicultural learning was a stated goal of the course, and students participated in exercises intended to spark reflection and discussion. Along with the three design projects, a phased conceptual design project was incorporated into the studio as a way to see how the students' ideas changed over the course of engagement. They were asked to voluntarily participate in a short-term longitudinal study of student perspectives. A subsample participated in a focus group discussion designed to provide a more complete description of the students' overall experiences in the studio throughout the semester.

## Evaluation through Design Work

One way to evaluate student learning is through their work products. Over the course of the semester, students worked hard to produce three usable designs for the community partners. The process was somewhat typical of a service-learning studio and involved gathering information from the site and community residents, discussing design ideas, and producing multiple renditions of design work to address community needs. Communication between students and residents was somewhat restricted due to the distance between campus and East St. Louis. In general, student work expressed the struggle between the design ideals they were learning about and the realities of East St. Louis conditions and needs. The resulting work was pragmatic and grounded in satisfying the residents' concerns and meeting site and budgetary concerns. During presentations to the community partners, students heard very positive feedback from residents who appreciated the attempts to understand their concerns and the illustrated design work.

Because the design projects focused primarily on producing good work for the community partners, other assignments were developed to encourage student reflection about cultural assumptions and learning. A theoretical design project was developed to provide markers of pre- and post-visit thinking about what was an appropriate park or open-space system for East St. Louis. "Park/City Vision for East St. Louis" was a four-phased exercise that responded to student experience over the course of the semester. Phase One occurred in the first two weeks of class and required students to develop a park system for a "new community" that, unbeknownst to the students, was set in the location of East St. Louis. No socioeconomic or demographic information about the residents was provided. Students had difficulty designing on a "blank slate" and tended toward traditional solutions—axial plans reminiscent of early twentieth-century city planning or large pastoral park systems. Grand overscaled gestures prevailed, with massive, naturalistic parks proposed as neighborhood parks, grand boulevards throughout the city, and multiple commercial centers to serve as civic nodes.

In Phase Two, still before the first visit to East St. Louis, students were told that their proposals were intended for East St. Louis, a community that many knew by reputation and a few had visited. They were asked to analyze the physical and social context based on data they could collect from printed and Internet sources prior to their first visit.[3] Using inventory and analysis techniques familiar to them from previous courses, most students were adept at acquiring and mapping census data, land use, environmental hazards, and locations of public services such as schools, libraries, and parks. From this inventory, they began to differentiate areas in the city in terms of hazards, opportunities, and constraints. Most students considered local assets to be the parks, the river, and the existing downtown, with liabilities being vacant land, highways, and industrial areas. In Phase Three they used this new knowledge to revise their initial park system designs to incorporate lessons from their analysis. These three phases occurred before the first trip to East St. Louis as a way to reveal prior thinking about park and city ideals, assumptions based on data collected, and how designers might frame solutions based on these sources of information.

The work produced prior to the first visit tended to fall into two categories, best described by one of the project reviewers as "tear it down and start over" and "tweak the edges and avoid the pitfalls." In the first case, students could see few opportunities to build on the existing poor conditions and proposed designs that would require razing and rebuilding large sections of the city. When asked what this would mean to the displaced residents, the students often reflected that with current conditions so bad,

why would someone want to live there, or they abstractly suggested reloca-
tion without acknowledging economic and social constraints to such efforts.
No students identified how or who would be responsible and tended to see
it as one grand removal and rebuilding effort. Most students would have
been introduced to criticisms of urban renewal in their history and social
factors courses, but parallels were not considered. The second tendency to
"tweak the edges" involved miniscule changes within existing conditions,
resulting in insignificant improvements. In these cases, the students seemed
to be paralyzed due to the scale and complexity of issues impacting the
community.

At the end of the semester, after three visits and many conversations with
community partners, students returned to the theoretical park plan exercise
for Phase Four. Given latitude in their final proposals, students developed a
wide range of proposals, many of which reached beyond the traditional scope

Prior to the students' presentation of four design proposals to the
41st St. Neighborhood Action Group, a student and resident talk
together about some of the design intentions. *Photo by Laura Lawson*

of landscape architecture. Design solutions tended to be less heavy-handed in terms of grand design solutions that looked good graphically but involved massive reconstruction. They tended to avoid comprehensive systems and focused more on phased approaches that would build gradually to improve the situation. Acknowledging the catalytic potential of community activism, many projects started from the perspective of small-scale, citizen-driven improvements that would build capacity and lead to bigger projects. Other students conducted independent web-based research on federal incentive programs and foundation grants that might bring investment back to the city. Instead of large parks as solutions, students felt that vacant areas could provide integrated community services, make connections between neighborhoods, provide economic development, and solve local flooding and crime prevention goals.

## Survey of Student Experiences

Student feedback was gathered at three points in the semester: prior to the first visit, immediately after the first visit, and at the end of the semester. The survey instrument was developed by educational psychology researchers and based on a series of established scales that measure racial attitudes, with additional open-ended questions to examine student expectations and professional goals (Spanierman and Heppner 2004).[4]

Survey participation was voluntary and kept confidential from the studio instructor. Fifteen of the sixteen students in the East St. Louis Design Studio participated. All participants, including nine men and six women, self-identified as white.[5] Fourteen were undergraduate students, and one was a graduate student. Student ages ranged from twenty to thirty years, with a median age of 22.4. All had taken at least one multicultural course as part of their undergraduate general education and most had been engaged in past service activities through religious affiliations, schools, or clubs. While specific information about the students' socioeconomic, racial, and ethnic status was not collected, in general, they were from socioeconomically and racially homogenous urban, suburban, and small-town communities in the Midwest.

### *Beginning of Semester: Assumptions and Expectations*

The first step was to gauge student expectations and attitudes coming into the studio. In general, the students had heard about East St. Louis before the class and knew that they would be working in a low-income African American community. When asked why they chose to take this particular studio, responses generally fell into two categories: interest in working in East St. Louis and a belief that it would enhance their professional development. In the first case, some students noted that East St. Louis was close to their hometown or that they wanted to learn more about it. One student wrote, "I have a vested interest in what happens in the St. Louis area, as it affects my family and friends. I also feel as a resident of the St. Louis area, I could not only contribute my knowledge about the area, but learn new things, meet new people, and help better my community." In the second case, students had career goals related to park design and redevelopment or considered the prospect of "a real life project" as an opportunity to develop their skills. Several students specifically stated desires related to working on issues of poverty, such as the goal to "open my eyes to the world and work in a real setting that needs assistance," and "being able to help people that may live in areas of poverty and racial injustice." A number of students expressed a desire to "learn strategies for turning around a misguided/unfortunate community" and "to solve all of East St. Louis' problems."

To uncover preconceptions prior to the first visit, students were asked what they expected to see. Most students had seen images in the media and expected to see closed factories, burnt-out buildings, and vacant lots. One student stated that he expected "a city that is in shambles that has great potential," while another expected to see a city that "has been ravaged by crime, corruption, and social injustice." For several, East St. Louis was notorious for crime. Others had heard about the residents' efforts to improve the community. One student stated that he expected to see "a lot of people whose optimism and spirit belongs to a better urban environment than that in which [they] currently reside." Conversely, another expected to see "a lack of interest by the community."

When asked how they expected the people in East St. Louis to react to their presence, most students thought that some community members would be appreciative and would perceive their work as helpful and receptive. Others responded with apprehension, fearing that their efforts might be met with disdain. For example, one student was afraid of being thought of as "the better than thou White man [who] has triumphantly come to fix their broken city." Another was concerned that they might be stared at, "making it known we're outsiders." Several students mentioned race specifically, noting that they hoped they would not be judged based on their color, and that they would not judge others.

To understand how general assumptions about their professional role might influence their experience, students were asked what considerations had to be addressed when designing a public landscape in a low-income community of color. Responses tended to stay within the realm of generalities:

safety, accessibility, social interaction, and community-based considerations about "sense of community," "respect for community," or "understanding community history and changing negative aspects."

To see if students were aware of racial inequality from a personal perspective, they were asked if they thought they had certain privileges because of their race. Responses reflected a continuum from awareness of privilege to denial and perceptions of "reverse racism." Two-thirds acknowledged some form of privilege and specifically mentioned educational opportunities, treatment in some contexts, and economic advantages. One student noted the success of his parents and grandparents who "elevated their social standing by using opportunities afforded to white people . . . I am a product of that system and benefit from it." Three students felt that they had some advantages but that minority groups also had privileges, specifically mentioning scholarships and educational opportunities. A couple of students responded that they did not feel they had privileges and stated their belief that everyone can be successful.

### First Visit: Experiences in the Field

In the survey that was conducted after the first visit, students expressed strong reactions to what they had seen and experienced. When asked how the first visit to East St. Louis compared to their expectations, over half responded that the city looked bad, citing such things as "burnt, vacant, and boarded-up homes." One student noted that he also saw rebuilt areas and areas that were nicer than he had expected. Several commented on how residents were committed to their community and to improving conditions.

When students were asked if they felt aware of their race in East St. Louis, all responded that they did. Several noted that most people they saw were African American or that people were curious about why they were there. One student said, "I didn't see any White people, and the community was depressed to a point below any that I had experienced." Another remarked that the only other white person in the area was a "White mail carrier." Many students reported that they stood out as white people, felt out of place, wondered if people would be friendly, and noticed how people stared at them.

Students reported experiencing a variety of emotions during their first visit that included pity, disgust, sadness, fear, excitement, happiness, hopefulness, and fatigue. A few noted no particular emotional response. One student stated, "I was feeling sorry for these people. They seem to be nice, decent people and to see some of them in such poverty . . . upset me." Another mentioned, "I felt very happy when talking to people in the community."

A number of students expressed concerns about their physical safety. For example, one participant mentioned, "I felt safe with the group, but when I wandered away for a minute I did feel a little uncomfortable when a group of three young black males approached." Another stated, "I felt scared sometimes, but those feelings were pushed aside by the emotions that came [from] talking with residents about their hopes." One participant linked emotion to race, responding, "I was fine in East St. Louis. Was I supposed to be feeling anything different because I was in this particular city? It's no different than Chicago and being White in a [B]lack area."

In general, students considered the most meaningful part of the experience to be meeting the people and talking about the projects, followed by seeing the sites that they were to design. They liked talking with community partners who tended to be very friendly, encouraging, and committed to community improvements. As one student noted, listening to the residents "provided more insight than just a map and statistics could." Even though some students were daunted by the complex environmental, social, and economic challenges facing the community, all expressed a strong commitment to addressing residents' needs and desires.

## Ending Perspective: Personal and Professional Reflections

After a challenging semester of design work and feedback, students were asked to reflect on their overall experience. Many mentioned that they better understood the complexity of problems faced by residents: "I knew from the news that the area was not in the best physical and social condition. I realize now that a lot of people don't want it to be like that but it is very hard for them to make a difference." Some students, however, reflected ambivalent attitudes and wondered how their work actually served the community. For instance, one student explained that her involvement made her proud to be of assistance while at the same time she felt discouraged about "attitudes of the residents" that would prevent community betterment.

The time spent in East St. Louis increased students' awareness of race, particularly their own awareness of being white. Several students observed how they had been the minority there: "With people out looking at us because we were the minority, we looked as though we were out of place." Some students noted that even though they stood out they felt welcome, but others felt the opposite: "I found out that racism is a bigger issue than I had expected. When we visited a couple of different neighborhoods, the residents felt as if we were in their territory." Their heightened sense of their own race did not necessarily influence student perceptions and attitudes about African Americans and racism. When asked whether the studio experience reinforced or dispelled stereotypes toward African Americans, students expressed complicated responses that indicated possible subtle changes or none at all. At one end of the spectrum a student wrote, "I feel like many residents in East St. Louis are content with the living conditions because they lack the want or motivation for change." At the other end, a student said, "It was surprising to meet individuals who were so dedicated to the future of their community." Some students expressed complex responses that revealed ongoing negative stereotypes as well as new perspectives resulting from their interactions. One student stated, "Stereotypes seem to be reinforced based on the people we met. Some people were very ignorant while others were helpful, hopeful, and understanding, welcoming us."

Most students did not feel their views on racism had changed as a result of the experience. Several responses stressed that they consider and treat all people as equals: "I was raised to treat people with respect and fairly no matter who they are." Two students commented on their perceptions of "reverse racism," and one wrote, "I feel less racist but am more aware of racism toward Caucasians."

At the end of the course, students were asked if they felt their professional education and design goals had been met. In general, all students felt that they had learned more about the profession, particularly related to park design, working with clients, social issues, and technical skills. One student explained how the experience had changed his approach to design, noting that he wanted to design for people, not to promote his own career.

## Multicultural Learning, Race, and Professional Training Beyond Design

We have structured our interpretation of the student surveys mentioned above in four categories: multicultural learning as professional rather than personal; minimal reflection on race and racism; limitations of the course and ESLARP structure; and reframing reflection beyond design.

### Multicultural Learning as Professional rather than Personal

Our analysis of student feedback and design work suggests that multicultural learning did occur as part of this design studio. However, it tended to be framed as professional training rather than self-reflection about race and racism. One of the most predominant findings is that students expressed a sense of professional responsibility to serve diverse groups and address community concerns. Many chose to take the studio because they believed the applied experience—the opportunity to work with a real client on real needs—would provide important professional training. Many felt it was their professional responsibility to improve environmental, economic, and social conditions for a diverse public.

Our survey results and changes in the design work reveal that the experience changed the students' approach to design. For most students, their understanding of the role of parks and open space expanded from aesthetic and recreational programming considerations to addressing broader community and environmental needs. Initially, students fell back on one-dimensional design responses that often included traditional approaches and complete reconstructions, with little attention to how such solutions might distress the existing community or how they would be achieved given the city's fiscal constraints. By the end of the semester, many of the students' proposals built on existing resources and community activism, addressed multiple community problems and desires, and proposed phased implementation strategies in response to resident concerns about feasibility. Students also grappled with ways to bring in external resources to address the bigger problems of hazardous waste, failing infrastructure, and lack of economic and educational opportunities. Most students realized the need to expand their knowledge of community history and existing conditions. In this way, they shifted their design process to respond to a different cultural context.

## Minimal Personal Reflection on Race and Racism

While appreciating the professional relevance of the studio, students failed to reflect on the ways in which race and racism informed their experience. Our analysis found that the students maintained subtle racist attitudes, such as continued negative racial stereotyping and paternalistic attitudes. In accordance with modern racism theory, many students denounced past acts of discrimination that had led to existing conditions but did not reflect on the pervasiveness of ongoing obstacles or their own reactions to racial-related experiences (McConahay 1986). This finding resonates with literature on white racial identity that understands racial identity as developmental, multidimensional, and dynamic (Spanierman and Sobel 2010). A developmental perspective acknowledges that students may be at different levels of awareness about their own racial identities and attitudes regarding other racial groups, and that development toward increased critical consciousness tends to occur through dissonance-inducing experiences.

The literature suggests that student responses might be understood as one or more of the following: silent racism, racial color-blindness, and active or selective nonengagement. *Silent racism* is unintentional negative stereotyping and paternalistic attitudes of well-meaning white people (Trepagnier

2006). Consistent with the multicultural service-learning literature on white students entering communities of color, participants tended to rely on stereotypes of African Americans to guide their experience and unconsciously perpetuated paternalism toward the people with whom they worked (Burnett et al. 2004; Novek 2000; O'Grady 1998). Another compelling framework is color-blind racial ideology—the belief that race does not and should not matter (Bonilla-Silva 2001; Neville et al. 2000). Students rarely acknowledged that race and racism had anything to do with the ongoing poor environmental or economic conditions of the city and demonstrated little awareness of societal racism. Many expressed the conviction that equal opportunity exists in the US, regardless of race, acted as if their whiteness was irrelevant, and blamed the victims for their circumstances. Race became much more personal only when students felt they were being stared at as outsiders or blamed for the city's condition, and this discomfort was sometimes perceived as racism against whites.

The third interpretation—*active nonengagement*—refers to students who use victim-blaming and negative stereotyping because they are not yet ready for or cannot deal with the incoming information (O'Grady 1998). Students may not have been prepared—intellectually or emotionally—to acknowledge the racial difference between the designers/professionals and the community and how this might influence interactions. While students may have read materials, examined statistics, and listened to lectures about the environmental and social problems associated with a low-income community of color, it remained outside their personal experience until the first visit. Prior knowledge that the city's population was 98 percent African American remained an abstract statistic until students were walking around neighborhoods and felt they stood out because they were white.

Rather than being actively nonengaged, O'Grady (1998) asserts that many will be *selectively engaged*. For example, they may confront the racist attitudes of others while avoiding their own white privilege. Students in the design studio viewed themselves as professionals commissioned to address a community need—pro bono work in the expert-outside-professional mold—rather than as collaborators. This fostered a paternalistic approach, showing that the relationship between student and community members can be defined in a variety of ways, ranging from charitable service to professional pro bono assistance to true partnership.

## Limitations of the Course and ESLARP Structure

Some explanation for these results can be found in the very structure of the design studio that focuses on design solutions and is not part of a larger multicultural learning curriculum. The focus on professionally useful knowledge and skills may have overshadowed opportunities for personal reflection about individual experience, the racialization of poverty, and other issues. The obvious need to improve local conditions, the enthusiasm of the community partners, and the short time frame were forces that kept students focused on design solutions rather than on larger societal issues that might have felt too big or abstract to tackle. Many students approached their work as problem solvers. They faced pressure to produce useful professional design work for the community partners. They did not question why East St. Louis became predominantly African American and poor or why hazardous sites still existed even though local activists had been trying for years to garner state and federal support for cleanup. Instead, encouraged by local activism and community pride, the students provided optimistic future visions that reflected what the residents wanted to hear, and were not necessarily equipped to judge their feasibility or the structural issues standing in their way.

An unexpected finding of our study is that students may not get the full meaning of their involvement because they are but one part of ESLARP's larger mission. The models set forth in multicultural education literature—assuring equal partnerships between students and community, shared decision making, and mutual learning—are central concepts to the ESLARP program as a whole and form the basis for the continuing work of faculty and staff. However, in order to make the most of semester-long courses, students may only see part of the overall effort. While faculty and staff work with community partners to define projects and outcomes, the students come in after many of these decisions have been made and therefore do not learn from the process. ESLARP serves as an advocate for East St. Louis and actively promotes the positive efforts of community partners, possibly downplaying discussions about stereotypes and structural oppression. Results from this and ongoing studies, however, have already been influential in changing individual courses and ESLARP practice, in general.

## Reflection beyond Design

The best resource for personal reflection among students ended up being our research, including open-ended reflection and focus group discussions. Several students commented at the end of the class that responding to questions about their experiences helped them focus on the issues. Focus group participants stated that they would have liked more opportunities to discuss racial issues; perhaps they felt more comfortable in these discussions with trained facilitators without the presence of their instructor.

Incorporating other forms of reflection—journals, discussion, role playing, etc.—may encourage more explicit discussion of race and poverty issues. Pre-service preparation could include discussion of how stereotypes occur and increase students' understanding of structural oppression. Throughout the experience, opportunities are needed for group discussion and reflection regarding how students are responding emotionally to what they see; further, this discussion should link their reactions to broader societal issues.

The design instructor may not be the best person to facilitate reflection. The relationship between design instructor and student, the general lack of training in multicultural education amongst studio instructors, and the studio's prioritization of design products are all reasons to question how multicultural education can be integrated in a community-engaged design studio. Interdisciplinary collaboration may be one solution. Another would be to incorporate critical self-reflection as part of ESLARP's outreach activities, facilitated by experts in racial attitudes among white students, outside the studio course. Finally, community members can be engaged to address issues of race and inequality as part of their discussions with students.

This study confirms the need for multiple forms of reflection but also the need to augment the studio experience with discussions about race, ethnicity, and class in the context of environmental history, design theory, and professional practice. Within design pedagogy there are opportunities to discuss cultural diversity, the structural factors that perpetuate inequality and racism, and personal and professional responses. Faculty and students can join in discussions on how the design and planning professions perpetuate or challenge injustice in the built environment (See Harris 2004).

This experience reveals potential conflicts between multicultural learning and the discipline-informed experience. The assumption that "real world" projects train students professionally while also enhancing their cultural competency has proven to be ungrounded. Professional, or discipline-based learning, tends to dominate student reflections. If multicultural learning is truly intended to be a learning outcome, it needs to be addressed explicitly through attention to how students contextualize knowledge, awareness, and skills—before, during, and after their experience.

## CHAPTER 5

# People and Place

## Communication and Community Development

*Keith Bartholomew and Mira Locher*

**The built environment** affects our everyday actions and our understanding of cultural values, social relations, institutions, and the distribution of power (Dutton and Mann 1996). The stories we tell about our everyday lives incorporate these concepts, yet few people in our culture are aware of the general principles of architecture and planning that underlie the design of our communities. While the lack of design literacy within the general population is perhaps understandable, the failure of many architects and planners to "hear" design-related information in peoples' stories and to effectively link design issues to community values leads to a number of urban dysfunctions, including socioeconomic segregation and the disintegration of cultural, commercial, and public spaces.

This seeming inability of architects and planners to learn from everyday stories should not be surprising, given that the skills that could foster storytelling and story-listening as part of professional practice are rarely included in the academic curricula of architecture and planning. To understand the disconnections and to cultivate ways of overcoming them, we developed a yearlong curriculum for entry-level architecture and urban planning students entitled *People & Place*. The course seeks to explore professional and societal values about the built environment in the context of community development service-learning projects. Through the use of narrative and laddering techniques, students explore how societal values can be translated and incorporated into planning and architectural designs, and how they can communicate the values inherent in those designs back to a broad range of community-based audiences. The first two years of using these techniques suggests that this strategy may be effective in closing some of the divides between the professions and the communities they are intended to serve.

## A History of Divisions

The disconnection of architecture and planning from each other and from society stems from a long history beginning in the seventeenth century when the first academic course in architecture was established, separating academic learning from practice. Industrialization spurred the split of planning from its parentage of landscape architecture, civil engineering, and architecture around the turn of the twentieth century. The 1930s saw an internal division in planning with the separation of physical and policy planning, leading to the development of a modernist predisposition toward procedures over outcomes (Throgmorton 1996).

The splits within the professions paralleled a split in the academy. In planning, theories and methods once part of traditional architectural training were cordoned off in distinct academic departments that, not infrequently, were housed in non-architectural academic units. Despite a more recent shift toward co-locating planning with architecture, planning programs tend to remain distinct and isolated from architectural programs.

While the professional and academic splits are regrettable, more alarming is the division of both profession and academy from the broader community. The value systems steeped in the history of the architectural profession have tended to serve the elite (Sutton 2001). Though its public health-inspired beginnings were more altruistic, planning, too, suffers from a similar patriarchal past. The continued use of theories and language that reinforce the role of the professions as privileged "clubs" make them even less accessible and understandable to the general public (Wheaton and Wheaton 1972).

## What Values Matter?

What are the values to which planning and architecture aspire, both in professional and academic spheres? Although planning's diversity has made the clear definition of a set of values problematic, general themes include: (1) betterment of the conditions for human settlements to meet the needs of the inhabitants; (2) identification of and engagement with linkages between large- and small-scale physical, economic, environmental, and social systems; (3) anticipation of future challenges and opportunities; (4) concern for public well-being and the equitable distribution of resources; (5) desire for effective public participation; and (6) interactive transmission of information between academy, profession, and community (Strategic Marketing Committee 1997). The standard curriculum in most university planning programs is not at odds with these themes. Using the University of Utah as an example, we see concentration on understanding the history and operation of urban systems, the environmental and societal impacts of policy, the provision of basic human and community services, and the information and decision processes necessary to achieve results that optimally respond to anticipated future conditions (College of Architecture & Planning 2008b).

Along the same line, the American Institute of Architects' list of value-based themes important to architecture include: (1) sustainable, healthy, livable communities; (2) incentives for affordable housing, green buildings, historic preservation, and brownfield renewal; (3) energy and water conservation; and (4) better, safer schools and civic spaces (American Institute of Architects n.d.). Again using the University of Utah's curriculum as an example, we can infer that most university architecture curricula incorporate these themes, offering courses that deal with architecture's connections to environmental/resource conservation and sustainability; cultural, environmental, and urban issues; the social and cultural constructs of the built environment; and design and the communication of design ideas (College of Architecture & Planning 2008a).

What are the values that are important to the broader community, and do they connect with the values of the planning and architecture professions and the academy? Although the answer to these questions will vary widely depending on environmental, social, and political conditions, researchers preparing for a regional planning process in the Salt Lake City region determined that the values most important to Utahans were self-esteem, family love, peace of mind, personal security, freedom, personal enjoyment, self-satisfaction, and accomplishment (Wirthlin Worldwide 1997). Citizens of central Florida expressed essentially the same values as part of a similar regional planning effort there (Harris Interactive 2005). These values, connected to a series of community attributes, indicate a significant divergence in the way citizens talk about values in the community and the ways in which professionals talk about values in architecture and planning.

## Objectives and Methods of People & Place

We created the People & Place course to begin the process of understanding the professional and academic values of architecture and planning, the values important to broader communities, and the possible methods of connecting these two "value fields." The introductory course facilitates exploration of these issues early in professional education with the hope that lessons learned in the class can frame subsequent explorations in theory and method.

The course revolves around a series of community development projects that the students work together on in small groups over a six-month period. The students begin the projects in mid-October, after they have had seven weeks of introductory work and study on topics including experiencing and understanding the built environment (and recording and communicating these observations through annotated architectural sketching), the history of urban design, methods of site inventory and analysis, placemaking, and the roles of values and narrative in architecture and planning. This introductory work is meant to give the students a general understanding of important issues and specific tools and skills that will enable them to "see" the study site in multiple ways.

The students work on the community development projects through mid-March, during which time they learn laddering and narrative interview methods, research design and practice, and presentation techniques. Readings and lectures during this period are focused on issues related to civic and urban spaces, with a particular emphasis on societal values and how those values are implicated by architectural and urban planning practice. These topics are meant to build on the students' initial learning and understanding of the study site by providing additional tools and methods for researching, recording, and communicating issues and ideas; a deeper understanding of the role of values in the built environment; and varied viewpoints on the design and role of urban space.

In mid-March the students present their research and work products in class, with models, drawings, and slide presentations. The next four weeks are devoted to learning how to translate and communicate the findings and values expressed in the projects for a broader audience in an exhibition format, and to understanding the projects within a broader regional urban and landscape context. The course culminates with a public exhibition of the students' work in the neighborhood the students have been studying.

The project groups are comprised of three or four students each. They are organized to have an equal mix of architecture, planning, and other majors (which have included environmental studies, international studies, history, political science, and bioengineering), and a balance of gender and culture/ethnicity. From essays the students write mid-Fall term, their specific interests often are apparent and are taken into account in the organization of the groups. All groups work in the same neighborhood, but each group is assigned a different research topic. During the first two years of the class, topics included affordable housing, civic space, community engagement, economic development, "greenfrastructure" (open space), historic preservation, neighborhood planning, small business development, social services, and transportation.

Each group is paired with a mentor—a local professional architect, planner, community organizer, landscape architect, or designer who has been selected for his or her specific professional knowledge and interest in the study area. The mentors and students meet weekly to discuss the students' ideas, progress, and trajectories as they identify a specific problem within their assigned topic. The groups meet with stakeholders and eventually choose a community organization or government agency as their client for the project. The students choose the client organizations based on how the organizations' goals fit with the students' project goals and the opportunities available through the partnership, such as association with an established community network, availability of a site (open land or existing building), access to nonprofit status, or assistance in getting funding. Client organizations have included the regional transit authority (for a pedestrian and bicycle network study and a light rail station naming project), the local city council (for a small area plan to guide future development), a homeless shelter (for a community garden), the city visitors bureau (for a walking tour of historic railroad sights), the city redevelopment agency (for a community park/greenway space and a shared parking development), a neighborhood elementary school (for a sidewalk and street-lighting improvement project), and a nonprofit city arts organization (for a community culture graffiti wall project).

Depending on the immediacy of the project's anticipated implementation, the students meet with their client organizations as often as twice a month or as infrequently as two or three times during the project. The students arrange meetings at the clients' offices or during previously arranged gatherings such as scheduled city council meetings. The students are counseled in preparation for all their meetings (with mentors and clients), organizing questions and agendas (when needed) and practicing interview and presentation techniques in advance.

Although each group is tasked with finding a solution to a problem discovered within their particular study topic, the overall objective linking the projects is the students' understanding and utilization of various means of communication to elicit and express societal values. As such, the community development projects generally fit into a problem-based learning structure. Based on Barrows and Tamblyn's (1980) research of medical students' learning processes, problem-based learning (PBL) has been shown to be an effective method for the development of problem-solving and lifelong learning skills in a number of disciplines (Savin-Baden and Major 2004). PBL is centered on three principles: (1) organization around problems rather than disciplines; (2) learning in small groups with both tutorial instruction and active learning; and (3) emphasis on the development of the skills and motivation that lead students to become lifelong learners (Walton and Matthews 1989).

Following these principles, the People & Place community development projects are designed to increase the students' social and political awareness, creativity, critical thinking and analytical skills, self-reflection and self-analysis, and ability to work in and lead groups.

> As future practitioners it is intended that students would be enabled to become questioning and critical practitioners—practitioners who would not only evaluate themselves and their peers effectively, but would also be able to analyze the shortcomings of policy and practice… Problem-based learning of this sort enables students to develop a critical position from which to interpret the practice of others, to (re)develop their own critical perspectives and thence to critique them. *(Savin-Baden and Major 2004, 44)*

To support the multidisciplinary approach, self-directed learning methods, and multivalent strategies inherent in PBL and in our community development exercises, the People & Place classroom curriculum incorporates readings from multiple perspectives, disciplines, and theories, including environmental history, landscape and urban design, law, art history, music theory, literature, political science, and sociology. We challenge students to explore the values represented in each discipline and ask them to identify ways in which their group projects might connect with those values. To record their observations, students write papers and maintain journals and sketchbooks. The sketch/journal exercises, readings, and class discussions build on the students' understanding of history, theory, research, and problem-solving methods while providing them with tangible skills to elicit value-laden information and ideas from community partners, and to communicate those values and information in multiple formats.

Student learning outcomes are evaluated in four specific ways during the two semesters. First, students are required to complete fourteen sketch/journal exercises during the year. These are reviewed by the instructors four times, at the midpoint and end of each semester. Written reflection on the completed exercise is part of each sketch/journal assignment. This allows instructors to judge what the students have learned from the exercise, student interest in the assignment, and the assignment's overall value (assignments are fine-tuned or replaced each year to better meet the goals of the course).

Second, the students prepare three project progress presentations as well as the final presentation in class. These presentations are slide-based, although other media also may be used. After each presentation there is a period of questions and discussion with the entire class. During this discussion, levels of student involvement and overall understanding of project issues become apparent.

The third method used to evaluate learning outcomes is the final public exhibition of the student projects. Since the information in the exhibition should describe the project completely, students must summarize the project, concisely convey the important points, and effectively communicate the results. The exhibition allows the instructors to evaluate how well the students understood the project processes and outcomes and how effectively they "tell the story" of and communicate the values inherent in their projects.

The fourth and most important method of evaluating learning outcomes is the reflection papers that the students write four times during the course (at the midpoint and end of each semester). The students are asked to reflect on the work they have completed up to that time; to relate it to class readings, discussions, and exercises; and to present it as a coherent essay. Because the students specifically are requested to discuss what they have learned and what it means to them, it is easy for the instructors to evaluate the learning outcomes, both in terms of successes and failures.

## Values in the Disciplines: Year One Results

Students in the first year of People & Place (2006-07) used their sketch/journal assignments as a means to point out various physical attributes of and problems with the built environment, initially addressing common problems such as cracks in sidewalks and poor signage, and attributes such as street trees and benches. In response to specific assignments, the students began to dig deeper into their understanding of the neighborhood, discovering issues of scale, materiality, and accessibility that either add to or detract from the ease and comfort with which people inhabit the neighborhood. In a series of facilitated focus group discussions midway through the year, the students indicated that social and environmental sustainability are important values to reflect in the built environment. They also voiced strong approval for respecting and protecting design and land use diversity. Another common theme was the issue of comfort in the design of buildings and urban spaces. They perceived a general disconnection between the values they understood as important to community members and those of policy makers. They also saw gaps in the level of understanding most citizens have in how values are (or are not) represented in built structures and civic space.

In a mid-project survey, the project clients mirrored some of these same perceptions, signifying only moderate confidence in the ability of architecture and urban planning to incorporate values they felt were important. The four (out of eight) clients who completed the survey indicated that the promotion of ethnic culture, a sense of history, social and economic inclusivity, and "a feeling of community" were important values that should be reflected in the built environment. They felt, however, that these values are "somewhat" to "not very well" reflected in the built environment. They felt the same way about the incorporation of those values in the current practices of architecture and planning.

These responses tend to validate the gap observed previously between the value statements of the architecture and planning professions (e.g., "engaging linkages between physical, economic, environmental, and social systems") and those articulated by members of the broader community, such as those involved in regional planning research mentioned above (e.g., "self-esteem," "family love," "peace of mind"). Interestingly, the People & Place students used neither the quasi-scientific terms of the professions nor the emotion-based values of citizens, focusing instead on community-based attributes (e.g., "cracks in sidewalks," "poor signage," "street trees").

While these three language positions—professional, community, student—seem disconnected, they are not necessarily incongruent. It seems plausible to have a planning initiative constructed to "engage system linkages," focusing on "sidewalks and signage," and resulting in an increased "sense of community." The gap, it seems, is not one of conflicting values per se, but is based more fundamentally in communication and language. Only after the profession, academy, and community are utilizing rhetoric that is understood and validated across boundaries can those boundaries be bridged and issues of value congruity be intelligibly engaged.

To take this step, in the second year of People & Place, we incorporated storytelling and story-listening both as strategies for communication and as methods of analysis. We chose these narrative techniques because they are ubiquitous in planning and architecture processes, although the stories are not always told with words. Still, we felt that the students were familiar with the formats and would be comfortable using them in a variety of contexts. To give the students a second tool to elicit values, one that would both complement and contrast the narrative analysis techniques, we also incorporated an interview method known as *laddering,* which uses a specific method of questioning to move from prosaic attributes to higher order values.

## Telling Stories and Expressing Values

Most public decisions are motivated or informed by a story line (Stone 2002). Because of their influence in defining the physical form of communities, the processes and products of planning and design are particularly underlain and influenced by stories. Narratives provide structure for understanding how the world operates. In the case of planning and architecture, the narratives are enacted and future oriented. Their validity is determined by their coherence—whether the story deals with the issues presented— and their fidelity—whether the story conforms to the audience's sense of truthfulness and reliability (Throgmorton 1996). The persuasiveness of a story, though, is framed by the degree to which the story resonates with the audience's values (Sandercock 2003).

However, stories are not merely metaphorical; they also are reflective of personal perception and understanding, both of which are framed by values (Beauregard 2003). The emotional elements of stories usually reveal the beliefs of authors and audiences by indicating what is important and what is not (Nussbaum 1990). This is why story-listening is just as important as storytelling. Architects and planners must learn to elicit, listen to, and properly evaluate individuals' and communities' stories, as these stories "reflect their tellers' ongoing search for value, for what matters, for what is relevant, significant" (Forester 1999, 57).

Professional storytelling is usually like academic storytelling: dry and emotionless (Finnegan 1998). "Emotion has been rigorously purged, as if there were no such things as joy, tranquility, anger, resentment, fear, hope, memory and forgetting at stake in these analyses" (Sandercock 2003, 197). This lack of emotion bolsters the myth of professional objectivity and technical expertise, both of which increase the divide with the community.

To help close that gap and to address qualitative and emotion-based types of knowledge, narrative methods have been incorporated into some professional education curricula, including design. Danko, Meneely, and Portillo (2006) report on an experimental use of narrative techniques in an interior design studio, where students used storytelling and story-listening at three distinct points in the design process (programming, concept development, and client presentation). After completion of the studio, students reported that the use of narrative methods heightened their sense of empathy for users of their designs, enhanced their degree of multisensory perception and visualization, and increased their level of holistic thinking (Danko, Meneely, and Portillo 2006, 19).

In a similar fashion, we challenged the People & Place students to incorporate both story-listening and storytelling into their project development and final products. After introducing the concepts to the students through readings on narrative process and rhetorical construction, the students were tasked with conducting interviews with community members that have a stake in the students' project, the study neighborhood, or both, and to identify narrative elements and embedded values contained in the interview responses. The students then attempted to use this input to inform their project work. The objective was to create products that reflect the stories and values from the interviews and to craft public exhibit pieces that effectively communicate those values back to the community.

In the first year of using narrative approaches students were moderately successful in accomplishing these tasks. The leading example comes from that year's transportation group, which focused on government decision-making processes for the alignment of a new light rail line. The group used information derived from their interviews to craft a set of user archetypes for the new line: e.g., a resident of a nearby city coming in on commuter rail and needing to transfer to the new light rail line to get to the airport to fly out of town; a teenage resident of the low-income neighborhood to the west of the study area wanting to use light rail to get to the high school within the study area; an employee of one of the manufacturers located near the airport who uses light rail to commute from a neighborhood south of the study area. The narrative nature of these archetypes allowed the students, community clients, and political decision makers with whom they worked to play through the advantages and disadvantages of the different alignment choices in a qualitative fashion that facilitated greater recognition of the values inherent in the decision. In their exhibit installation, the students used these archetypes, integrated with more traditional quantitative data, to demonstrate the alignment options and to invite exhibit audience members to engage their own stories.

Another example comes from the greenfrastructure group, which worked on the development of a community garden at a homeless shelter. The group recorded their interviews with various persons involved with the shelter—residents, case workers, neighboring business owners—and edited the pieces to create an audio collage of stories they played through

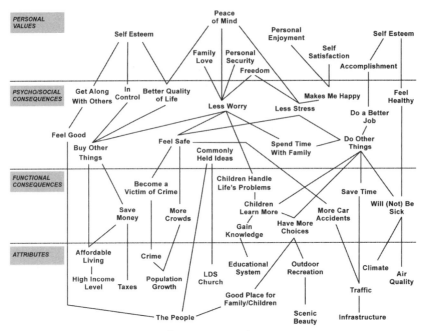

Figure 1. Hierarchical values map from a regional planning process in Salt Lake City, Utah. *Illustration by Wirthlin Worldwide 1997*

headphones that were integrated into their exhibit. In a number of stories, shelter residents shared values that they associated with the idea of having a community garden:

**Resident #1**: I think it's an excellent idea and also even the older people. Because I've heard many older people say things that they had a garden all of their lives and then in their later years they had to live out of a paper sack. Meaning that they had to go to the grocery store for everything. So, they would also be interested.

**Resident #2:** I think it'd be a great idea. I think a lot of people could use it here. It really gives you a sense of responsibility. It gives you a sense of taking care of yourself. You don't have to worry and depend on other people so much. When you get it growing and you're going to eat it and you sit down and eat it and you say "Look, I did this; man, this is great." You know what's in it. You don't have worry about what kind[s] of chemicals were put in it. You get a good feeling inside when you're eating your own stuff.

**Resident #3:** I like watching things grow. Digging into the soil and watching it, nurturing it, growing it. And knowing that I grew it, and it was a great feeling of accomplishment of what I could do. I wasn't such a numskull, dummy. I was ok, I could do it.

## Laddering

In addition to narrative approaches, we identified a marketing-based interview technique called *laddering* as potentially useful for eliciting community values and making connections between those values and planning and design processes. Derived from means-end theory, the laddering technique is founded on an understanding that consumers do not make purchase decisions based just on the observable attributes of a product but on the higher-order values consumers associate with that product (Olsen and Reynolds 2001). This is true, in part, because consumers are not selecting a product per se when they make a purchase decision but are choosing a set of consequences that the attributes of the product help to effect (Peter and Olsen 1999). The attributes, which in isolation are irrelevant, become meaningful when they are associated with consequences through behaviors pursued by the consumer to achieve some goal or desired outcome. These goals or outcomes are themselves frequently associated with higher-order values (Olsen and Reynolds 2001).

Though laddering originated in marketing (Howard and Warren 2001), it has been adapted for a number of regional planning initiatives, including the two regional initiatives referenced above, in Salt Lake City and central Florida. In the Salt Lake City example, researchers interviewed eighty-three individuals in 1997 to elicit opinions about community attributes and tie those attributes to physical and emotional consequences and, ultimately, to basic values (Wirthlin Worldwide 1997). Following the typical laddering questioning sequence, the first questions asked respondents their opinions on attributes related to community economic and social health and the challenges and opportunities related to growth and the future. Respondents then were asked to specify functional and emotional consequences connected to those attributes. Finally, they were asked to articulate the basic values associated with those consequences. The key values respondents indicated—self-esteem, family love, peace of mind, personal security, freedom, personal enjoyment, self-satisfaction, and accomplishment—were connected to community attributes that included cost of living, crime, population growth, education, outdoor recreation and beauty, climate, air quality, and traffic (see Figure 1). Planners used the output of this laddering analysis

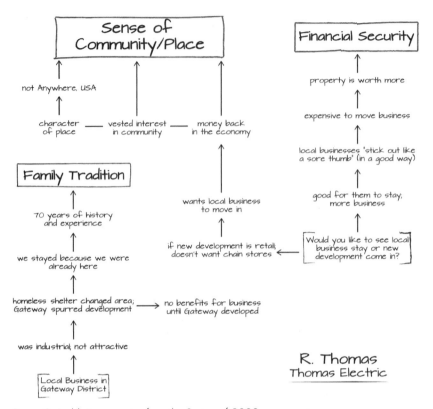

Figure 2. Laddering exercise from the Spring of 2008
People & Place course. *Illustration by Bartholomew/Locher*

to build a regional planning process that has had remarkable success in connecting planning outcomes to community based values (Coalition for Utah's Future 2007).

Having seen its effectiveness demonstrated at a regional planning scale, we adapted laddering to a neighborhood scale for use in the People & Place course. We began by having students read and discuss several leading articles and book chapters on the subject, which provided the basis for a series of mock laddering interviews in class. We then sent them out to conduct three laddering interviews on their own. They started by interviewing a friend or family member. This gave them a practice run with the technique so that they could become more at ease with the process and understand the types of questions that elicit effective responses. For their second exercise, students interviewed their project group mentors. This provided the chance for deeper exploration into substantive themes while still in a comfortable setting. For their final exercise, students interviewed an individual associated with the organizational client for that student's community development project.

After completing the laddering interviews, we gave the students additional direction on how to combine the data from multiple interviews into hierarchical values maps. The students were asked to combine the results of the client interviews from all members of their group and then individually create values maps based on the results. Given that these maps would be drawn from just a handful of interviews, there was no expectation that they would be representative of broader community values or even necessarily the values of the client organization. Nevertheless, it was hoped that the exercise would heighten the students' awareness of how values connect to some of the community attributes being addressed in their projects (Figure 2).

From the laddering and values mapping exercises, students discovered that financial security/economic stability, family tradition, physical comfort, a sense of place/community identity, a peaceful society, and environmental justice were important values for their clients. In reflecting on the laddering interviews, most students remarked that they found the interview process uncomfortable but rewarding. In one student's words:

> It made me examine my values . . . and why we are really doing this. The thought process and resulting values that came out of it are beautiful and encouraging. I was disheartened at first by all of the work involved in these interviews, but I am finding them to be helpful in the broader scheme of things. By hearing other people's values, I examine my own and can then better communicate the strengths of [my group's project].

Some student groups clearly addressed the values from the laddering exercises in the final outcomes of their community development projects. For example, the greenfrastructure group's homeless shelter garden plan would provide opportunities for residents of the shelter to grow some of their own food, thereby increasing their sense of ownership and self-reliance. The connections between the project and these higher-order values were suggested, in part, by the group's laddering interviews, which demonstrated associations between growing one's own food (an attribute), a greater sense of community (a psychosocial consequence), and environmental justice and a more peaceful society (values). These results provided the foundation for the group's installation at the public exhibit.

Although the laddering results were evident in the work of the greenfrastructure group, the influence of laddering in the other projects was not apparent. There are several possible reasons for this. Some students felt the laddering interviews were invasive and uncomfortable and did not complete the interviews in time to fully incorporate the information into their projects. Other students found it difficult to transform the abstract concepts represented by the values information from the interviews into concrete physical responses to the community development problems they were working to resolve. Still others were unable or did not recognize the need to find a method to communicate their value-laden responses to the community development problems back to society in ways that would be easily understood.

From this first trial of laddering, we learned that it is necessary to develop one or more communications-based methods to help students make the leap from the conceptual to the real. One method for accomplishing this leap is *reverse-laddering*. In this process, the values inherent in the students' architecture and planning-based projects are connected back to consequences and attributes through a series of interview questions with the objective of translating the values into attributes that are easily communicated to and recognized by laypeople. The use of reverse-laddering in subsequent years of the People & Place course has shown it to be reasonably effective in achieving these results.

## Conclusions

In the People & Place course, we have observed that while students are generally comfortable interviewing their clients using open-ended methods, they tend to be reticent when asked to use more directive interview techniques. Hence, most students find the narrative analysis methods less stressful than laddering. Nevertheless, student experience shows that laddering's structure enables them to identify more easily the interviewees' values. Both narrative analysis and laddering have been important catalysts for the student groups' incorporation of values into their community development projects. However, most groups have focused on one technique over the other and have shied away from in-depth exploration of either method (presumably because of the perceived time obligation and personal discomfort with the interview processes).

For both the narrative and laddering interviews, we found that the best way to improve the effectiveness of the techniques is through practice and reflection on the process. The more familiar the students are with the methods, the more comfortable they are interviewing their clients and the more successfully they complete the interviews. Effective use of the techniques in reverse to convey the values in the students' projects, however, has been more challenging, as the students have tended to focus on communicating the ideas of the projects rather than the values expressed within the projects. This can be remedied, we propose, with classroom skill sessions on specific methods for communicating values (with both text and graphics) followed by class brainstorming sessions related to effectively elucidating the values in each of the groups' projects.

The results of our research suggest two primary requirements for reconnecting architecture and planning with society. First, professionals and academicians need to learn more about what values are important to the members of the communities they serve. Narrative analysis and laddering technique are examples of two methods to elicit this type of information. Narrative analysis, especially in the form of story-listening, provides a familiar platform that can be applied to architecture and planning in various formats, while laddering utilizes a particular interview method that can be used to focus in on specific kinds of information. Second, similar techniques need to be used in reverse—i.e., storytelling and reverse-laddering—to frame and translate the content of architectural and planning projects into values that are comprehensible and easily conveyed to laypeople. Logically, this would increase the potential for effective communication by reducing the use of elitist jargon. It thereby would increase the potential for effective education regarding the function of design in the making of spaces and communities, while giving voice to those stakeholders who—for reasons of language and politics—have traditionally felt left out of the process.

# PART TWO

# Learning to Reflect and Evaluate

## Editor's Introduction

**The 2008 Erasing** Boundaries Symposium revealed that many design and planning educators evaluate their service-learning experiences by judging how well students developed their professional skills. They consider whether students learned how to assess needs, organize participatory processes, incorporate context in their analysis, develop programs, and make professional presentations. Opportunities to reflect and evaluate are usually limited to brief essays or surveys at the end of a course, or the submission of journal entries. While these approaches may be laudable, they often fail to take advantage of other valuable evaluation methods that can be integrated throughout the whole service-learning experience and evoke deeper reflection that has a lasting impact on the practices of future professionals.

The focus on professional learning alone limits opportunities to critically interrogate more complex issues faced by the professions: relevance to community needs and values, ethical dilemmas, and broader social, economic, and political dynamics. The unilateral focus on professional practice often misses opportunities to fully engage multicultural learning and address difficult questions of racial inequality and social justice. Often faculty themselves are not trained to organize and conduct this kind of analysis and reflection. There must be room for issues of class, race, and multiculturalism alongside design theory, environmental history, and professional practice. This requires expanded and multidisciplinary discourses and dialogues.

Reflection by students, faculty, and community members is a vital aspect of service-learning pedagogy. Of critical importance is how it is organized and coordinated with substantive coursework and how it may utilize new and established evaluation techniques. The chapters in this section invite us to explore approaches to reflection and evaluation and tailor them to learning experiences in design and planning. When reflection becomes a fully integrated component of the educational experience, a set of powerful dynamics are set in motion: academic learning and service experiences are linked, critical thinking is activated, personal development is stimulated, and over time the potential for deeper transformation is expanded. Reflection offers students an opportunity to process thoughts and feelings related to their experiences while helping them to become increasingly aware of their own biases and assumptions.

*Susan C. Harris* and *Clara Irazábal* use reflection and evaluation methods to awaken what they call the "transformation of subjectivity" in their students. Through service-learning experiences they hope to increase their students' capacity as collaborators, doers, coeducators, and socially responsible professionals. They developed a methodology for the evaluation of outcomes by students that contrasts the value of the service component with the value of the learning component. The students themselves analyze the projects to help develop a better understanding of the factors contributing to productive service and learning.

*Michael Rios* aims to increase the social and cultural reflexivity of future professionals. Reflexivity, derived from Paulo Freire's concept of "conscientization," or critical consciousness, is achieved through a mutually reinforcing cycle of dialogue, engagement, and reflection. This cycle of inquiry fosters openness to new possibilities for improving the human condition. In an increasingly plural society, argues Rios, design education and practice stand to benefit by embracing service-learning's central pedagogical goal—self-reflection or greater reflexivity through praxis. With increased reflexivity professionals gain in their capacity to advocate for "others," achieve greater cross-cultural understanding, and uncover new possibilities for improving the human condition through praxis.

In this section, *Peter Butler* and *Susan Erickson* recount how at the Iowa State University, a third party, the PLaCE program coordinator, assumes responsibility for project evaluation and record keeping geared towards understanding how students are assimilating community values and priorities in their projects. This approach enables design and planning faculty to focus on teaching their students about participatory community design, active "listening," and cultural sensitivity alongside the more typical skills related to design, mapping, and analysis. But this model is not without its challenges and limitations; after over seventy projects completed through their PLaCE program, Iowa State is poised to reconsider how evaluation and reflection can be better integrated into their curricula to benefit both academic and community partners. PLaCE program leaders recognize the need to more fully understand the impact that their work is having on the communities they have served. Without such knowledge and understanding, service-learning courses, projects, and research may fall short of meeting the goal of mutually benefiting and supporting both academic and community arenas.

How can we expect faculty to integrate reflection into their courses when they have to keep up with theory and practice in their professional fields and meet their institutions' requirements for publication, administration, and community service? Design and planning educators who embrace service-learning may also find themselves challenged by the time demands of studio-centered curricula. As noted in the contribution by *Laura Lawson et al.* in Part One of this book, faculty at the University of Illinois sought assistance in the reflection and evaluation process from a discipline other than their own—educational psychology—to help them better understand the level of multicultural learning among students.

Even among those who recognize that reflection is essential, there has been little assessment of the long-term impacts of service-learning experiences on students in the design and planning disciplines. The contribution of *Lynne M. Dearborn* helps us understand how the East St. Louis Action Research Project (ESLARP) has impacted its alumni's professional career choices, personal development, and civic responsibility over the long term. This can help us to develop the standards and measures for long-term assessment that are, for the most part, lacking. In her teaching, Dearborn promotes a transactive exchange between students and instructors, students and community, and subject matter and learning environment. This leads to an iterative dialogue that reflects upon the service-learning program, the learning process, and the concrete results.

## Prescriptions for Change: Learning to Reflect

When planning and design educators adopt service-learning pedagogy, they find themselves seeking alternative teaching, learning, and evaluation strategies. They search for ways to gauge their students' learning and development in each particular experience. However, many modes of knowledge delivery, assessment, and evaluation used in design and planning are designed to support professional skill development. Yet service-learning experiences offer learning dimensions unique to a real community context where complex forces—people, processes, structures—interact and dictate what unfolds. What one learns from a community context is directly influenced by the way each experience is mentored and guided. The vital and integrated role that reflection plays in service-learning pedagogy cannot be overestimated.

To be effective in their efforts, design and planning educators need to fully embrace reflective practices and methods for evaluating the impact of service-learning experiences on all parties involved—students, faculty, and community partners. They need to share and develop strategies for reinventing their learning environments (studios and classrooms) and transforming them into vibrant and interactive experiences where social issues, practitioner ethics, and both personal and professional challenges can be reflected upon and understood.

## CHAPTER 6

# Transforming Subjectivities

## *Service that Expands Learning in Urban Planning*

### *Susan C. Harris and Clara Irazábal*

**I n a recent** service-learning course we taught at the University of Southern California (USC), our goal was the "transformation of subjectivity," as students traversed their own paths from students to professionals, learners to doers and coeducators, and from experts to collaborators. Our intent was to minimize the boundaries separating classroom and community. We encouraged students to bridge the gap between disciplines (urban planning, public policy, public management, public administration, and real estate) and sought to help them become collaborative and socially responsible professionals. We also tried to change the role that community partners usually play in service-learning partnerships. Many public agencies and nonprofit organizations welcome the assistance of students but do not see themselves as educators. We entered each partnership with the goal of becoming coeducators with them. Students were also made explicitly responsible for coeducating their peers on the different project areas they were working on, as they needed to give updates to the rest of the class throughout the semester and their grades were partially assigned by their peers.

The transformation of student identities or subjectivities was a central objective of both the service-learning instructors and providers. It was also a major factor in our methodology. We used student evaluations to assess the value of service-learning experiences, and the evaluations were basically a test of whether the transformation we hoped for actually occurred. We used student journals, interviews with community partners, course evaluations, and other course documents to assess this change.

As a result of our experience, we offer practical suggestions to urban planning faculty and others who are interested in developing meaningful, sustainable service-learning partnerships that minimize the boundaries between campus and community, student and professional, learner and educator, expert and collaborator, and academic and practitioner. We suggest a pathway to service-learning experiences that can transform the subjectivities of all those involved.

## Service-Learning at the USC Joint Educational Project

The USC Joint Educational Project (JEP), established in 1972, is housed in the university's College of Letters, Arts and Sciences. JEP partners with instructors who wish to offer their students the opportunity to work in communities for course credit. The organization places an average of 2,300 students each academic year. As a "full service" service-learning center, JEP staff develop and monitor service-learning assignments, design curricula, and evaluate students' service and academic performance.

Historically, JEP has placed most of its service-learning students at public schools in the predominantly Latino and African American working-class neighborhood surrounding the campus in South Los Angeles. More recently, JEP has partnered with nonprofit organizations and government entities to design service-learning projects. In addition to its work with undergraduate courses, JEP supports a small number of graduate students, "Salvatori Community Scholars," whose dissertation work contributes in some way to the public good, connecting them with undergraduate service-learning students who receive course credit for serving as research assistants for the Scholars.

## Integrating Service-Learning and Urban Planning Pedagogy

In the Fall of 2007 and Spring of 2008, JEP partnered with the USC School of Policy, Planning, and Development to develop new service-learning assignments for students in Professor Clara Irazábal's introductory urban planning course. This chapter focuses on the first semester of this experience, Fall 2007. The course had five primary goals: (1) introduce students to urban planning and development and the theories and methods underlying planning processes; (2) introduce substantive subfields of planning (e.g., community planning, transportation, housing, urban design); (3) expand students' analytical, problem solving, and public presentation skills; (4) develop the capacity for reflective and socially responsible practice; and (5) develop research and collaboration skills (Irazábal 2007). Although the instructor had taught this course several times, she had never integrated a community service-learning experience before 2006. Similarly, JEP had limited experience working with courses outside of the College of Letters, Arts and Sciences, or with placing service-learning students at nonprofit organizations or government agencies.

Irazábal and JEP staff identified the following goals for the service-learning assignments:

- Provide introductory students with pre-professional experiences in the same areas of urban planning explored in class;
- Allow students to use the theories and methods learned in class to address real urban planning problems;
- Encourage reflective practice and effective presentation skills by requiring weekly journals and periodic presentations;
- Develop students' capacity for teamwork and collaboration through their interactions with the staff of complex (and, in some cases, multiple) organizations and through their work with peers on group projects;
- Encourage the transformation of subjectivity and identity while developing professional urban planning skills.

With these goals in mind, JEP contacted the staff at a variety of organizations to discuss the possibility of developing a service-learning partnership. Rather than "cold calling" organizations, the instructors drew on existing relationships and contacts at sites that either the professor or JEP staff knew to be receptive to student interns and university partnerships. Ultimately, five new partnerships were established for the Fall 2007 course. These are outlined below.

1. **Community Redevelopment Agency of the City of Los Angeles (CRA/LA).** The CRA/LA is a public agency established to address conditions of blight in Los Angeles. Its mission is to "make strategic investments to create economic opportunity and improve the quality of life for the people who live and work in our neighborhoods" (www.crala.org/). Five students worked with CRA/LA staff on a mapping project of downtown Los Angeles aimed at identifying strategic locations for "greening" public space by adding landscaping, pocket parks, street furniture, bicycle facilities, pedestrian amenities, crosswalks, and other street improvements.

2. **Los Angeles Department of City Planning.** Five students worked on the department's campaign to increase citizen participation. The

students designed a flyer to provide information about the city's General Plan, especially with regard to housing, and to inform the public about upcoming town hall meetings. Students also developed a directory of neighborhood councils.

3. **Association of African American Professionals (AAAP), California Elder Care Initiative.** The AAAP is a nonprofit dedicated to raising awareness about issues of concern to the African American community. Its Elder Care Initiative "aims to make systems more responsive to the needs of older adults in underserved communities, and also helps these seniors make more informed choices about health care, safety issues, financial management, housing options, community involvement, and supporting the educational needs of young children in their care" (www.aaprofessionals.org/, accessed 2007). Five students conducted research on nursing homes and other health services available to low-income, minority senior citizens in Los Angeles County. They also documented various city departments' planning projects related to the elderly.

4. **Inquilinos Unidos (IU).** Inquilinos Unidos (United Tenants) advocates on behalf of tenants to improve housing conditions in Central and South Los Angeles. Four students worked with IU to help them broker a partnership with the Human Relations Commission (HRC) of the City of Los Angeles, which shares the goal of increasing access to affordable housing in Los Angeles.

5. **William C. Velasquez Institute (WCVI).** WCVI is a nonprofit educational and research organization that studies ways to "improv[e] the level of political and economic participation in Latino and other underrepresented communities" (www.wcvi.org/). Four students worked with the Institute to plan the National Latino Congreso, an annual gathering of activists designed to develop policy agendas on a wide variety of issues affecting Latinos nationwide.

In addition to the placements at nonprofits and government agencies, ten students opted to develop urban planning "mini-courses," working in teams of three or four to teach fifth and sixth graders in the Los Angeles Unified School District (LAUSD). Their lessons covered such topics as mapping, land use, transportation, and the environment. Eleven students worked as research assistants for Ferdinand Lewis (JEP's 2007-08 Salvatori Community Scholar), a PhD candidate in the School of Policy, Planning, and Development whose research considered the factors that inhibit or encourage the use of public parks by children. Lewis trained the students in the use of an audit instrument designed to collect field data about safety, pollution, traffic, noise, and other factors that affect children's willingness or ability to play in urban parks.

Each of the service-learning assignments required sixteen hours of service over the course of the semester; the number of hours per week varied significantly by project, although most required two hours on-site every week for eight weeks. JEP asked students to rank the service-learning assignment options they preferred, and made placements based on student preferences, availability of the student and site staff, and student access to transportation for distant sites.

## The Study's Evaluative Methodology

Because this was a new experience for both of us, we wanted to consider as many factors as possible to help evaluate the successes and failures of the course. Our data sources include students' weekly reflective essays, midterm and final oral presentations, final written reports, student course and program evaluations, student grades, and site evaluations (i.e., agency staff evaluations of the students). Forty-four students enrolled in the course and each submitted weekly essays, resulting in over 300 essays. We conducted post-course interviews with site supervisors and a small number of students to get additional feedback about their experiences.

It soon became clear that some of the service-learning assignments were more successful than others in eliciting effective service and learning from the perspective of students and community organizations. We use "service" and "learning" in an expanded sense here, with implications beyond the academic tasks of the course. Rather, we followed an integrative approach to learning and service that includes the students' own characterizations of service and learning success.

One of the students in the class provided us with a useful tool that we adopted to categorize our findings. In her paper she observed that her service-learning assignment—teaching a mini-course to local elementary school students—resulted in what she deemed a "high service/low learning" experience:

> The JEP program places USC students in local K-12 schools to teach 'mini-courses' as one alternative to placements in community agencies or nonprofits. The structure of this program is doomed to produce high-service/low-learning outcomes for the USC students. Regardless of their

enjoyment, and the intrinsic rewards, of their role as mentor, the USC student is still only parroting their own coursework, and at a less sophisticated level of understanding.

For this student, serving the community by teaching children was a personally rewarding experience but one with little educational value. While not all JEP mini-course students agreed with this assessment—indeed, many years of JEP program evaluation data suggest quite the opposite experience for most mini-course students—this particular student's way of examining service and learning as separate components proved to be very useful for analyzing the outcomes of the course. Expanding on the student's framework, we created four logical types to explore the strengths and weaknesses of each service-learning project: (1) high service–high learning, (2) high service–low learning, (3) low service–high learning, and (4) low service–low learning.

After getting a general sense of which service-learning assignments fit into which category, we used an inductive analytical approach to identify the key features of each type. Our impressions of the "high" and "low" learning outcomes associated with a particular assignment depended on how we defined "learning." Similarly, our sense of what constituted a "high" or "low" service project became more complicated when we considered the perspectives of agency staff alongside those of the students.

Since the majority of our data come from student sources, our analyses focus primarily on the impacts and outcomes for students. However, we incorporate the perspectives of our community partners when relevant as well as our own reflections; our objective is to understand how the course transformed the subjectivities of all those involved.

## High Service–High Learning

Our research identified several key elements that contribute to—or detract from—a successful service-learning project and make it more or less likely to transform student subjectivity.

### Clearly-defined, significant projects

While students' experiences varied at each site, three of the service-learning projects for the introductory planning course generally fit the "high service–high learning" profile: the CRA/LA, AAAP Elder Care Initiative, and Urban Parks projects. These three assignments shared several characteristics. First, they involved mutually beneficial service projects with well-defined tasks, producing results of great significance to the student, the site, and beyond.

The day-to-day tasks for these projects tended to be clear, concrete, and proportionate. For instance, *Jay*,[1] a student assigned to CRA/LA, describes his group's project:

> My first week at the Community Redevelopment Agency was very produc-
> tive and insightful . . . Our first order of business was to create a schedule
> of how we wanted to spend our time so that we could accomplish all our
> goals and still have time in the end to prepare for our presentation . . .
> Our task is to: identify places where sidewalks can be extended without
> impacting traffic, identify places where landscaping, art, street furniture
> could go and to identify locations for mid-block paseos.

As *Jay* notes, this group understood the assignment and had a clear schedule for completing each task.

Students also enjoyed doing work that contributed to the "big picture." For example, the team assigned to Ferdinand Lewis's Urban Parks project hoped their research would have a wide-reaching impact. In their final report, the students wrote:

> As a group we were determined to have our results serve a specific
> purpose besides the advancement of Mr. Lewis' degree. Our goal was to
> have our data as well as our analysis of the park situation in Los Angeles
> to be used by the city in future planning. We have already discussed
> amongst each other that we would like to submit all of our findings to the
> City Council as well as to the City's Parks and Recreation department.

The students working for the AAAP's Elder Care Initiative were also able to realize concrete results during the semester. The team produced a comprehensive map of nursing home services in Los Angeles County and at the end of the project, one of the students presented his team's work to an audience of over 200 policy makers. While the student, a junior policy, planning and development (PPD) major, learned a great deal from the experience, his team's efforts also informed the work of many who advocate on behalf of minority elders in the city.

These projects were beneficial for the hosts as well. Ferdinand Lewis (2008) noted the benefits of working with service-learning students:

> First, the [Salvatori Community Scholar] Fellowship has given me a way
> to work out my methods in a "real world" situation that I could not have
> done by myself. Developing the research "instrument" is one of the hardest
> parts of the dissertation, and testing it in the field is a big part of the pro-
> cess. Having a research "team" gave me a way to find out what works,
> and what doesn't, much more efficiently than I could have done alone.

Also, the undergrads brought much more than their commitment and enthusiasm to the table—they also brought alternate perspectives and opinions, which I would not have had on my own. Equally important, though, is the opportunity I've had to train undergraduates in the process of advanced research. There is an aphorism that "teaching a subject is the best way to learn it" . . . Training the undergrads for my project has trained me for this research, more effectively than I could have imagined.

### High level of support from on-site staff

The students in these assignments received a relatively high level of mentoring, supervision, and training from the project staff. The staff viewed their work with service-learning students as an investment in their programs and many saw themselves as coeducators for the students. They took time to meet individually with students, answer their questions, and provide training and guidance. These projects had support at the highest levels of the organization; the department's deputy chief helped design the service-learning project for the CRA/LA, and the executive director of the AAAP served as the students' supervisor.

These professional urban planners were passionate about their work and eager to impart their knowledge and enthusiasm to students. The deputy director who oversees the CRA/LA department in which the service-learning students served described his goals for the project:

One is that we want to create an environment in which there is the opportunity to learn. Two, we wanted to see that there is a way that what they're getting the academic training in can be applied—[a] practical application side to the academic training.

This exceptional group of supervisors taught the students professional skills related to their work as planners and gave them access to experts with these skills. Students at CRA/LA, for example, were introduced to a GIS mapping software program, and Lewis taught his research assistants a variety of data-gathering techniques, including the use of instruments designed to measure the environmental features of public spaces. The students recognized and appreciated the support provided by their site supervisors. *Spencer*, a sophomore PPD major, stated:

Both of [our supervisors] have been very helpful in giving us books and printouts which would be pertinent to our project. Actually, it came as a pleasant surprise that they actually took a lot of time *to help us.*

## Close connection between service and course assignments

A third characteristic of high service–high learning projects was a close alignment between the deliverable for the agency and the research project assigned for the course. We discovered this primarily through our review of student evaluations of other projects that did *not* relate closely to the course. For example, the team assigned to work with the Los Angeles Department of City Planning wrote the following:

> Overall, we were unfortunately unable to obtain primary or secondary research and actually contribute to the revision process. We felt that we were underutilized by our supervisor and her colleagues, and wish we could have contributed a more substantial amount to the organization.

## Transformed subjectivities

These high service-high learning assignments were the most likely to transform the subjectivity of students, encourage them to see the world and themselves as urban planners do, grasp a more comprehensive realization of the challenges and opportunities faced by professionals in the field, and become more informed and sensitized about social responsibility and ethics in the profession. Even as early as the first week of the assignment, some students felt the impact of their experiences. *Paula* describes her first week at the AAAP:

> On my first day . . . we talked about personal goals and the goals the Initiative is trying to achieve . . . I walked away feeling important, professional, and also with the idea that I was finally going to be able to make a difference and have an impact on the lives of other individuals.

At the end of the semester, the same student reflected:

> These past weeks working with the AAAP and their Elder Care Initiative have been an exhausting, however amazing, experience . . . I learned that planning is one of the most important aspects of life . . . it is the basis of organization within cities. I also learned that planning is not an easy job, especially when dealing with a large city like Los Angeles. It requires a lot of research, thought, telephone calls, and driving! Through this program though, I have discovered that this is the job for me. It was a solidifying aspect in my choosing to be a PPD major.

*Carlos*, who worked with Lewis on the Urban Parks research project, described what he learned from his experiences in two journal entries near the end of his eight-week assignment:

Echo Park is a large, beautiful park with so much potential. I attended the park my whole life, however, when I attended the park with Mr. Ferdinand Lewis I was taught to see the park in a completely different light. (Week Seven)

To begin I would like to say I didn't know what my future with a degree in PPD would be. I have enjoyed PPD 227 and all the activities we have participated in so much that I wish to pursue a career in planning and development. When I look at cities I see them differently, as I have gained knowledge about [what] the city planners may have thought before it was constructed. (Week Eight)

## High Service–Low Learning

In these assignments, the service projects were of great help to the agency but generally did not provide the opportunity for students to learn or apply new skills related to the course. Three projects fell into this category—the Department of City Planning, the William C. Velasquez Institute, and the LAUSD mini-courses. The fundamental problem with each assignment—from the students' point of view—was that the work involved mundane or simplistic tasks that were unrelated to course objectives.

Despite the lofty goals of the major projects in which they were involved—e.g., to increase civic participation or to convene a national policy-making forum—the actual work of the students often involved basic, low-skill tasks that are essential to an organization but not reflective of the professional work performed by urban planners. Students spent much of their time finding contact information for individuals, confirming speakers, or entering information into a database. Put simply by one student who worked for the City Planning Department: "All the tasks and errands I did could have been done if I worked at Kinko's rather than City Hall."

Similarly, some of the students placed in the Los Angeles Unified School District complained that their assignments—teaching young children about urban planning—made it difficult to engage with course concepts in a "sophisticated" way. The process of developing lesson plans more closely mirrored the work of teachers than urban planners. This was a source of frustration to some students who had no intention of becoming schoolteachers or professors of urban planning.

At the William C. Velasquez Institute, the initial plan was for the service-learning students to work on the Institute's "Greening of the Los Angeles River" project. However, as one of the lead sponsors of the National Latino

Congreso, the agency needed more help to organize the conference, which occurred midway through the semester. *Lauren*, a junior, describes her assignment at the Velasquez Institute:

> After the orientation and tour we were given a list of officials, CEOs, politicians, and other important figureheads in the Latino community, and we were instructed to call them (or their assistants) and find out if they would be able to speak at the Congreso or if they had to decline the invitation. I was disappointed with the assignment that [I was] given, but at the same time I did not have any expectations . . . Although I understand that what I did on Monday was very important in securing speakers at the Congreso, I hope that as the weeks progress my tasks will be more exciting.

The supervisor at WCVI acknowledged that the project was not ideal for students:

> It probably exactly wasn't what the students were looking for in the end. You know, I know that we did the best that we could. When they first negotiated, I believe they negotiated for river project stuff. So this is slightly different . . . With the nature of how short a time they had per week and then the nature of us in a frantic organizing mode, we couldn't quite give them, you know, a project they could call their own.

The students who benefited most from these assignments made efforts to go above and beyond the initial scope. Unlike his teammates at the Department of City Planning, *Robert* took time to talk with urban planners about their work and learn more about the goals of the project. He wrote:

> Everyday we came out of the office, I felt a sense of accomplishment knowing that, however small our progress was for that day, we were still able to make somewhat of an impact. Going into the experience my ultimate goal was to come out with knowledge of an aspect of the field of urban planning. I feel that I've accomplished this overall goal as I have obtained knowledge regarding not only what [my supervisor] does in regards to city planning, but also an overall knowledge of the goals of city planners and the work that goes into planning a city.

*Robert's* comments contrast with those from *David*, another student at the site:

> I am by no means a negative person, however, the work I did for City Hall really had nothing to do with the planning class that I'm currently enrolled in . . . I really had no premeditated goals going into the semester

therefore I was not upset when I came to find out our job was simply "busy work" in a planning type environment.

These examples show that while the assignment design is important to student learning outcomes, so is the attitude of the individual student. Students who took advantage of the resources and experiences available to them were more likely to have positive learning outcomes, regardless of the scope of the service-learning project itself. These depictions also suggest that "learning," to a large extent, is in the eye of the beholder. Nevertheless, it is very likely that the students would have benefited more had these projects involved consistent, pre-professional experiences that were closely aligned with the goals of the course.

## Low Service–High Learning

Two service-learning projects had "low service–high learning" outcomes for most students. These projects benefited the students personally and academically but provided little apparent service to the organizations. The staff at Inquilinos Unidos, for example, initially tasked the students working with the city's Human Relations Commission to develop a joint effort to improve affordable housing options in Los Angeles. The broader mission of the organization inspired the service-learning assignment: "Our objective in this project is to not only find a way to produce more affordable housing, but more importantly to make affordable housing more equitable," explained one student. "The work we are conducting will help improve the quality of life of these tenants who have been exploited and forced to live in unsanitary conditions," noted another. However, the steps necessary to reach these considerable goals were unclear. As a result, the students initially struggled with the placement since the "service" component lacked direction and structure.

Over the course of the semester, the students settled into a "participant-observer" role, interviewing the staff, observing meetings, and shadowing the work of their supervisors. The agency staff mentored the students, developing enriching experiences for them that deviated from the typical service-learning project. For example, the staff at the HRC and IU took the students on tours of public housing and new multiuse developments and arranged for them to interview tenants and landlords. They spent considerable time meeting with the students and sharing their professional experiences and wisdom. They connected the students to colleagues in other city departments and organizations. These impromptu tours and interviews, and the reports and other materials they gathered, were a rich source of "data" for the research paper assigned for the course. In short, these professional urban planners were an invaluable resource for the students, who used what they learned from their experiences to produce "A"-quality work for the course.

The contributions to the organizations were less tangible, however. Regarding the benefit of the collaborative project for IU, *Evan* concluded:

> As for Inquilinos Unidos and their relationship with the HRC, I feel both organizations would greatly benefit from future collaboration.

Evan cited the value of the experience and suggested that she learned about the resources available in city government regarding public housing. However, she also suggested that the students did not contribute in a meaningful way to IU, which presumably already knew that the "HRC has great resources" and had hoped to establish a collaborative plan of action.

We include the William C. Velasquez Institute in both the low service-high learning and high service-low learning categories. While the students felt that they learned little about urban planning through their service-learning assignment at the WCVI office, actually attending the National Latino Congreso turned out to be a highlight of the semester. Yet the experience at the Congreso was a "bonus" unrelated to their actual service-learning project. We comment on it here to highlight the inherent unpredictability of service-learning and to encourage readers to be on the lookout for such unplanned "teachable moments."

*Lauren* explains:

> At first, I did not think any of the stuff we were doing at the Institute was relevant for the course, but when we actually attended the Congreso we were able to learn a lot . . . We were able to generate a lot of ideas for our final project.

*Araceli* concurred:

> Although I did not learn much through the planning process of the Congreso, I did learn a lot when I got to sit in on some of the workshops for the Congreso . . . Something great we also got out of the Congreso was the many contacts and great people we met through the Congreso.

The ability to attend the Congreso at no cost was a reward for all the "busy work" the students did for the WCVI. The volunteer responsibilities at the Congreso were minimal so they were able to take full advantage of the professional conference. The greatest learning—both personal and academic—for this group of students was only indirectly related to the service provided to the organization. However, service-learning pedagogy is fundamentally about mutually beneficial partnerships, not just positive student outcomes. Indeed, the first "principle of good practice" that has guided the service-learning field for more than two decades states that an effective program "engages people in responsible and challenging actions for the common good" (Honnet and Poulsen 1989).

## Low Service–Low Learning

The fourth type of service-learning project results in few benefits to either the organization or student. Fortunately, none of the assignments in our course had this outcome, but our review of other types allow us to surmise the factors that are likely to characterize "low service–low learning" assignments: (1) poorly-defined projects, (2) little direction or support by site staff, (3) little initiative by students, and (4) unclear connection between service projects and expected learning outcomes.

Notwithstanding the inherent unpredictability of service-learning outcomes, the risks for "low service–low learning" results can be greatly minimized with appropriate pre-course planning and in-course monitoring. Similarly, post-course evaluation can assist in identifying problems in order to make changes that will promote "high service–high learning" experiences in the future.

## The Challenges of "High Service–High Learning" Projects

The goal for service-learning should be to create high service–high learning projects. However, the organizations that clearly benefited from the service provided by students identified several challenges. Many were related to the short-term nature of service-learning assignments, which can be difficult for organizations that do not operate on a semester calendar. It can be taxing for organizations to craft a project that is limited in scope yet meaningful to both the students and the site.

### The "Perfect" Service-Learning Assignment?

The Green Mapping project at CRA/LA was a perfect service-learning assignment from the point of view of the students. They learned valuable new skills as they walked the streets of downtown Los Angeles, identifying potential green spaces and documenting them with cameras and GPS equipment. They received expert mentoring from professional staff and their written product served both the organization and the course. Indeed, this service-learning assignment was the envy of the class—or at least for those students in "high service–low learning" assignments who felt short-changed by their experiences. One student expressed this sentiment in an anonymous course evaluation:

> The big problem was that some class members had the opportunity to work with organizations doing professional planning work, to learn professional skills, and to network with professional planners, while others had to teach fifth graders and do research on education issues, rather than planning issues, per se.

From the point of view of the CRA/LA, managing a service-learning project—even a "high service" project—is a challenging endeavor and requires a significant investment of time and resources. The CRA/LA staff supervisor, who has hosted other service-learning students and who happens to be a former graduate student of the course instructor, commented:

> We've spent a lot of time coming up with a project that would be meaningful to the CRA/LA . . . [and] meaningful to the students . . . It's not especially hard but it's time consuming and so we've spent a lot of time making sure that what they're doing is something that's valuable all the way around.

In the end, the CRA/LA staff contributed nearly as many hours to development and support of the project as they received from the service-learning students.

Another high service–high learning project, at the Association of African American Professionals, also struggled with time management issues. The supervisor worked directly with the students and invested considerable time and energy into ensuring that they had meaningful experiences. She set high standards for herself and extended these to the students with whom she worked; just as she committed far more than a few hours per week to the project, she expected the same from the students.

## Practical Steps for Transforming Subjectivities

We offer a list of questions for urban planning instructors and community partners to consider in order to cocreate truly transformative and mutually beneficial service-learning assignments.

**For the university instructor:** Begin by thinking about the goals for your course and the learning experience that you seek for your students. Consider what the students might learn in a community context that they are unlikely to learn in a classroom.

- What type(s) of service-learning assignment is (are) most likely to help your students achieve the learning objectives of the course? Do these projects lend themselves better to individual or group work?

- Will the service component be required or optional? How much credit will be assigned to the service component? How will the work be assessed?

- What kind of pre-service training or orientation will be provided for the students and who will provide it? What information about the course and project needs to be included in that training? Could the training take place during class time? If not, when and where?

- What special skills are required for the service-learning assignment (e.g., direct contact with a Spanish-speaking population, the opportunity to practice certain technical skills)? Are there any prerequisites for the course?

- How will the students' work at the site benefit the organization?

- What are the short- and long-term goals of the service-learning project for the students?

- How will the instructor facilitate the delivery of research findings and final reports to the community partners after the service-learning projects end?

- What are the mechanisms for keeping track of student work (time sheets, attendance slips, sign-in logs, journal entries, etc.)?

- What are the mechanisms for discussing challenges with community partners?

- How will you incorporate the students' community experiences into classroom activities (e.g., reflection, course assignments)?

- Be sure to leave space to take advantage of teachable moments, as the inherent "messiness" and unpredictability of the pedagogy is often what leads to the most meaningful outcomes for students.

**For the community organization:** Begin by thinking about the work of your organization and break it down into concrete tasks. Understand the skills and time required to accomplish each task. Identify the additional assistance, skills, and knowledge that would benefit your organization and consider how service-learning students (in particular disciplines, such as planning) might help you fill this gap, breaking it down into concrete tasks. How much time does each task take? What skills are required to do the work?

- What type(s) of service-learning assignment would best serve the organization (e.g., direct service, consultation, research)?

- What will the students do, specifically, for the organization? Provide as many details about the project as possible.

- What special skills are required, if any? What kind of pre-service training or orientation will be provided for the students and who will provide it? What information about the organization and/or project needs to be included in that training?

- How many students can the organization adequately manage and in what roles?

- How much on-site training and supervision are the students likely to require? How many hours per week will the staff have to mentor students?

- What will students learn from their service experiences? How does this link to the course goals and requirements?

- What are the intended short- and long-term goals of the service-learning project for the organization?

- How can the service-learning project further the organization's mission?

- How will the organization implement the recommendations, use the research findings, or sustain the service outcomes after the project ends?

- How can the organization build on the project for future service-learning courses (in either the same or a different discipline)?

- What are the mechanisms for keeping track of student work (time sheets, attendance slips, sign-in logs, etc.)?

- What processes are in place for discussing challenges with university partners?

- How else could the organization contribute to the class (e.g., guest lecture, attend or host student class presentations, assist with student/project evaluations)?
- What other kinds of assistance could the organization use to more effectively manage students? Is this assistance available elsewhere at the university or in the community?

## CHAPTER 7

# Operative Sites for Dialogue and Reflection

*The Role of Praxis in Service-Learning*[1]

*Michael Rios*

> Education is an act of love, and thus an act of courage. It cannot fear the analysis of reality or, under pain of revealing itself as a farce, avoid creative discussion.
>
> Integration with one's context . . . results from the capacity to adapt oneself to reality plus critical capacity to make choices and to transform that reality. —*Paulo Freire*

## Introduction

Within the disciplines of architecture and landscape architecture, the service-learning model of education can teach students the civic relevance of practice, facilitate interdisciplinary learning and collective problem solving, foster professional ethics, and introduce diversity issues into experiential learning. University-based assistance helps community groups build local capacity, make key decisions, and identify resources for implementation, and serves as a mechanism for developing agreement and support for locally-driven projects. Also, projects and studies carried out by service-learning activities often include recommendations that can lead to changes in policy and regulation, in addition to physical improvements in neighborhood settings (Rios 2006). However, integrating this activity with self-reflection is often lacking as an explicit pedagogical goal. Moreover, attention is typically given to the development of technical skills and to providing assistance, with little or no emphasis on student reflexivity—the recognition of one's location with respect to others and how this affects the production of knowledge and power.

Reflexivity is a relatively recent innovation in academia. Some see it as a "deconstructive exercise for locating the intersection of author, other, text, and world, and for penetrating the representational exercise itself" (MacBeth 2001). Others see it as a dialogue between the analyst and the intended audience about the various personal values and biases brought to the work by, in this case, the design professional, and how this situatedness can alter or suppress certain points of view (Gergen and Gergen 2000; Behar 1996; Kiesinger 1998). The mutual engagement between practitioner and community is a form of reflexivity that allows participants to move beyond the binary relationship of expert and client. A turn toward reflexivity suggests greater emphasis on process in design education to allow for different and multiple viewpoints to emerge. In the context of learning, knowledge is mutually constituted and the position of the self is best described as dialogical rather than the idea of a core, essential self (Hermans 2001). The dialogical self can be contrasted with the Cartesian self, which is based on a dualistic relationship not only between body and mind, but also between self and other (Hermans and Kempen 1993).

In the following pages, I argue that service-learning is a pedagogy that enables the teaching and learning of reflexivity and, in particular, a greater consciousness of students as citizen designers—as advocates for marginalized groups and facilitators of cross-cultural exchange. In other words, reflexivity in service-learning allows students to draw connections among what is being studied, who is affected, and the larger political implications. This is critically important inasmuch as design education is more often focused on product. Technical and formal considerations are privileged over an understanding and aim toward social change. Today, we live in an increasingly diverse world that will have a significant impact on the social, cultural, and physical landscapes of regions and cities, suburbs and towns. For example, it is projected that non-Hispanic whites will become a minority in the United States by 2050 (Passel and Cohn 2008). How will the design profession respond to this social transformation, and what is the role of educators in preparing students to practice in a multiethnic society? Using Paulo Freire's concept of praxis, the case described in this chapter illustrates the possibilities for service-learning in creating greater social and cultural reflexivity among students as future professionals. The case centers around a semester-long student exchange program involving several Brazilian and US universities, including the University of Brasília, the Federal University of Rio Grande do Sul, the State University of New York College of Environmental Science and Forestry (SUNY ESF), and the Pennsylvania State University.

## Service-Learning as Critical Pedagogy

The contributions of Paulo Freire (1921–1997), a Brazilian educator who worked with the poor, provide a theoretical framework from which to consider service-learning as a pedagogy that enables the teaching and learning of reflexivity central to design education in an increasingly plural society. Freire is considered one of the most important education thinkers of the twentieth century. To Freire (1970), the purpose of education is liberation and the attainment of self-consciousness. As opposed to the "banking" concept of education where knowledge is transferred from teacher to student, Freire proposed a problem-posing concept of education that enables individuals to reveal their own social realities and raise critical questions about their positions in society. Working with poor urban and rural populations throughout Brazil in the 1950s, Freire developed a methodology of informal education that begins with the learner as the subject of knowledge production and learning as a process of discovery that reveals the structural conditions—the object—surrounding the learner. Freire used structured dialogues about social "situations" rather than standardized forms of instruction (such as curricula) to identify ways to improve the lives of the poor. Central to Freire's theory is that one can know only to the extent that one problematizes the realities in which one is immersed.

The dialectic between self and society is critical to the process of learning. However, reflexivity without action is complicity in the social reproduction of inequity. Thus, a second contribution of Freire relevant to the discussion of service-learning concerns praxis. For Freire, the ultimate goal of learning is praxis as the mutually reinforcing relationship between reflection and action to change the world. Praxis "remakes the conditions of informed action and constantly reviews action and the knowledge which informs it" (Carr and Kemmis 1986). From this perspective, self-actualization of one's position in society not only engenders greater reflexivity, but also impels one to change the very same conditions being revealed in particular situations. Moreover, praxis is not to be conceived in the abstract but rather drawn from real-life experiences of participants and the everyday struggles people face in society. As informed action, praxis promotes both individual and collective change.

Praxis—and the reflexivity embodied in it—is one of the strengths of service-learning over other forms of pedagogy. Service-learning is becoming increasingly popular, with increased support to balance applied and theoretical research in the academy (Furco 2001). A review of service-learning in architecture, landscape architecture, and planning programs reveals educational benefits for students, faculty, and communities alike (Forsyth, Lu, and McGirr 2000). However, service-learning is not always recognized and understood by those unfamiliar with its nontraditional education methodologies. As a form of pedagogy, service-learning is derived from a theory of democratic education and schooling developed by John Dewey (1859–1952) in response to aristocratic ideals about western education and society that had persisted into the twentieth century (Harkavy and Benson 1998). Dewey was one of the first theorists to challenge the Platonic view of the universe and society. Plato conceptualized the universe as a perfect and unchanging ideal, and society as an immutable class system of the ruling elite and the masses. For Dewey, knowledge is power that can be used for the good of society. From this perspective, human progress can be measured by the degree to which the larger public participates in and contributes to real-world problem solving and the production of knowledge beneficial to society in general. Dewey never wrote directly about service-learning, but into the twentieth century he championed an intellectual critique of the philosophy and ideals of the "Old Education" in the American school system and advocated a new public education steeped in student engagement and reflection. Dewey advocated for experiential education that focuses on transactive processes between teacher and students involved in hands-on learning. According to Dewey, reflection on the experience and context of problem solving increases the student's capacity for future intelligent thought and action.

As Dewey believed reflection begot action, Paulo Freire (1970, 1973) advocated consciousness that concerns itself with political, social, and economic contradictions and the actions to be taken against human oppression and suffering. Freire's concept of "conscientization" is not only an expansion of Dewey's ideals for humanizing the public and building participatory knowledge into another cultural context, but also a substantiation of education as part of the global process for an organic transformation of society. The Freirean influence on community and participatory education has been to push the debate about education beyond the state's interest in producing a skilled labor force to a global consciousness about radically improving the human condition (Gadotti 1994; Miller 1998; Steiner et al. 2000). Freire's ideas have expanded to include education (Spener 1992; Giroux 1997), health promotion (Wallerstein, Sanchez-Merki, and Dow 1997), and community development (Arnold et al. 1991), among other disciplines. Freirean praxis is also implicit in a number of approaches to community capacity building and citizen participation (McKnight and Kretzmann 1988; Sanoff 2000). For example, McKnight and Kretzmann's "asset-based community development" assumes the existence of latent human capital and that an explicit focus on these assets provides a foundation from which to develop community-based strategies for social change. Moreover, assets provide a resource base that builds on a community's strengths rather than its deficits, its capacities rather than its problems. In design schools, Freirean praxis has been advanced under the rubric of critical education theory, or critical pedagogy (Dutton 1991; Chrysler 1995), which is concerned with

> providing teachers and students with the skills and knowledge to expand their capacities to both question deep-seated assumptions and myths that legitimate the most archaic and disempowering social practices that structure every aspect of society and to take responsibility for intervening in the world. In other words, critical pedagogy forges critique and agency through a language of skepticism and possibility. (Giroux 2006)

Over the past twenty-five years, architectural educators such as Thomas Dutton have been experimenting with transformative forms of critical pedagogy that aim to integrate existing social relations in the design studio through collaborative projects with inner-city Cincinnati neighborhoods. For example, in the Over-the-Rhine neighborhood, students design and build site-specific installations that draw attention to issues of public significance, stimulating dialogue and reorienting consciousness.

With few exceptions, critical pedagogy in design education has focused on the interactions between teachers and students in the studio setting, with little mention of service-learning as an explicit pedagogy that enables greater reflexivity. Moreover, little has been written about immersive community-based service-learning as a purposeful vehicle for social praxis. It is the Freirean model of praxis that drove the pedagogical goals of the Consortium for Sustainable Urbanism.

## Consortium for Sustainable Urbanism

A central goal of the Consortium for Sustainable Urbanism was to instigate greater social and cultural reflexivity among students. The idea for the Consortium began in 2001, when Marta Romero, a professor of architecture at the University of Brasília, was a visiting scholar at the Hamer Center for Community Design at Penn State University. Dr. Romero's main objective was to study university outreach initiatives to identify ways Brazilian universities could begin implementing service-learning into curricula more significantly. As the director of the Hamer Center, I was equally interested in expanding and deepening service-learning experiences offered to Penn State students given the lack of representation and exposure to cultural diversity within the student body. This mutual interest led to conversations with colleagues in architecture and landscape architecture programs at SUNY ESF and the Federal University of Rio Grande do Sul. The collective discussions resulted in the creation of the Consortium for Sustainable Urbanism, a four-year student exchange program at each of the four universities, from 2003 to 2007, that focused on urban poverty and community engagement in Brazilian and US cities. Students were encouraged to engage in hands-on experiences in community settings through curriculum-based projects and independent studies.

At each university, a local community where a series of service-learning experiences could be structured for the students was identified as a partner. Service-learning activities included supportive technical assistance for community and neighborhood planning and design, small-scale construction, and undergraduate thesis projects. Within the instructional setting, activities were organized through a reading seminar and studio-based instruction. The former introduced students to theories of poverty, community empowerment, and urban design. The latter served as a collaborative workshop to focus learning and apply it in community settings.

Given the uniqueness of each academic program at the four respective universities, the seminar and studio were supplemented with additional courses as required by each home institution. Penn State students were required to take a three-credit independent study while participating as exchange students at either the University of Brasília or the Federal University of Rio Grande do Sul. Curriculum exercises were introduced to facilitate observation and reflection. Students were required to make regular entries

Students were encouraged to conduct fieldwork using participatory methodologies. *Photo by a student*

University students, working with *favela* youth from Porto Alegre building a shade structure. *Photo by a student*

into a sketchbook journal, conduct three guided field studies, and submit a bimonthly e-mail progress report. One goal was to help students draw connections between the urban landscape, socioeconomic factors, and the impacts of planning, development, and urban growth. While technical assistance and small construction projects allowed progress to be made toward improving several of the targeted communities, the limited time period for student participation in community settings did not allow for deeper relationships to develop—a prerequisite to developing social capital and building community capacity. However, the modest efforts of Consortium activities did provide individuals a unique learning experience to develop skills and reflect on their roles as future practitioners interested in improving urban conditions.

Exposure to conditions faced by Brazil's urban poor instigated self-awareness about social, class, and material differences from similar communities in the United States. As one student wrote in his journal about Eldorado do Sul, a displaced community outside Porto Alegre:

> Community members have little to no income. Basic shelter takes precedence over new construction when it comes to available materials. And time and energy would be considered better spent doing something that would make money. These constraints were all new to me. I have worked on a budget before, but never without one at all. I have worked with communities with limited resources, but not without any at all.

Drawing from these reflections, students responded to the stated needs of *favela* residents despite the lack of resources. As necessity is the mother of invention, these situations provided an opportunity for practical, but creative responses and specific actions:

> In order to help the problem of security at night [on a dark road], we came up with a system of illumination involving torches, or small lights run on used car batteries. Another group was working on creating a social capital map to locate and record resources that existed within the neighborhood. We were hoping that this map would produce someone with an understanding of electrical systems, and his or her knowledge could be utilized to benefit the community as a whole.

By contrast, other students proposed theoretical interventions that responded to larger structural issues discovered through their reflections about the city itself. One architecture student developed ideas to improve the public spaces of Brasília, Brazil's modernist capital. Recognizing the unrealized potential of infrastructure to provide places for social interaction among Brasília's different populations, she proposed reclaiming portions of Brasília's nonoperational metro stations, known as "ghost stations." From her perspective, the underground stations provided an opportunity to re-integrate fragmented aspects of city life through a variety of uses that could be shared equally by Brasília's upper and lower classes:

> Brasilienise society has become an archipelago of (class-based) enclaves, and the question should not be how to hold back the inevitable transfor-mation into archipelagos, but what possibilities this spatial and social reality offers for the creation of new and interesting forms of the public domain.

This student's experience illustrates aspects of praxis. The decision to focus on the larger issue of uneven development grew out of her situation as an exchange student living in Brasília without a car and her daily obser-vations of spatial segregation and a transportation system skewed toward Brasília's upper and middle classes. Reflecting on these issues compelled the student to identify ways the planned city of Brasília had exacerbated class divisions and to search for solutions to the everyday struggles faced by individuals relegated to second-class citizen status. This instigated a cycli-cal pattern of inquiry between reflection and action, ultimately leading to a reconceptualization of the underground stations as a new public realm that, in addition to improving transit, would provide a setting for different classes of people to socially interact with one another.

Whether focusing on practical solutions in *favela* communities or pro-posing larger interventions at the urban scale, recurring themes evident in the students' work clearly centered on community engagement, citizen partici-pation, and social responsibility—key elements of service-learning. Several student journal entries illustrate this point:

> Prior to class, I had submitted a comment to the studio blog offering my opinion that a sustainable city can never be built without the approval of its people; and in order to reach this approval, sometimes so-called professionals need to listen and learn while at other times they need to educate and convince. Silvana's (a *favela* resident's) experience made me want to add that professionals also need to be meticulous observers of culture, language, use of space, etc., in order to be able to come up with ideas that will be suitable for their city's population(s).
>
>    The neglect that the residents of Vila Jardim receive from their munici-pal government despite the Brazilian law that cities must develop a plan for sustainable, poverty-reducing development is further proof that raising

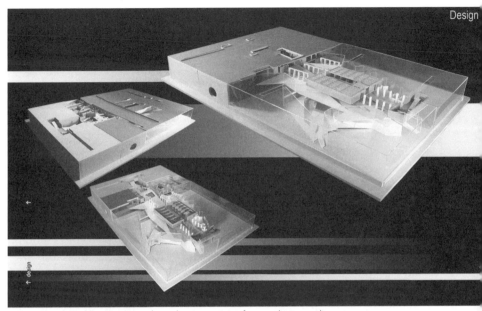

A Penn State student proposes the adaptive reuse of an underground metro station into a public space to be shared by a diversity of social groups living in Brasília (project by Andrea Zalewski). *Photo by Michael Rios*

consciousness among citizens is much more important than creating laws on their behalf since only the will of the people can uphold the law in the first place.

Working in these community settings provided, in Freirean terms, social "situations" that instigated student reflection and created a space to discuss and brainstorm ways to improve the material conditions of Brazil's urban poor.

Facilitating this learning were structured activities such as required journals meant to stimulate critical reflection about personal experiences. Every two weeks students sent reports via e-mail comprised of a "description of place and culture" as well as a "study critique." The latter was intended to focus reflection on students' observations and on the interpretation of specific situations each had experienced. These reports served the purpose of connecting disciplinary understanding, observation, and reflection with larger social and political questions. Central to this exercise was the critical incident technique, a structured approach to writing about incidents and used to reflect upon, monitor, and evaluate one's actions and experiences (Stanton 1995). Each student was asked to write about incidents based on the degree of impact on the student's reasons for engaging in, or being present, at the time.

In addition to the bimonthly reports, students were asked to keep a regularly updated sketchbook and complete a series of field studies to document, in visual terms, the social, cultural, and physical landscape where they were working. Some of the field studies included cognitive maps of how places are perceived experientially, spatial investigations of environmental justice, the material manifestations of power and inequality, and site observations documenting social and cultural patterns of use and behavior.

Together, the journals and the field study exercises helped to structure the students' experience while facilitating personal reflection and engagement with the larger world, an important goal of critical pedagogy espoused by Freire. As important, student reflections also stimulated novel responses to place and site-specific conditions. While limited in scope, the structured exercises and activities helped to connect disciplinary understanding with an awareness of civic and social relevance. This is not to suggest that the

Students present their ideas to local youth in a community workshop in Eldorado do Sul, Brazil. *Photo by Cheryl Doble*

individuals participating in the Consortium were not already inclined to make these connections. Rather, the Consortium provided an opportunity to deepen students' experience of the links connecting learning and engagement, reflection and practice.

## Implications for Service-Learning Pedagogy

In this chapter, I have argued that dialogue and reflection promote a cyclical pattern of inquiry that leads to the formation of new social imaginations of self and other. Praxis in service-learning provides students with knowledge that differs from, but also complements, classroom learning. By explicitly incorporating dialogue and reflection into learning experiences, students become acutely aware of the material conditions of specific places other than their own and gain a deeper understanding of the complex social, political, and economic factors that define community life. Also, the immersive experience of being in a community exposes students to a different world and helps them gain cultural competencies—tools necessary for understanding diverse perspectives and communicating across racial, cultural, and class differences. As future professionals, these skills are crucial to developing an ethics of engagement, especially in an increasingly plural and multiethnic society defined by greater social disparities. As a landscape architecture student who spent a semester in Brazil poignantly states:

> I am taking something home with me that will never fit in a bag. I am packing Brazil. This country has fed and housed me for the last half of this year. It has shown me poverty at levels beyond [anything] I have ever experienced, and a contradicting wealth that exists within well confined and controlled areas. It has shown me the most amazing natural site I have ever seen, where life erupts from the earth in a spectacular display of water-works within a lush green environment. Brazil has shown me large vibrant urban centers, and quiet gaucho countryside. It has shown me white sandy beaches with warm waters, and pine forests that cover mountains that open up to wide valleys with white rivers cutting through. Brazil has shown me richness of culture and pride in history. It has shown me samba. It has shown me a fanatic enthusiasm for *futebol*. Brazil has shown me what Brazilians think of America, and their relationship within the world. Brazil has shown me about popular participation, and political involvement. Brazil has shown me cold windy winter nights, and hot humid summer days. It has shown me how to drink *mate*, and eat *churrasco*. It has shown me how to greet new friends, eat late, and party

even later. It has shown me hope among disparity, and charity among affluence. Brazil has shown me myself.

While student experiences differed in context, duration, and level of community engagement at the respective universities, this case underscores the importance of learning in diverse sociocultural settings and emphasizing learning experiences that focus on dialogue and reflection. Praxis in service-learning offers pedagogical value through this mutually constituting dialectic. Going beyond the classroom and into community settings instigates self-reflexivity. Reflexivity in these settings forces students to confront their own relationships to the production of inequality. Upon further reflection, such awareness can lead to individual and collective action as students or later as practicing professionals.

The case also illustrates the fact that reflexivity can lead to greater understanding of the exchange between different forms of knowledge and power. Praxis in service-learning instigates reflexivity that is at the center of Paulo Friere's concept of "conscientization," or critical consciousness, leading to liberation and the potential for radically improving the human condition. From this perspective, students can consider how their present and future work either reinforces existing social and institutional relations or, by contrast, keeps open the possibility of new political projects. Reinforcing this learning is a design pedagogy that provides a physical and social space for discourse to consider issues of material relations, cultural identity, and empowerment. This space also enables negotiation and the exchange of different forms of knowledge, deepens social understanding between students and community members, and deepens students' understanding of the settings that surround these experiences. In sum, praxis in service-learning provides "operative sites" for students to personally engage the larger world around them and develop the skills necessary to tackle complex problems that they will face in their professional lives.

---

## CHAPTER 8

# Potential and Limits of the PLaCE Program's Design Extension Studio Model

*Peter Butler and Susan Erickson*

**I**ntegrating outreach and engagement in design program curriculum as sustainable practices has grown to be an international directive. Sustainable design depends on collaboration with the public in the design process. From the community's perspective, participation in the process engenders stewardship, longitudinal engagement, and provides stimulation towards action. Faculty members, especially within the realm of land-grant institutions, satisfy a need for service and through engagement may embark on outreach driven research. From the student's viewpoint the relevancy of their role in facilitating design, envisioning place through participatory processes, builds ethical and moral values and confidence. The academic infrastructure to implement and direct such programs is a great challenge to administrators and faculty. This chapter describes an alternative infrastructure model of a design outreach program as established at Iowa State University and takes a critical, reflective look at past experiences with a view towards future improvements.

Iowa State University's Department of Landscape Architecture provides a curriculum that prepares students for landscape architectural practice in a manner that recognizes the role of the designer in relationship to those with whom they work—communities and clients become collaborators. As a result, particular areas of skill development related to community design are integrated into the curriculum. Those skill sets include communication (including "listening"), cultural sensitivity and awareness, interpretation of community input, methods of participatory design, expression of input through design, and understanding of collective processes and critique.

In the department's overall curriculum, participatory community design and related topics are learning objectives of specific second and fifth year courses. In the second year, The Social and Behavioral Landscape course (LA 274) exposes students to specific methodologies, practices, history, and theory related to the collection and analysis of observation and participation in design. A companion studio course, Site Planning and Design I (LA 202), devotes its final four to six weeks to applying principles learned in LA 274 to a community park design project. Later, during the fifth year capstone studio, Community Landscape Design (LA 401), students are challenged to use participatory methods on a more complex community project. While other courses in the curriculum may address topics related to participatory design, they are not predominant learning outcomes.

## Working with PLaCE to Advance Curricular Goals

The department of landscape architecture works with the College of Design's PLaCE program to teach and learn theories and practices at the core of its second and fifth year curriculum. The Partnering Landscape and Community Enhancement program (PLaCE) provides an institutionalized unit within the College of Design (COD) for directly responding to requests for assistance and linking those requests to faculty and their courses. It replaces what had become an informal outreach agenda with a narrow range of projects, and an often unfair distribution of resources and assistance. A lack of information related to community needs had limited the opportunities for advancing new faculty research and outreach activities and supporting curricular teaching and learning goals. Furthermore, a lack of record keeping, chronicling, and evaluating outreach activities meant that the contributions of the COD's activities to advancing knowledge remained largely undocumented, and upper-level university administration remained unaware of the extent or impact of the college's community outreach activities.

The turning point for the COD came in the late 1990s, when then Dean Mark Engelbrecht created the PLaCE program to link the college's resources and curriculum with community assistance. As a program of the college's Institute for Design Research and Outreach (IDRO), and its Extension program for Community and Economic Development, PLaCE seeks to engage with communities throughout Iowa "in collaborative efforts to understand, envision and promote a fundamental enhancement of their physical environment."

By 2000, the PLaCE program was underway but without the staff to administer it, a situation that was remedied in 2001 when Extension stepped in to create and support the position of a part-time program coordinator. PLaCE's first program coordinator brought a background in landscape architecture, multidisciplinary private practice, collaboration, and networking, and set to work with the COD's four departments: Architecture, Art and Design, Community and Regional Planning, and Landscape Architecture.

The PLaCE program continues to grow and currently receives about 120 requests per year, of which ten to twelve typically result in a university outreach project. Between 2002 and 2009, seventy PLaCE projects, distributed geographically throughout the state, were successfully completed. While all four COD departments have contributed to the PLaCE program, the two smallest departments—Community and Regional Planning and Landscape Architecture continue to maintain the highest level of engagement.

PLaCE project types vary according to project availability, course offerings, teaching assignments, and faculty preferences. Typical projects include small town comprehensive plan updates, park designs, therapeutic garden designs, trail plans, wayfinding graphic design plans, storefront redesigns, and cultural district plans.

Financial transactions and transportation arrangements for PLaCE projects are handled with support from the Institute for Design Research and Outreach office (IDRO). PLaCE projects usually generate report and/or poster products for the community partner, copies of which IDRO subsequently archives by geographical location. PLaCE records become a part of Extension's central database, making information related to outreach efforts and outcomes readily accessible to communities, students, and scholars.

## The Coordinator's Role

The PLaCE program relies on the pivotal position of the program coordinator whose initial charge is to respond to incoming requests for assistance and filter them using the following criteria:

- Applicability to academic departments;
- Potential for information gained to benefit other Iowa communities;
- Fit to learning outcomes of specific courses;
- Potential for student and community engagement;
- Potential source of best service.

If the program coordinator finds that PLaCE is not the source of best service to a community request, he or she redirects it to other resources on or off campus. The PLaCE program coordinator assists studio instructors with tasks that are often difficult or cumbersome for faculty focusing on delivering course content. Project recruitment, budget preparation, negotiation of fees, contract writing and execution, and report finalization are handled by the program coordinator who prepares contracts outlining reasonable expectations for both academic and community parties. Such an approach clarifies expectations and helps to avoid disagreements and misunderstanding related to the quality and quantity of deliverables. The program coordinator attends faculty meetings a few times each semester to create and maintain relationships with faculty who are interested in integrating outreach projects with their courses.

## Integrating Academic and Community Goals in the LA 202/PLaCE Project

The LA 202 studio is structured each academic year to integrate a PLaCE project wherein sophomore-level landscape architecture students collect and interpret community members' concerns and observations regarding the design of a community park. As LA 202 is the students' first site design studio, the learning outcomes for the course are primarily introductory in nature. For the LA 202's PLaCE project, "A Park for a Small Town in Iowa," the learning outcomes, developed over time by all course instructors, include the following:

1. **Knowledge and Contemporary Issues:** Focus on public parks, community analysis, site analysis, rural Iowa, play space/connecting to nature, narrative design, and environmental psychology.

2. **Design Process and Drawing:** Focus on conceptual and iterative spatial design, program development, site phenomenology as design media, sectional drawing in design analysis, community engagement in design analysis, regional and local context-sensitive design.

3. **Relevant Overall Course Learning Outcomes:** Understand landscape design as a process that begins with a site problem/opportunity and evolves through a series of visual explorations; explore giving conceptual ideas, experiences, and programs (functions, uses) order, form, and space; articulate relationships between form/space and experience/emotion; develop skills in mapping and analyzing landscapes; understand and use contextual influences on design; consider the complexity of topographic articulation and manipulation; consider the uses of plants in creating space; and develop skills in articulating a landscape narrative and interpreting landscapes.

Participatory design literature informs the specific community design approach taken by LA 202 course instructors. In Henry Sanoff's *Participatory Design: Theory and Techniques*, Frank Wulz devotes a chapter to his multistage framework for critically examining a project's participatory forms (Sanoff 1990). While the LA 202 studio project is not specifically conceived according to Wulz's framework, it unfolds in a parallel manner.

Wulz identifies a cadre of stages or forms of participation including representation, questionary, regionalism, dialogue, alternative, co-decision, and self-decision. Stage One, *representation*, commences at a project's onset. When a PLaCE application is received at the COD, it includes a park program developed by a local park committee tasked to oversee and steward the project during and beyond the LA 202 studio's involvement. The park program identifies practical features, elements, and concerns for students and faculty to consider and account for in the design process. For example, the park committee for Earlville, Iowa, identified a desire for their park to include active and passive recreation, an access road, shelter, restrooms, a twenty-vehicle parking lot, and trails and paths. In representing the community client, the LA 202 studio starts with achieving an understanding of the stated community needs while developing familiarity with characteristic park elements.

Stage Two, *questionary process*, involves the collection of "objective material, observable and statistically comprehensible" (Wulz 1986, 41). LA 202 includes community site visits to inventory and analyze site characteristics and impacting factors. Quantifiable information related to the demographic evolution of Iowa's rural communities are also queried to determine issues germane to specific user groups including elderly, immigrant, and 'bedroom' communities. Helping students who are future design practitioners develop awareness and sensitivity regarding the rural population's unique and complex needs is a core learning dimension and desired outcome of the project.

*Regionalism,* or Stage Three, invites awareness of understanding and engaging the specific geographic and cultural situation of a project. Students read and review literature and information related to the region's identifying geology and landform qualities. They study the patterns and features of settlements, buildings, agriculture, industry, and man-made infrastructure constituting Iowa's cultural landscape over time. The studio relies on site visits to observe and record cultural factors shaping the rural landscape while stressing their value to developing context-sensitive community park designs.

Stage Four, *dialogue,* asks designers to seek knowledge from the source—the people with whom one works. Generally, as in the LA 202 project examples cited (New Virginia, Earlville, Charles City, and Allison), the distance between Iowa State's Ames campus and the selected LA 202/PLaCE community project limits the amount of time spent in the community. A typical site visit includes traveling to the community, convening an evening of community meetings and meals, camping overnight, participating in a morning community meeting and tour, and pairing students and community partners in dialogue sessions. The community-student dialogue sessions include formal and informal interviews and are guided by a set of general questions provided by faculty. The questions seek to gain understanding of specific community habits, behaviors, preferences, and desires. Such questions include: What do people do to play and socialize? What are the community concerns? What are the community's annual and traditional celebrations? Many of the specified questions seek to prompt atypical thinking and surface unvoiced or subconscious qualities unique to the community and region. Students are also encouraged to engage in open-ended conversations to foster greater exchange, relationship building, and dialogue. While the level of exchange during the dialogue sessions is participant-dependent, students indicate an increased sense of intimacy with their community partners and, in some cases, eventful exchanges and stories provide "innovative impulses" for their designs. Often a particular community narrative collected by a student forms the basis of an entire park design concept. Greater dialogue fosters an increased sense of responsibility and accountability by students and community members alike. For sophomore design students, such interaction provides both increased motivation and heightened anxiety related to creating successful, useful, and community-relevant design proposals.

In Stage Five, community participation extends to "*alternative*," "*co-decision*," and "*self-decision*." Stage Five is crucial to a community design process, and difficult to achieve in the duration of an LA 202 studio/PLaCE project. In LA 202, following the dialogue phase, students prepare "alternative" park designs and present them to the community at a final community meeting. Communities typically receive a report with quality illustrations and visualizations of potential projects. After that time, faculty and students disengage and communities are left to complete critical Stage Five steps on their own or with assistance from academic or private sources. As faculty and students move on to new projects and new semesters, the program coordinator is often only able to provide limited follow-up consultation with a community. In follow-up meetings involving the PLaCE program coordinator and community park committee, participants are often able to work together to evaluate "alternative" designs and recommendations and reach a level of "co-decision." In the New Virginia community's PLaCE project, a graduate student continued working with community partners during the co-decision stage. "Self-decision" involves working in a more focused manner with the PLaCE program coordinator, and, ideally, with a graduate or upper-level undergraduate student. A high level of commitment by community stakeholders to steward the project from this point forward is required. If the project has proceeded with limited community leadership and involvement, it is often not likely to advance to the next step.

An unspoken barrier to project continuity and Stage Five realization through academic means involves private sector practitioners. On occasion, practitioners have taken students' conceptual work to the next level of design development through contractual agreements with communities. Channeling work from the studio to practice is an opportunity for mutual benefit. Some in practice see themselves in competition with the university for this work. They argue that academic partners should not take projects beyond the theoretical level and should instead leave them for private firms and practitioners to develop and complete. A potential for the "handing off" of projects post-studio adds another layer of complexity to the academic process.

## Learning from LA 202 and PLaCE

Valuable learning is resulting as the number of PLaCE projects and LA 202 courses integrating them increases. The following discussion draws from survey data as well as the cumulative experience of this paper's coauthors—one being a former LA 202 faculty member and the other being the PLaCE project coordinator. The focus of reflection is the period of 2003-2008 and the experience of LA 202 studios being led by teams of two or three instructors undertaking PLaCE projects with their students in small Iowa towns with populations under 5,000. Locations of PLaCE projects include New Virginia (2003), Earlville (2004), Charles City (2006), and Allison (2008).

### Students and Community Participants

A Post PLaCE Project Survey administered to students and community members, who participated in one of four projects occurring between 2003 and 2008, provides evidence of the PLaCE project's impact on its participants. The Post PLaCE Project Survey was administered to determine success in achieving student outcomes and enhancing their learning experience; success in satisfying community expectations, and how the community has applied what they gained through the process; and how to better the design process to satisfy community and student needs.

The Post PLaCE Project Survey asks each group, student, and community member a specific set of questions.

### Fifth Year Landscape Architecture Student Questions

- Do you remember the community park design project completed in Landscape Architecture 202?
- What do you remember about your interaction with the community?
- Was it a positive experience or a negative experience?
- Did your design for the park reflect the community's needs?
- How could the community's involvement be better integrated into the project?
- Has the community design project influenced how you have approached more recent projects?
- In what way has it influenced more recent projects?

### Community Park Committee and Other Local Citizen Questions

- What were your expectations for the community park design project?
- Did the project meet your expectations?
- What do you remember about your interaction with students?
- Was it a positive experience or a negative experience?
- Do you feel that student designs addressed your community's needs?
- How could the community's engagement with students be improved?
- How has your community proceeded with park development?
- What, if any, influence did the students' involvement have on the park development?

*Student and Community Reflections*

The Post PLaCE Project Surveys completed by fifth year landscape architecture students indicate positive attitudes toward the LA 202 experience and feelings of having acquired knowledge and experience related to public input in the design process, one of LA 202's stated learning outcomes. Many students indicate an awareness of the importance of integrating social context in the design process and of developing sensitivity to community needs and desires. Many express newfound confidence in their abilities as designers, especially in terms of representation, and a desire to seek more integrated approaches to design. In hindsight, students mention other methodologies and approaches to community engagement such as focus groups, community-wide surveys, and working with local children. Their more sophisticated view of the engagement process arose from later exposure in the curriculum, particularly in the capstone community design studio.

Informal follow-up discussions with students after their survey submissions reveal that students don't always understand how different learning outcomes and skill sets continue building through the curriculum. For many students it becomes clear over time that what had been an introduction to participation and community engagement in the LA 202 experience continues in the ensuing years of their landscape architectural courses and studios. With hindsight they are able to make critical observations and suggestions about how to enhance LA 202 projects by inviting participation from a more diverse range of community members such as the youth and elderly, and by administering community-based surveys.

Community members responding to the Post PLaCE Project Survey also regard it as a positive experience. They mention that being provided with "outside the box" solutions assists in stimulating action and change within the community. While they feel that students are indeed able to express community and participant desires, values, and aesthetics through their designs, they also feel that some proposals are overly outlandish and unrealistic. Overall, the blending of more modest, program-driven park proposals with those that challenge expectations result in provoking dialogue, choice, and energy in both the committee and community at large.

## LA 202 Faculty Reflections

LA 202's learning outcomes related to conceptual thinking and exploration through the media of spatial design challenge students to think beyond convention and preconceived notions of how rural public space is designed. In community design projects, these learning outcomes often create conflicts and tensions between academic and community partners. Community expectations are grounded in experience and being a "rural Iowan" equates with being practical, economically sensible, realistic, and efficient. LA 202 students, many of whom come from rural Iowa, share this general profile. The imaginary bubble of design studio provides students with a supportive and exploratory learning setting for most of their second year. For their final six weeks, they are thrust back into a rural community context. Such a tug and pull between "convention" and "creativity" challenges faculty, students, and community members and is further impacted by the project's short duration and its alignment with academic expectations. During preparatory meetings for the Earlville Park, a committee member shared photos and plans for a more "conventional" park shelter with the LA 202 instructor whose goal was to challenge his students to design a "creative" shelter using vernacular forms and materials. The instructor subsequently withheld sharing what the community had already pre-imagined for the park with his students in order to direct them toward unconventional solutions.

Over time the LA 202 studio has incorporated design representation modes including photomontage and image editing, which are helping to elevate student comfort and confidence in representation. To communicate the complex issues informing the park's design, a final report including student-generated information is prepared for the community. This enables community members to "follow along" and gain a better grasp of the student's design proposal. Students are required to adhere to an outline that guides the preparation of their concept statement and accompanying design drawings. Such a process helps students communicate more persuasively both verbally and visually. While "out of the box" design projects may remain obscure, for the most part, their accompanying written and visual components aid in their comprehension.

The studio project limits collaborative efforts with community members because of both the learning outcomes mentioned above and travel and financial constraints. The project is usually a four- to six-week project that again limits collaborative opportunities. Success is achieved when an environment is created in which both students and community members are able to understand more deeply their physical, social, and cultural environments. Community members are able to see their place in the world through a new lens. Generally, individuals may not consider the glacial form of the Paha hill as an inspiration for the design of a public space. If students successfully execute their designs, they may reveal alternative environmental values to participating community members. By the nature of the projects, they do envision and promote enhancement of the community's physical environment. However, the relevance of the envisioned designs to the community may be lacking. The promotion of the concepts within the larger community may also be weakened because of the relative skill levels of the second-year student. Overall, the projects emphasize the genius of place, and the inspired student will inspire the community towards a new potentiality for rural public space. The value of student PLaCE projects may not reside in plans for a new park, but in the students' design process—where value is built into the community and revealed to the audience.

## PLaCE Coordinator's Reflections

From the PLaCE program coordinator's perspective, the key to resolving differing expectations is communication. Communities that request studio outreach projects rarely exit the process with the product they were expecting when they made their preliminary inquiry. As mentioned earlier, the program coordinator screens incoming requests and directs them to appropriate sources of assistance. Requests with the potential to be integrated into a studio as outreach projects proceed to the next step, which involves a phone interview to determine the level of community engagement, the fit with the university academic calendar, the availability of funding, and a frank discussion regarding the community's expectation of project outcomes. Community partners learn from the project coordinator that students are in the midst of their education, and that it would be unrealistic to expect a product comparable to one generated by a professional design office. PLaCE project applicants are informed to expect a wide range of student-generated projects representing varying levels of design ability and promise. They are led to expect design and planning proposals offering stimulating, fresh, and often unexpected strategies and approaches to community development. Finally, it is underscored that LA 202 studio projects result solely in conceptual development schemes and not construction documents.

As the first official studio design course for landscape architecture majors, LA 202 teaches students to generate design products that clearly communicate concepts while being comprehensible to a community audience. A challenge for students is visually and verbally communicating complex and layered relationships to their audience. Many students recall in their Post PLaCE Project Survey that their lack of advanced representational skills led them to feel particularly uncomfortable in presenting to the public.

Over the five-year time span of this study, processes have changed to better serve all parties. Effort has been made to more strongly integrate community members into the process. One example is the community visit. Local stakeholders are asked to find accommodations for the studio class, set up meeting arrangements, and issue invitations to appropriate community members.

The importance of the final presentation to the community cannot be overlooked. Each final presentation takes on its own form, but a big finish to the project is important to students and community partners alike. Students may travel back to the community and present their findings to the community at large, or community partners may travel to the university and attend the presentation of final designs. Having a reason to visit the university is often a rare treat to residents in outlying areas.

## Taking Stock: Future Directions

Continuous attention to program improvement has been an important reason for this program's sustainability. The PLaCE program began with a goal of creating more effective university responses to community requests for assistance, while maximizing the benefits of university assets and resources to students and citizens throughout the state. As service-learning's value to higher education increases, this program is ideally positioned to develop and advance in ways that increase its ability to integrate educational and outreach goals. Tai, Haque, McLellan, and Knight (2006) suggest the following methodology for landscape design projects with a service-learning component: research and analysis; planning and design; implementation and action; and sharing reflection, celebration, evaluation, and recognition. Transitioning to a service-learning model will require refocusing course energy and approaching outreach projects in new ways. Specifically, the components of reflection, evaluation, and recognition have not been systematically developed and integrated into PLaCE projects. Vision for the future of the PLaCE program includes conducting a model studio incorporating a full service-learning methodology and monitoring the results that accrue to students and to the community.

### Toward a Service-Learning Model for the PLaCE Program

Iowa State University's PLaCE program would benefit by making the role of reflection more prominent in its PLaCE projects. Henry Sanoff (2003), one of the great pioneers of community-based design projects, acknowledges the importance of reflection activities. Robert Coles (1993) states that "Our institutions of higher learning might certainly take heed, not only by encouraging students to do such service, but by helping them stop and mull over, through books and discussions, what they have heard and seen." Eyler and Giles (1999) also underscore the importance of structured reflection activities to the service-learning process. Inclusion of reflection activities in studio coursework has been less than optimal and might significantly enhance learning that occurs in community outreach. By administering exit interviews and surveys, the PLaCE program could quantify the effect of outreach projects on student development in the areas of community design and service-learning. Another opportunity to measure effects would be to survey alumni on the impacts of the program on professional development and career choice.

An integrated service-learning curricular approach could provide ongoing engagement, over the course of a four- or five-year accredited landscape architecture program, between academic partners (faculty and students) and community partners in a specific community or region. For example, a small community-based second-year design project could be followed in the third year by a regional design studio addressing the larger community context. A fourth-year construction technology course could focus on designing specific community elements while design/build courses could collaboratively construct, with community assistance, student-generated designs. In the final years, the focus could be on increasingly sophisticated long-term visioning projects, senior level community-based research projects, and interdisciplinary projects collectively involved with problem-based service-learning in the community.

Committing to a service-learning curriculum structure strengthens and reinforces partnering between the community and the academy. Such an approach increases the possibility of making lasting contributions, resulting in building local capacity and bringing forth positive community change. It also strengthens landscape architectural education and practice by promoting professional efforts and practices designed to foster increased environmental and community sustainability.

## Adding Value to Communities

As the PLaCE program matures and grows, program leadership is interested in monitoring the value of outreach studio projects to their partnering communities. The question of community impacts resulting from service-learning has received little attention from researchers. Cruz and Giles (2000) see this as a social justice issue: "There has been no cry from the community to research community impacts. This is a constituency without a voice in academia and therefore has been silent." Brouwer (2002) indicates that the community benefits from outreach projects either directly (as a result of the project) or indirectly, from a greater awareness by students of community needs in general. While this makes sense intuitively, evidence-based study of this concept might yield valuable information about ways to enhance learning and impacts for all parties. Community recipients of PLaCE studio outreach projects indicate that student-produced visualizations aid them in sharing the project vision with others, generating interest, gaining support, and preparing grant submissions. Such community input remains largely anecdotal. Future plans for PLaCE include developing assessment tools for measuring program and project impacts and guiding its ongoing evolution. Other visions for program development include broadening the university constituency to include participation from a wider range of faculty, and working to more fully incorporate all steps of Tai's methodology, with particular attention to the steps of celebration, evaluation, and recognition.

## Conclusion

As a component of the paradigm of sustainable design, community outreach and engagement methods and pedagogy take great steps toward creating a more equitable environment. Putting all the pieces together by supporting faculty in service-focused research initiatives, providing administrative infrastructure to facilitate engagement and community connections, and enhancing, deepening, and enriching the learning opportunities for students, the PLaCE program will continue to be a positive force for Iowa communities. As design is an iterative process, the molding of the program will continue indefinitely, providing more opportunity for reflection and action.

## CHAPTER 9

# Moving from Service-Learning to Professional Practice

*ESLARP's Impact on its Alumni*

Lynne M. Dearborn

> The biggest thing I learned through my ESLARP work that
> has made a difference in the way I work is learning to listen.
> —*Alumnus, architecture undergraduate program*

**S** **ervice-learning in** professional architecture, landscape architecture, and planning programs can be particularly beneficial because studio and workshop courses that already provide experiential education offer important opportunities for formal reflection (Forsyth, Lu, and McGirr 2000, 251). Reflection can itself be instructive and deepen students' understanding of design and planning, particularly with respect to social and community issues. But does this learning last and is it sustained in the practice of the future professionals? Are there beneficial long-term outcomes for alumni who enter professional design and planning practice?

## The Study of ESLARP Alumni

Since 1987, the East St. Louis Action Research Project (ESLARP) at the University of Illinois at Urbana-Champaign (U of I) has provided a program of mutual learning and assistance that has been an important part of the growing neighborhood revitalization movement in East St. Louis and other Illinois communities (www.eslarp.uiuc.edu/). (See Chapter 4 for additional information about ESLARP.)

Over 500 alumni were involved in courses in architecture, landscape architecture, and urban planning that included an ESLARP component during the time period of interest, 1992-2003. However, the faculty and staff within ESLARP knew of outcomes for only a select group of "star" alumni, whose career choices have resulted in leadership roles providing service to distressed communities and underserved populations at both the local and national levels. The choices made by these stars suggest that involvement in service-learning courses has a long-term influence on the choices alumni make and where they choose to practice. However, anecdotes from ESLARP's star alumni offer no concrete understanding of the relationship between ESLARP experiences and the choices alumni make about how and where they will practice their professions (i.e., long-term outcomes). This led to three research questions:

1. What are the long-term outcomes of participation in ESLARP service-learning courses in three areas: personal development, civic responsibility, and professional choices?

2. Does involvement in ESLARP service-learning courses impact the choices that alumni make about how and where they practice within their professions?

3. Can alumni who have become fully involved in work with distressed communities and underserved populations identify particularly pivotal educational processes, projects, and/or experiences that influenced their perspective?

A mixed-methods study was employed to investigate these questions. Because no comprehensive database of ESLARP student participants existed, one had to be created before beginning the study. Class lists were obtained for architecture, landscape architecture, and urban planning classes known to have included ESLARP components between 1992 and 2003. All available lists were used to create a database of students involved in ESLARP service-learning courses. The alumni office provided current contact information. The survey of service-learning outcomes for ESLARP alumni, created for this study, was mailed to 525 individuals.

The survey included eighty questions in the following seven categories:

1. Alumni educational information;

2. Alumni experiences with service-learning when they were students;

3. Current employment and service work of alumni;

4. Skills alumni use and activities they engage in as professionals;

5. Alumni opinions about how society works;

6. Alumni reflections about themselves as members of society and as professionals;

7. Alumni recollections about their ESLARP experiences.

One hundred and thirty-three surveys were completed and returned. These data were analyzed and used to generate a focused interview guide for telephone interviews. Survey respondents were asked to provide contact information if they were interested in taking part in a follow-up telephone interview about their particular experiences with ESLARP. From the list of those willing, thirty interviews were conducted, ten from each discipline. The open-ended telephone interviews lasted between thirty and sixty minutes.

While this is one of the few examinations of student outcomes from service-learning in architecture, landscape architecture, and planning, we note its limitations so that in future studies they may be overcome. The study was limited by a lack of ESLARP-related course documentation. There was no database of ESLARP-related courses or student enrollments before this study was initiated, nor was there any ongoing and integrated evaluation or periodic tracking. Thus, when students graduated or when faculty and staff moved on, no systematic record of ESLARP's history of class and student participation remained. The database included fewer landscape architecture alumni because fewer landscape architecture course rosters were available. Thus, it is not surprising that survey respondents were much more likely to have been enrolled in architecture (46%) and urban planning courses (43%) than in landscape architecture courses (11%).

The lack of documentation also impacted the study, because some of the limited funds received had to be used to generate a database and contact list. The survey could have yielded responses testable with a greater degree of statistical rigor if it had been administered to a control group of alumni who had not taken part in ESLARP-related service-learning courses, as originally intended, but that was not possible as funds had to be used to create a database. Data from a control group could have offered even greater insights into the impacts of ESLARP service-learning experiences.

## Educational Background and Experience with Service-Learning

The 133 survey respondents had earned degrees primarily in the three departments of architecture (50%), landscape architecture (10%), and urban planning (28%). The remaining respondents (12%) had earned degrees from a range of other units across campus, including community health, geography,

| Department | Relevance of Community Service to Coursework | | | |
|---|---|---|---|---|
| | Related (n=117) | Tangential (n=40) | Not Related (n=9) | No Answer (n=19) |
| Architecture (n=80) | 60% | 28% | 5% | 7% |
| Landscape Architecture (n=20) | 55% | 15% | 5% | 25% |
| Urban Planning (n=85) | 68% | 18% | 5% | 9% |
| All ESLARP-based Courses Noted (n=185) | 63% | 22% | 5% | 10% |

Table 1. Relevance of ESLARP-related service to coursework. *Illustration by Lynne M. Dearborn*

and forestry. The respondents who had earned degrees in architecture, landscape architecture, and urban planning had received both undergraduate (61%) and graduate degrees (39%).

Study respondents had broad exposure to community service as a course requirement both through ESLARP-based service-learning and through other courses. Sixty-two percent had taken at least one ESLARP-based course while 38 percent had taken two to five courses. Thirty percent had taken courses with non-ESLARP-based community service as a course requirement; nearly all (95%) of these courses were in architecture, landscape architecture, and urban planning. Thirty-eight percent of respondents participated in community service that was not part of required university coursework.

After respondents were invited to give specifics about their ESLARP-based service-learning courses, they were asked to reflect on the relationship between the service component of their class and coursework (see Table 1). These were categorized by respondents as *related* (for example, a studio where the major design project involved a community partner as client); *tangential* (related in topic but perhaps not the major focus of the coursework); or *not related* (community service which had nothing in common with coursework). Eighty-five percent of all respondents indicated that the community service performed was either directly or tangentially related to the major topic of the course.

## Current Employment, Service Work, and Skills and Activities as Professionals

Typical of what might be expected of alumni from programs in architecture, landscape architecture, and urban planning, a majority of respondents

| Characteristic | Better than Most People | Much Better than Most People |
|---|---|---|
| Respecting the view of others | 55% | 21% |
| Thinking critically | 46% | 33% |
| Communicating my ideas to others | 43% | 18% |
| Ability to compromise | 42% | 20% |
| Listening skills | 40% | 28% |
| Moral or ethical judgment | 43% | 25% |
| Thinking about the future | 42% | 31% |
| Tolerant of people who are different from me | 48% | 29% |
| Effective in accomplishing goals | 51% | 25% |
| Ability to see the consequences of actions | 50% | 27% |
| Empathetic to all points of view | 45% | 19% |
| Ability to work with others | 53% | 30% |
| Knowing where to find information | 42% | 30% |
| Knowing who to contact to get things done | 44% | 20% |
| Ability to lead a group | 44% | 23% |

Table 2. Respondents' comparison of themselves with others. *Illustration by Lynne M. Dearborn*

(63%) were employed in traditional design firms and planning departments. An additional 16 percent held positions in engineering, firm management, construction-management, and in community development, areas peripheral to but supportive of the design and planning professions. The remaining 21 percent were employed in fields such as information technology, human relations, and health care. When respondents' employment was classified by sector, the striking difference between individuals with design majors and planning majors became clear. Planners were mainly employed in government-related work (61% of planners, as compared to 29% of landscape architects and 14% of architects). However, architects and landscape architects are primarily employed in the private sector (71% of architects and 63% of landscape architects, as compared to 18% of planners). Some respondents worked in the nonprofit sector (6% of architects, 4% of planners) and a few respondents were educators (4% of architects, 4% of planners). This is not necessarily surprising, but should be borne in mind when considering the remaining study findings.

Respondents were asked to provide their perceptions of themselves in comparison with "most other people" for twenty-two characteristics that might impact their professional conduct: for example, communicating their ideas to others, listening to others, and speaking in public. The results generally suggest that respondents believe they make decisions ethically, communicate well, think critically, and work well with others. Table 2 provides a more complete representation of their thinking, illustrating results for the fifteen characteristics where at least 60 percent of respondents rated themselves better than most or much better than most. These responses and those that follow in this section provide a snapshot of respondents' evaluations of themselves regarding their strengths as professionals and as volunteers. While the survey's introduction noted that its goal was to understand how the ESLARP experience had influenced former participants, the part of the survey discussed here did not specifically ask respondents if they felt that their strengths were related to their ESLARP experience. Nonetheless, the next part of this chapter, based on follow-up interviews, illustrates possible linkages between these assessments of strengths and ESLARP experiences.

There were no statistically significant differences in the opinions expressed by those with design degrees in architecture and landscape architecture; however, significant differences were evident between those with planning and design degrees. Respondents whose major was planning ranked themselves higher on the scale, as compared to individuals with design degrees, when considering their ability to speak in public, knowing who to contact to get things done, and engaging in public service to change public policy. Also, respondents who took two or more ELSARP service-learning courses, regardless of their degree, ranked themselves much higher in their ability to speak in public than those who had taken only one course.

When asked about their current participation in community service and volunteering, 58 percent indicated that they had participated in community service in the past year, substantially more than the 44 percent of American adults who volunteer annually (Independent Sector 2001). Thirty-one percent of respondents said that they volunteer in their community at least monthly.

## Opinions about Society and Their Place in It as Citizens and Professionals

Respondents described themselves as an aware, thoughtful, and engaged group overall. They suggested that they had an improved understanding of the complexity of social problems, with 68 percent agreeing or strongly agreeing with the statement, "Social problems are more difficult to solve than I used to think." When ESLARP alumni were asked to provide their opinions about how society works and individuals' responsibilities within

| Descriptors | Describes me well | Describes me very well | Total % Indicating Describes well or very well |
|---|---|---|---|
| Before criticizing somebody, I try to imagine how I would feel if I were in his or her place | 48% | 18% | 66% |
| I usually take a long time to consider things before I make up my mind | 33% | 21% | 54% |
| I often discuss political or social issues with my friends | 50% | 21% | 71% |
| I often try to persuade others to take my point of view | 28% | 11% | 37% |
| I have testified in public hearings or spoken at meetings held by public agencies | 15% | 28% | 43% |
| I read a newspaper of watch news shows daily | 37% | 41% | 78% |
| I always vote in national elections | 22% | 61% | 83% |
| I always vote in state and local elections | 33% | 32% | 65% |
|  | Does not describe me well | Does not describe me at all well | Total % Indicating Does not describe well or at all well |
| I sometimes find it difficult to see things from the other person's point of view | 45% | 18% | 63% |

Table 3. Respondents' assessment of themselves. *Illustration by Lynne M. Dearborn*

society, their answers suggested that they were quite empathetic toward those in society who had fewer resources than they did. For example, they disagreed or strongly disagreed 61 percent of the time with the statement, "People who receive social services largely have only themselves to blame for needing services." Their responses indicated that they felt strongly that community members had a responsibility to volunteer their time and expertise to help individuals in need, address community problems, and improve the community. As a group, they held opinions that implied that they felt empowered to change the social status quo through community service or by becoming a community leader. They suggested that they were focused more on improving their community and volunteering to help others than they were on their own personal success. Further, demonstrating their receptivity to diversity, 70 percent of respondents disagreed or strongly disagreed with the statement, "I feel uncomfortable working with people who are different from me in such things as race, wealth, and life experience."

The survey asked respondents to assess themselves with regard to twelve descriptors. Their answers connote that they are generally empathetic, nonjudgmental, and politically and socially engaged. Table 3 gives an overview of the aggregate assessment by respondents with regard to nine descriptors.

Sixty-six percent felt that the statement, "Before criticizing somebody, I try to imagine how I would feel if I were in his or her place," described them well or very well. Nearly an equal number felt the statement, "I sometimes find it difficult to see things from the other person's point of view," did not describe them well at all.

At the end of the survey, respondents were asked to reflect back on particularly vivid memories of their ESLARP service-learning experiences. They were asked to analyze the impact of these experiences to identify their most compelling aspects. The survey then invited respondents to provide additional detail about these experiences and connections to strategies that their service-learning instructors employed. The following section uses reflections of respondents and analyses of these experiences to investigate pivotal educational events that have influenced respondents' professional and personal lives. The discussion builds a richer understanding of the impact of ESLARP-based service-learning on the decisions alumni have made as professionals and citizens.

## Reflecting on ESLARP Service-Learning Experiences

A majority of survey respondents had positive recollections of their service-learning experiences within ESLARP, but also provided a substantial critique of aspects they felt were unsuccessful. The reflections provided here, interpreted in the context of material presented previously in Table 2, suggest links between ESLARP experiences that respondents deem transformative and their assessments of their social consciousness.[1] In addition, respondents believe that service-learning courses helped them develop leadership abilities and offered them skills and experiences that have been valuable for their career development. A series of four survey questions asked respondents to recollect ESLARP experiences that were particularly pivotal in their understanding of:

1. Experiences of those who are different from you;
2. Issues of social justice/injustice in relation to the physical environment;
3. Your role as a professional designer or planner;
4. Responsibilities and opportunities for professional designers/planners to change socially/physically unjust conditions.

Answers to these four questions demonstrated that ESLARP provided this group with memorable and pivotal experiences in each of these areas, with 67 percent to 77 percent affirmative responses for each question. In each of these four areas, personal interaction with others and observation of the environment were most often noted as the most compelling aspects of ESLARP service-learning experience. Providing a more detailed response, one survey respondent wrote, "Listening to residents' concerns and ideas pointed out things that I never would have thought impacted their lives." Another said, "I realized that I can do all the planning and design in the world but it will go to waste if the community doesn't respect it."

Respondents indicated that their instructors' comments were also influential in their understanding of those who were different from themselves and in their understanding of issues of social justice as related to the physical environment. One respondent wrote that his instructor's comments and lectures gave him an understanding of the entire history of East St. Louis, which helped him see that, "East St. Louis is a perfect example of how people use zoning and political influence for their advantage and the disadvantage of others." Respondents indicated that their own personal reflections were pivotal in their understanding of their roles as professionals and their understanding of responsibilities and opportunities for professional designers and planners to change socially and physically unjust conditions.[2]

The impact of ESLARP-based service-learning coursework was also explored through open-ended interviews with just over 20 percent of survey respondents. Interviewees were randomly selected from among respondents who indicated a willingness to take part in follow-up interviews. Interview responses demonstrated that ESLARP components of coursework impacted participants' choice of jobs and the way they conducted themselves both professionally and in their daily lives. A number of interviewees indicated that because of their ESLARP experiences they chose to work in community-focused jobs and to seek out employment with interdisciplinary firms and organizations. Moreover, for alumni from all three professional programs, ESLARP experiences had brought into focus the importance of sensitivity to client needs, client communication, and a better understanding of the constituencies who are left out of design and planning processes. Interviewees also indicated ways that ESLARP experiences had modeled the importance of involvement in and support for the community both in everyday life and in leadership roles. Interviewees pointed out connections between particular ESLARP experiences and their civic-minded actions as citizens.

Open-ended interview responses provided feedback about particularly effective service-learning strategies. Interviewees also highlighted experiences that gave them a deeper understanding of Metro East St. Louis, the life there, and insights into their professional roles in such places. Analysis of interview responses revealed five principal themes bridging these areas: (1) realizing the complexity of the urban fabric; (2) recognizing the impact of structural forces on the environment; (3) understanding the perspective of residents; (4) re-envisioning themselves and their chosen profession; and (5) contending with the pace of change.

### Realizing the Complexity of the Urban Fabric

ESLARP-based coursework facilitated students' understanding of social, economic, political, and physical intermingling in Metro East St. Louis. Interviewees stressed that those courses where there was a focus on inter-disciplinary processes and those that provided a sense of the bigger picture helped in understanding and addressing complexity. One alumnus of a studio that included architecture, landscape architecture, and urban planning students in interdisciplinary teams noted, "Working in the interdisciplinary way that we did in this studio helped me to see that the problems were complex and couldn't just be solved from the perspective of standard landscape architecture design. It broadened my perspective on the causes and solutions to what I saw and experienced in East St. Louis." Another said, "I realized that there was something bigger than me here. I needed to prepare, understand and analyze. I needed to spend time on the whole—the big picture—the social and political context were critical to work in that place."

Interviewees also described their "ah ha!" moments when they began to see East St. Louis as different from the stereotype they had of a disadvantaged community and to understand the multiple forces at work there:

> There were a few interesting things that I observed that made me realize things were not what I expected . . . I met the mayor at one point in my time in East St. Louis. I was really surprised that the mayor of a town where there were so many abandoned buildings and where there was so much poverty would arrive in a fancy car and have gold rings on every finger. It just didn't make sense to me . . . That was when I realized that this was not like the place I grew up. It was a lot different and from then on I didn't expect that I could imagine what it was like there.

Finally, when the complexity became overwhelming, "pointing out the positives" helped keep students focused and engaged:

> It is also important that the instructors and staff point out the positives to the students . . . The students doing the neighborhood surveys, they realize that these people are people like in any other neighborhood or place. I think when we hear over and over again, people say they feel safe and

like they belong in their neighborhood, it makes us realize that the physical qualities are less important.

These reflections show that as students began to understand the complexity of the environment where community service-learning took place, their stereotypes about life in physically declining urban neighborhoods were invalidated. They also began to realize that the physical conditions were connected to a longer history and to resulting structural forces in place in the region.

### Recognizing the Impact of Structural Forces on the Environment

Clues to the history of social and economic policies, and the history of local politics, are often visible in the physical fabric of small industrial cities like East St. Louis. This history, with both national and local components, continues to influence what students see on site visits and what they hear from residents. Faculty who taught ELSARP-based service-learning courses between 1992 and 2003 used a variety of techniques to reveal this history to students. One alumnus who had been a teaching assistant for Urban Planning 101 noted the effectiveness of reflective essays:

> The students had a reflective essay that they were required to hand in after the weekend [in East St. Louis]. It was clear from reading those essays that for many students this was a life-changing experience. They saw things that they had never seen and gained new understanding of why things were as they were. There was still the one or two students who didn't get it and simply wanted to know why people didn't just move. But most of them came to understand the social justice perspective.

This alumnus went on to note that in successive semesters, reflection exercises were incorporated into Friday night discussion sections after students had spent the day working with community members. He felt this was a more successful reflection strategy than having students reflect in the isolation of their dorm rooms back on campus. For an alumna who had been a graduate student in an architecture studio, reflecting on the opportunity to talk informally one-on-one with residents while engaged in community projects gave her a sense of the impact of city politics on the physical environment:

> I pretty clearly understood what the nature of the power structure was after talking with residents . . . Money would be invested and money would disappear. Also there were big signs announcing who the city manager and the mayor were. Next to the signs were falling down houses. So it

was clear that there was little regard among politicians and leadership for changing [physical] conditions there. They seemed to be oblivious.

An alumnus of the undergraduate landscape architecture program provided an overall assessment of how his realization of the impact of structural forces on the environment affected his long-term outlook with regard to his professional role:

> It really changed my whole perspective because I began to understand the impact that the local government, and the federal government policy as well, had on what we saw there. It became clear that policies and corruption impacted what is there now and why it is physically the way it is . . . Because I came to understand the structural conditions at play in East St. Louis, I have been able to better interpret and see similarities with other distressed urban areas.

### Understanding the Perspectives of Residents

Student interpretations of the physical environment in places like East St. Louis are often formed and re-formed through exposure to community residents, politicians, service providers, and the course instructor. However, student responses can vary from being overwhelmed by the conditions, outraged at the injustice, or figuring out how to work for change. Nevertheless, students are expected to respond with design and planning proposals incorporating not just their own interpretations but also those of the residents. An alumnus of the graduate planning program described how he gained insight into one resident's perspective and how it differed from his own:

> The ninety-minute interview that we did with the resident was probably the best introduction to how residents felt about their neighborhood . . . The woman we interviewed was older and was born and raised in East St. Louis. She told us the story of her life—how she saw the neighborhood change before her eyes. I was struck by how calm she was. She was so matter-of-fact in her representation of her life experiences and how things in the city fell apart around her. I would have been more upset. She didn't seem pessimistic at all as I would have been or as I would have expected . . . There was a degree of culture shock when you realized what life was like for people there and how different it was from what I experienced every day.

An alumna of the landscape architecture graduate program explained how understanding the residents' perspectives impacted her design work:

I did one interview with a resident who had lived in East St. Louis for fifty years. I asked her why she stayed there. She had these very fond memories of how it used to be . . . The younger kids don't really care about the neighborhood the way the older ones do. I tried to incorporate that generational difference into my design for the park. I gave the seniors who still live there a particular place and designed the area particularly for their needs and provided something different in a different area for the younger kids.

Finally, an alumna of the planning graduate program talked about how these personal interviews helped to undo stereotypes that students often have about residents of poor communities:

The door-to-door interviews I think are very eye opening for the students. It lets them make a connection with the residents because they are often invited inside their homes. Students get to know the residents and find out "they are just ordinary people" and that "the situations that they are living in are not their fault" . . . I also think it was particularly effective when you [faculty] talk to the students about political action and let them know that you are not going into this with a value-free perspective—put that out there on the table for them so they see that you are committed to making things better and that you see the injustice in the conditions.

### Re-Envisioning Themselves and Their Chosen Profession

When alumni described ways that their ESLARP-based service-learning course experiences have affected their lives after graduation, they provided examples of three types of impacts: recognizing the importance of people in design and planning processes, re-envisioning themselves and their responsibilities as professionals in society, and understanding their chosen profession in new ways.

In comparing their ESLARP-based studio work with other studios, alumni of the architecture and planning programs noted that the work in East St. Louis helped them recognize the importance of people in design and planning processes and helped them hone listening skills that they use in their professional lives. One alumnus of the architecture graduate program states:

My experiences with ESLARP made me realize that people are an important part of architecture. In other design projects we basically ignored the people who would be using the things we were designing.

Through this design studio experience I learned that I am really nothing like the people who might be using the spaces I design. Before I had always designed things the way I would like them to be. I learned some techniques for asking questions and listening to people that are helpful in my professional life.

Another alumnus of the joint architecture-urban planning graduate program talked about developing tools that he now uses professionally:

My ESLARP time helped to broaden my perspective on social justice as well as the methods by which designers and planners can and should work with neighborhoods . . . My current firm is involved a lot in community planning and design. I use a lot of tools developed during my ESLARP experiences . . . We do a lot of listening before we ever start any project.

Interviewees also discussed ways that their ESLARP experiences helped them re-envision themselves as professionals in society:

The second important lesson that came from my time with ESLARP was the notion that my professional life is not just about going to the office. As a professional, I have a responsibility to be a volunteer. We [architects] have a lot of knowledge that could be very useful to those in need.

An alumnus of the planning undergraduate program got a chance to see planning in action:

ESLARP outreach weekend helped me to see what planners do. It helped me to see that planners DO THINGS! It helped me to see that planners are active and involved and help to bring the community together to see what has to be done. Unlike other intro classes where I was given theory, theory and more theory, this class gave me a good idea of the profession.

An alumna of the undergraduate landscape architecture program stated that her interdisciplinary ESLARP service-learning studio helped her see the breadth of possibilities for practicing landscape architecture and influenced the types of professional offices where she sought employment:

The interdisciplinary studio structure greatly impacted my understanding of the broad nature of landscape architecture practice—how landscape architects are often the "middleman" in these types of urban design projects. I saw how the professions could and should work together in professional life. This experience motivated me to seek work in an interdisciplinary office and to push that office to take a more integrated approach to planning and design whenever feasible.

*Contending with the Pace of Change*

The last important theme that ran through the interview responses of alumni is connected with the slow speed at which positive change happens in distressed, low-income communities. Alumni from all three programs mentioned that their ESLARP experiences highlighted the fact that other professional coursework had given them an unrealistic sense that physical change in the environment happens at a very fast pace. One interviewee stated succinctly, "I realized that things happened slowly over time. Making change anywhere doesn't happen over night." The following statement from another alumnus illustrates that gaining a more realistic sense of the pace of positive change was important but sometimes difficult to accept:

> I would always go away from ESLARP outreach activities with mixed feelings. On the one hand I got demoralized about how to make substantial and large-scale change. Usually the apathetic residents that we came into contact with were the ones who most needed our help. On the other hand I learned that incremental change has value. I hoped that if those who were most involved got help and improved their situation that it might show others that there was hope and that they too would participate because they saw the benefit it had had for others . . . I developed a philosophy that affects my professional work today. Basically, you do what you can do to make things better for whomever you can.

## Reflection

Alumni responses to both survey and interview questions suggest that their history of participation in experiential education through ESLARP-based service-learning courses influenced their actions as professionals and as community members. They indicate that they are more likely than the average person to carefully consider and critically reflect on a situation before acting. They tend not to take things at face value but to gather information and look under the surface. They intimate that they are inclined to use their professional skills and talents to promote the common good. This group of attributes, examined in the context of respondents' comparisons of their ESLARP-based service-learning courses with other design and planning courses, suggests that participation in ESLARP courses prompts different and more socially conscious professional actions than other experiential education that design and planning students encounter while at the University of Illinois. One planning alumnus described this difference quite well by comparing his ESLARP experience to another service-learning course:

> The most effective thing that the professor did [in the community orga-
> nizing class] was to use examples from experiences in East St. Louis to
> illustrate principles of community organizing. It really gave the opportunity
> to see the principles applied to situations that the class had become
> familiar with . . . The service project in [another] course was to do a study
> of Urbana to facilitate the siting of an SRO. That approach developed
> skills needed for professional planning work. It was really about learning
> to operate within the system to accomplish a goal . . . But the community
> organizing class and the service in East St. Louis was about student ex-
> posure to the realities of the lives of others that they were not familiar with
> and weren't previously exposed to. It allowed students to develop a level
> of empathy with the residents that the other approach did not.

The interviews suggest that the ESLARP experiences involved more
than just interactions between students and others and between students
and the environment; the experiences incorporated transactive processes.
Transaction implies a mutual exchange between two entities (Itin 1999, 95).
The description of ESLARP experience provided by the planning alumnus
above illustrates such a transaction, where the student and residents of a
neighborhood in East St. Louis exchange knowledge with each other. Alumni
responses to our survey suggest that transaction distinguishes ESLARP-based
experiential education from some other experiential professional education
at the University of Illinois. First of all, within ESLARP the subject matter
of environmental design is broadly considered. Students engage the complexity of environmental design. Second, the learning environments are
expanded beyond campus to include settings in East St. Louis that offer
readily apparent links between physical, social, political, and economic systems. Third, the teaching process offers a high degree of mutual exchange
between student and instructor; they learn from each other. The transactive
nature of these relationships offers students the opportunity to engage and
reflect on both the subject matter and the learning environment. Students
engage in transactive relationships with the neighborhood through two-way
exchanges of information with residents and through observations of and
actions in the physical environment. Students engage in transactive relationships with the subject matter of environmental design where they reflect on
their preexisting knowledge, modify their conceptualizations, apply, and
reflect again. Finally, alumni responses to our survey indicate that the cycles
of reflection by teacher and student offer the possibility for the kind of long-
term learning outcomes cited by alumni.

# PART THREE

# Crossing Borders

## Editor's Introduction

**P**rojects that cross national borders often demonstrate both the powerful possibilities and substantial challenges of service-learning. Students and faculty can learn how to work effectively in a world of diversity and increasing interdependence. By understanding other peoples and nations, they can deepen their understanding of themselves. However, they are first challenged to understand and engage in places and communities they are unfamiliar with, grappling with different languages and cultures, ways of living and values. It may be even more difficult to know "the other" when real and imagined distances are so great. Brief encounters may be very intense, and without adequate preparation and reflection, lessons can be quickly forgotten and communities involved summarily abandoned. Nevertheless, well-organized and carefully conceived international projects can cross many boundaries, sustain collaborations, and mutually benefit communities and academic institutions.

In this section, *Lynda Schneekloth* and *Scott Shannon* discuss the University at Buffalo, the State University of New York's collaboration in Monteverde, Costa Rica. Since 1991, university students from North America have joined a team of seasoned design educators and local community partners in a place-based research collaboration. The participants are immersed in a local environment as part of a program combining professional service and learning. The program emphasizes relationship building between people and in the communities where they live. This leaves designers vulnerable and open to unfamiliar ways of knowing, participating, and learning while providing a service. As professional and local knowledge combine and interact, alternative futures and scenarios—not fixed master plans—emerge.

In *Daniel Winterbottom's* design/build capstone studio at the University of Washington, students apply their design learning to a public service project either locally or abroad in Mexico, Guatamala, and, most recently, Bosnia. Building strong relationships and fostering community empowerment are core principles of the design/build studios that aim to confront and address complex social and ecological problems and community needs. The largest dump in Central America is now home to Guatamala City's Children's Garden of Hope, a design/build collaboration between Safe Passage, Winterbottom, and his students. This park embodies the multicultural process of its making, and marks yet another site where students gained exposure to new ways of thinking about their role as designers. It is what Winterbottom calls alternative "compassionate design" practice that is aimed at addressing social injustices.

## Prescriptions for Change: Crossing Borders

The two international programs discussed in this section underscore the importance of working with local partner organizations and communities to develop, facilitate, and comanage international service-learning programs. Partner organizations play a community advocacy role, help to mediate and foster relationship building, and provide continuity over time. Coordinated efforts and institutional structures with stable staffing and financing are needed to develop long-term partnerships and ensure that service and learning goals are realized by both community and academic partners.

Effective, mutually beneficial collaborations are necessary for all service-learning but especially critical in international and cross-cultural learning projects. International projects are apt to expose the structures and conditions that differentiate, define, and divide cultures and nations. They should also help all involved achieve a greater understanding of global inequalities. Design and planning educators need to pay special attention to "the other" and promote reflection on the different perspectives, expectations, and interpretations emerging from diverse histories and cultures as they are encountered in the world.

International service-learning programs dislodge all participants—faculty and students alike—from the academically secure and delimited on-campus studio environment. The "studio" becomes a community-bounded space populated by students, faculty, and community partners where differences extend across diverse cultural, social, and economic boundaries. This forces both teachers and learners to negotiate and practice in ways that are often unfamiliar and unexpected. Design and planning educators need to understand and explore the potency of this unique studio space and rethink their own agency and the agency of their students and community partners. Success will be measured by the degree to which it encourages and empowers greater intercultural learning, reciprocity, and exchange. The knowledge of design and planning learned in one place must confront the local history, wisdom, energy, and exigencies of other places.

## CHAPTER 10

# Easing Boundaries through Placemaking

*Sustainable Futures Study Abroad Program*

Lynda Schneekloth and Scott Shannon

## Introduction

**The Sustainable Futures** study abroad program was initiated by the School of Architecture and Planning at the University at Buffalo/SUNY in 1991 and institutionalized in 1993 in collaboration with the Monteverde Institute (MVI). MVI has been managing study abroad courses for US students since the mid-1980s, beginning with a focus in tropical biology. The addition of a design/planning-based study abroad program that was integrated with the community, not just the forest, brought challenges to everyone. Within a few years, a US-based consortium included the Landscape Architecture programs at the University of Maryland and SUNY/ESF at Syracuse, the Urban and Regional Planning program at the University of Illinois at Urbana-Champaign, and, most recently, the Architecture program at Ball State University. Each summer for ten weeks, students from these programs and disciplines/professions travel to a rural area in Costa Rica to study, learn, and participate in this service-learning course.

### The Place: Monteverde, Costa Rica

Monteverde, in the province of Puntarenas, Costa Rica, is an extraordinarily appropriate place to experiment with this type of practice and to engage students in facilitating the making of the place. The small community was founded in 1950 by Quakers from the US seeking to live in a country without an army. They built a meetinghouse, a school, a dairy plant and cheese factory, and lived peacefully with the Costa Ricans who also inhabited the area. Along with the Ticos[1] they have been true placemakers—they built the entire community and managed it through a town meeting for many years. Members of the community served on the road committee, the burial committee, and on the board of the co-op or dairy plant; they taught, they farmed, they painted, and they made music. And when they found out how unique the ecology of the region was, they developed institutions and raised funds to protect the forest.

Over the years, the diverse group of people who live in Monteverde have articulated a shared vision of the future—one in which the unique ecological qualities of place have formed the foundation for future community development. In most locations the phrase "uniqueness of place" is used primarily as a rhetorical devise; in Monteverde, where the local ecology of the cloud forest produces one of the most biodiverse locations on Earth, uniqueness is more than enthusiastic local boosterism.

The remarkable ecosystem found in Monteverde is due to a number of factors; most particularly, the unusual juxtaposition of steep mountainous terrain with elevations ranging from 2,600 feet to 6,000 feet over just a few miles, its local situation astride the Continental Divide, and its regional situation within the Central American isthmus between the North and South American continents. As a result, there is an unusual concentration of both indigenous and migrant species.[2]

With the emergence of ecotourism as an unmistakable economic phenomenon by the mid-1980s, Monteverde's economy shifted dramatically from agriculture and dairy to a dominant focus on tourism and hospitality-oriented service businesses. Since that time, the main attraction to the area remains the Monteverde Cloud Forest Preserve, a 10,500 hectare privately owned and protected natural area administered by the Centro Cientifico Tropical/Tropical Science Center (CCT). Today, over 75,000 people visit the preserve each year to hike the trails and hope to catch a glimpse of some of the most notable species found there.

### The Program

> . . . working with other students in the program, with people who are just as passionate about the health of the earth—whether or not you know each other—you can make a difference. That was one of the greatest feelings about being a part of the program while I was there. —*Sustainable Futures end-of-course student participant response*

Sustainable Futures has been one of the most visible and interactive programs sponsored by the Institute. The interdisciplinary program is centered on a service-learning pedagogy and, therefore, the students are highly visible in the community of approximately 6,000 people. Each student receives credits for a design or planning studio, a seminar in sustainable design, and an independent study credit that includes the requirement to capture their own experience in the context to include Spanish, journaling, and participation in the local culture. The first week is an orientation, followed by an intensive four-week "semester" (eight a.m. to five p.m. each day). The students are encouraged to travel during a weeklong break, and then participate in a second four-week semester. The students work with their local client(s) and present their findings to the entire community at the end of each of the semesters.

Students and faculty from Sustainable Futures have provided design and planning assistance to a variety of local not-for-profit groups and institutions, local government, and even private landowners seeking opportunities to develop easements and management plans for the conservation of local ecosystems. All of our projects are initiated from within the local community, and each year we select what might be most appropriate given the urgency of the project, the structure of the requesting parties, and the composition of our student groups and faculty who are participating.

Students work in interdisciplinary teams on all projects—planners, architects, and landscape architects—and struggle to understand and appreciate the methods and aims of their sister disciplines. Depending on the project, we have used focus groups, social science methods of interviews and surveys, and, occasionally, we have held large public meetings. But most of the collaborative work is done in small groups in which community members bring their local knowledge to teach us, and where they willingly engage the "professional" knowledge that students and faculty bring to the table. Each year, fifteen to twenty graduate and undergraduate students participate in a range of community projects, live with Costa Rican families, study Spanish, travel by foot, and learn to live with new flora and fauna.

## The Aims and Purposes of Sustainable Futures: The Practice of Placemaking

The program was built on the theory and practice of placemaking developed by Schneekloth and Shibley (1995, 2000). All practices are embedded in theories, even if unacknowledged and tacit, and all theories result in particular actions and not others. Placemaking is a fundamental human activity: both a theory about the world and a practice that changes the world.

Theories and practices rely on aims, purposes, and beliefs. The foundational belief of placemaking is that all people desire to live in a *beloved place* and people everywhere care about their places; they want places they can love, places that are healthy for working, building community, and raising families. Our second belief is that inherent in the practice of placemaking is the assumption that people purposefully work, individually and collectively, on their places, and that they are *competent* to engage in such work. The third belief is that the unit of work, or of analysis, is *people-in-place*, not just people, and not just place. This is a practice concerned with constructing relationships—of people to place and people to people in those places. Placemaking builds on the literature and theory of place; but it is a verb, not a noun, and does not reify the essentialism that is often embedded in place theory.

All professions have practices that include a range of agreed upon skills and insights. For designers and planners, it is a stated goal to improve the lives of people we serve through accommodating their needs while creating beautiful places. We share a code of ethics that outlines our responsibilities to our clients, to the places we make, and to our profession. Even so, the placemaking theory shifts the focus of practice from the place or client to the relationship of the people to the place. This practice expands what has been treated as the technical work of "public participation" to a co-practice that facilitates mutual influence. In this definition of practice, *all* people engage in placemaking; architects, landscape architects, planners, engineers, and so on are simply the "professional placemakers."

Specifically, placemaking practice engages three tasks: opening a space for dialogue; confirming and interrogating ideas, beliefs, and attitudes; and framing action. The primary responsibility of the professional placemaker is to engage those involved in any intervention in a conversation that seeks to learn about the place, to share local and professional knowledges, and together frame the goals and issues at hand. The second task is based on the idea that everyone's ideas make sense to them; consequently, confirming people's ideas and perceptions of place is critical. Confirming, however, doesn't necessarily mean agreeing. If trust has been developed in the dialogic space, then it is possible to challenge the ideas of others—including the professional. As the conversation deepens and thickens, the participants seek to frame action by identifying all who need to be involved, deciding what kind of actions should be taken, and what types of interventions are appropriate.

Working on community projects was the most rewarding part of
the experience. This service that we provided gave meaning to my
academic work. —*Sustainable Futures end-of-course student participant
response*

These tasks are not unusual in any professional intervention, but the
attitude with which they are engaged can vary from a strategy of co-optation
of a client to the true engagement of the local population in decisions affecting their lives. In the latter context, it means making our professional
knowledge vulnerable to local knowledge and working in the open space of
dialogue to share an interpretation of the context and ways of proceeding.
This is probably the most difficult lesson to teach in a traditional university setting, and forms the base of a rationale for the inclusion of service-
learning opportunities as a fundamental part of professional education. We
teach students many things in our universities and engage them in widely
varied studio design projects, but to learn how to engage people-in-place
in a collaborative relationship, in which students both learn and provide
service, requires them to actually participate in-place, most often with faculty and professionals who can model this kind of practice and share their
experience and tacit knowledge. Doing this away from campus provides
an individual space for students to reflect on their own professional and
individual "truths":

Living in Costa Rica where I was separated from my culture and my environment and introduced into a completely different lifestyle allowed me to
open my eyes and view back upon myself and everything that I believed I
was familiar with . . . Being away from the world that I knew allowed me
to really understand things about myself that I may have never found out
otherwise.

The imperative to be inclusive and interactive does not relinquish any
responsibility of a professional in the conduct of practice—the designer
has to continue to address and use his or her experience of other places, of
knowledge, of processes, and of facilitation. But it does sometimes mean
that the quick and easy response that could be applied in a traditional studio, without interaction, is not appropriate. The practice of placemaking
erases boundaries between professionals and local people, between expert
knowledge and place knowledge, and sometimes even between whom you
thought you were and who you might be; it even raises questions of why
we engage in our various professional practices.

## Placemaking as the Collaborative Construction of Place

The placemaking orientation has implications for the academic practice of service-learning. The recognition that the work of "experts"—be they registered professionals or students—is embedded into life, shifts the focus of work from design product to process. As a result, in the Sustainable Futures study abroad program, our engagement in a myriad of projects over many years is always done with the consciousness that each particular intervention is a part of past and future projects, as well as a part of the everyday life of the people in Monteverde. At the same time, this engagement is clearly a way of learning more about the practice of design and planning, the practice and skills of an interventionist profession, and the complexity of integrating local and professional knowledge.

### Framing a Future with Local Communities: Scenario Planning

How does this work? Of all the projects we've engaged, perhaps it is the ongoing Scenario Planning in the Monteverde zone that best describes the impact of this theory on the learning and on the service we bring to the community. Scenario Planning is a community planning technique used to explore alternative futures for a place, municipality, or region by posing the question, What is likely to happen given the current conditions, trends, and various pressures to change? (Peterson, Cummings, and Carpenter 2003; Avin and Dembner 2001; Harwood and Zapata 2006). This process is significantly different from master planning or visioning processes that present the question, What do you want to have happen? As with all scenario planning exercises, the same volume of physical growth based on historic patterns are proposed for alternative scenarios, but with different community design patterns and densities in order to illustrate the difference between different values and probable futures. In Monteverde we have also tried to incorporate typical Tico development patterns into each of the alternative scenarios.

We began the scenario planning at the request of some members of the local community and the Institute due to the rapid growth of the community and the lack of a local municipal government in Monteverde that might ordinarily provide structure for planning. Although this community had engaged in placemaking for years, including a visioning process in the late 1990s called *Monteverde 2020*, there was no official governing body to construct or implement any plan. Even today, after the institution of a local municipal government in 2003 (*Distrito Monteverde* was formed only following a change in the Costa Rican constitution), they have yet to complete or implement a *Plan Regulador* (the Costa Rican equivalent of a comprehensive plan and corresponding zoning and development ordinances).

In the initial year of Scenario Planning (2001), the Monteverde community members who worked with us in our ongoing conversation about the possible futures of Monteverde identified alternative probable futures they thought could emerge in their community depending on decisions that would be made in the next few years. Living there gave them insight into historic trends, multiple voices and tensions in the community, and possibilities of alternative futures. The three scenarios jointly developed in our conversations can be summarized as: (1) a future driven by a *business as usual* approach to growth, development, and regulation (or lack thereof); (2) the continued growth and focused reliance on *eco-tourism* as the predominant economic base, and (3) a *diversification* of the economic base to protect the community from disruptions.

Sustainable Futures brought a set of fresh eyes, precedents and comparative knowledge, and planning and design skills to these scenarios. Nevertheless, the challenges were particularly complex in Monteverde because the data on which to base future projections were not readily available. There were no historic maps that could give us growth patterns, no centralized demographic material on which to base projections, and no communal economic data to analyze—only fragmented information held by various institutions and businesses. To calculate the historic annual growth rate for the Monteverde region since its inception in the 1950s required using a combination of federal census data and local municipal records from the health clinic and water board. With this information we were able to suggest that the region had grown approximately 7 percent annually, with a local economy that, after a brief post-9/11 lull, seemed to be expanding even faster. Using early "tourist" maps, historic aerial photographs, and even an embroidered wall hanging of the region dated 1972, we identified patterns of settlement and calculated the physical growth on which to project the potential expansion of housing and commercial building for 2010 and 2020 in each of the primary communities in the region. We started in the small area of Monteverde and Cerro Plano in 2001, then Santa Elena in 2002, Cañitas and Los Llanos in 2003, and San Luis in 2004. Areas of Cerro Plano, Santa Elena, and Los Llanos have been revisited and given more in-depth study from 2005 to 2007.

The power of enlarging the dialogic space of placemaking was particularly apparent in 2004 when we had architecture students from the University of Costa Rica participating. With this opportunity, we expanded our dialogue into the very small community of San Luis to include meetings with women and children, extensive interviews with a wide range of community residents, and a variety of informal gatherings including several soccer games and a dance at the local community center. When some students had difficulty divorcing themselves from their predominantly North American-suburban design prejudices in considering various types of community forms, a rich dialogue challenged their knowledge to enable their ability to incorporate the requirements and desires of the community. A strong consensus emerged underscoring a need for more and improved housing, better infrastructure in the form of water, electricity, and roads, more community services, greater economic opportunity, etc., as well as an overarching desire to maintain a truly rural character in the San Luis Valley where almost no tourism-based development now exists.

To accomplish this, we needed the professional skills of planners, architects, and landscape architects—each making an important contribution to the data and/or images of possible futures. That doesn't make these collaborations easy, but it does reflect the complexity of people-in-place and their desires:

> One of the planners spoke of some tension between the designers and planners, and the complexity of having to work in realms outside of your own expertise or ways of working. Yet the lesson learned was "although our projects may be vastly diverse in subject, our ultimate task is to provide tools that can be used by the community in order to promote equity and sustainable, healthy growth."

For our students, building the scenarios enabled them to learn about the place and the people of Monteverde, to engage the local community in a conversation that they now realized had been going on long before they arrived and would continue long after their departure. The exercise was built on student capacity for research and analysis and form-giving through diagrams, designs, and maps. Students offered their emerging professional capacity to the dialogue about proposed alternative futures. Many grappled with new insights and methods they were just learning; they envisioned new questions not considered during traditional coursework. They learned that communities are complex and varied with many views of what the future should be. Most importantly, they learned that they could support the community conversation and negotiations through insightful questions and through professional representation in analysis, drawings, maps, and narratives. But it remained the *community's* discussion. At one meeting, a student made the comment: "We decided . . ." and a community member immediately responded, "Thank you very much for your work, but you don't get to decide, we do."

Students and residents viewing and discussing the characteristics of the San Luis Valley. This small rural community collaborated with students to develop a set of scenario plans incorporating small-scale sustainable tourism facilities. *Photo by Scott Shannon*

From a pedagogical perspective, scenario planning, like most of our projects, has not had discrete beginnings and endings. Sustainable Futures work has rarely begun with a single well-defined problem or approach that was maintained throughout because we learn so much each year in the process of engagement and because of power shifts and new knowledge within the community itself. Underlying this approach, however, are the core principles of developing good scenarios toward the goal of a sustainable future that are built on sound analysis of existing conditions and trends in community demographics, local economy, environment, and physical growth.

The difference between more traditional forms of community participation and placemaking is the difference between giving community members the opportunity to respond to proposals versus the responsibility of the placemakers to open and maintain an ongoing dialogue where the professionals and community jointly frame the "problem" and structure the resulting responses. In this ongoing conversation, we are able to more completely understand various perspectives and, therefore, can confirm everyone's interpretation of the issue. We also question and interrogate these same issues because we bring different experiences, knowledges, and visions. Although

Sustainable Futures students work on assembling a bamboo structure in San Luis for the local women's paper recycling cooperative. *Photo by Scott Shannon*

we are the "outsiders" in this community, the openness of the conversation and structure of placemaking enables a collaborative construction of place to which students and faculty can contribute to the lives of the people on the mountain.

### The Value of Local Partnership

Our local partner, the Monteverde Institute, makes the Sustainable Futures service-learning experience possible. The Institute (MVI) was formed in 1987 by several members of the local Quaker community who hoped to foster greater opportunities for education, research, and cultural exchange between the local community and Costa Rican and North American colleges and universities. Since 1991 Sustainable Futures has been one of the more significant programs sponsored by the Institute. This community-based educational institution is an active participant in Monteverde and, therefore, provides the continuity essential to, and inherent in, placemaking. It permits us to be "interventionists" and to come and join them each year with our experience, insights, and professional skills. It positions our "expert" knowledge within the local knowledge of this particular place and community. The program was greatly facilitated by the vision of Nate Scrimshaw, former executive director, who understood the power of placemaking but also understood that it would only work if our activities were supported by an ongoing presence in the community provided by the Institute.

In the last five years, we have introduced the role of a staff course coordinator who, as a part of their many responsibilities, works part-time throughout the year to maintain the momentum and progress of various projects and initiatives under way in the community. Our current MVI course coordinator, Anibal Torres, is a fourth-generation local resident who has studied and traveled in North America, but returned to Monteverde to build a life in the place he knows and loves best. Although only in his mid-twenties, he knows everyone in the community on a first name basis, he is fluent in both English and Spanish, and he moves between the Tico and Anglo communities with ease.

Having a person like Anibal involved as an integral part of the dialogue with the local community changes some of the traditional dynamics between "expert design professional" and "lay client." Anibal straddles the dividing line in this relationship, often acting as an informal first sounding board for design or planning ideas, as well as an interpreter of not only language, but of the subtle cultural differences that can muddy understanding of what students are seeing, experiencing, and designing. It forces students (and faculty) to rethink some of the traditional roles of the designer in the placemaking process—from that of creator to facilitator, and from expert dispenser of technical knowledge to that of interpreter and participant in a more democratic process. The course coordinator's job is critical, and requires a great deal of energy and hard work, a wide range of organizational and communication skills, broad knowledge of the local community, and a knowledge of the projects, previous work, and players who preceded the current student group. Ultimately, the Monteverde Institute as a respected and embedded institution and the course coordinator as a liaison are exceptionally important to Sustainable Futures.

Another project, the Enlace Verde (Green Necklace) helps to describe another type of Sustainable Futures / Monteverde Institute relationship. The goal of this project is the establishment of conservation easements on properties to connect forest fragments and conservation areas in Costa Rica, a country that is just beginning to establish laws regarding easements and how they might be applied. The importance of these easements is clear as many altitudinal migrants such as bellbirds[3] and quetzals need continuous forest to access food throughout the year. Working with local conservation biologists, the students learned much about the local ecology and its threatened status. The result has been a substantial effort to identify, create, and protect critical biocorridors, not only within public land and private reserves, but also on key parcels of private land.

We were encouraged to consider the added value of new biocorridors for other avian species and also arboreal mammals such as the white-faced monkey, three-toed sloth, and howler monkey (Saunders, Hobbs, and Margules 1991). Students and faculty, assisted by Institute staff, have met with local farmers and institutions to develop land management plans for individual properties with the mapping information available. The Institute, helping both to facilitate our teaching and benefit the community, has brought legal advisors to the region to work with landowners.

As the Enlace Verde project proceeded, it became obvious that this was also an opportunity to create a regional trail system extending from the Continental Divide in Monteverde to the Gulf of Nicoya, and elements of access and small hostels became a part of the planning. Each year, new landowners and small communities, such as San Luis, have begun to plan to host walkers along the trail, now known as the *Sendero Pacifico* (Pacific Trail). This project has been, in many ways, a project of the Institute, one for which we provided a variety of professional services. Each year students learn what has happened in previous years, and they add new insight, new possibilities, and new energy to the invaluable work of conservation and forest/ habitat sustainability. Knowing the biologists and walking the land makes it present and real for the students. The interest of the Institute and US-based universities gives credence in the project to local people. Like many of the projects, the interdependency is vital.

The local partner also provides insights that keep our North American bias in check, at times mediating between the kind of knowledge and experience we bring, and the knowledge and experience of the people of the Monteverde zone. One of the most complex issues confronting Sustainable Futures has been the issue of "the road" and increasing traffic. There remains only one road leading into and through the community that ends at the Monteverde Cloud Forest Preserve. For a community such as Monteverde, this is a much more complex issue than meets the eye. The existing minimally improved dirt road was built and maintained by local individuals and nongovernmental organizations for many years. For local residents of Monteverde, mud in the rainy months and dust in the dry season are a part of daily life; access and delivery of goods in an expedient manner is economically vital (especially with milk delivered to the cheese factory every day). The recent act of paving this road is almost unanimously viewed an improvement and a public good. What is perhaps overlooked or voiced by only a few residents is that this road, the *only* road, has served as the living room of the community for over fifty years—it is the place where people meet, stop and talk, do business, send children to school, and travel by foot, horse, motorcycle, car, and other imaginative forms of transport.

From a North American experience, where roads have been essentially taken over by cars, the loss of this public space threatens to tear at the heart of the community. More traffic and improved driving conditions have already increased the 5-10 kph speed, the norm on a bumpy, curvy, gravel road. As predicted, increased speed has created hazardous walking conditions and more accidents. The Sustainable Futures program has addressed the issue of the road in many ways and participated in community conversations on this issue since our initial programs in the early 1990s. Each year, the road improves—some sections are paved and have improved drainage, more and more Ticos are able to afford cars, tourism increases bring more and bigger buses—and each year there is less social interaction on the road and traffic moves with faster speeds. Sustainable Futures has done a number of studies requested by members of the local community and, more recently, the municipality has prepared design proposals for efficient circulation that would engender safer roads. Some have been implemented, such as a change of traffic patterns in Santa Elena, and some plans are being seriously considered, such as pedestrian walkways between Cerro Plano and Santa Elena. But the separation of traffic is very complex given the terrain and drainage issues.

Whether we work on scenario planning, conservation easements, building design, or the road, all of our service projects rely on our local partner, the Institute, to identify opportunities for us to work with the local community and provide continuity to the Sustainable Futures program in our absence. They, at times, play a pivotal mediation role and always embed our experience and concerns into the various voices representing local experience. Even when values conflict, such as in the ongoing road discussion, it is clear that there are no right answers or correct positions. There is only the need to be respectful of the various perspectives and to embrace the tension, a task greatly facilitated by the Institute.

## Cross-Cultural Immersion

Unlike many study abroad programs, Sustainable Futures was founded on the idea of cultural engagement as an integral part of the learning process, not just a way of providing an interesting setting for, or a backdrop to, geographically themed coursework. Our students become immersed in discovering the critical and interconnected nature of the Monteverde region's people and their cultures, as well as the unusual qualities of the physical place—the geology, the physiography, the climate, and the remarkable ecology. In order to be responsive to place and to the people in place, we have woven a variety of opportunities to introduce practical applications of appropriate theory, particularly sustainability and landscape ecology, as well as various approaches or techniques specific to community planning, including drawing on local experts as instructors.

### The Value of Dislocation

There are a number of conditions that make this type of educational experience exceptional even though it has been complex and somewhat difficult to implement. The first condition rests in the foundation of placemaking as discussed above. A second condition that facilitates student learning is the very unfamiliarity of the place. The anthropologist Edmund Carpenter once said, "We don't know who discovered water but we can be sure it wasn't a fish." That is a good description for the student's immersion in the culture of Costa Rica, in general, and Monteverde, specifically.

Working within a placemaking perspective in a service-learning situation dislocates many of our students from the educational practices they have relied on for many years. This is especially true for students who have been immersed in the cultural indoctrination that occurs in studio-based professional schools. This tacit, or informal learning, often called the "hidden curriculum," is important for any type of practice. While it facilitates learning in some ways, it also constrains us into thinking that our attitudes and expectations are the norm. All of this goes away in a cross-cultural learning experience if students are paying any attention at all. This can be upsetting and exhilarating—and usually is both:

> Upon my arrival, it appeared that this country was foreign to me in a variety of ways. In fact, intimidation, not mystery, is what I felt initially.

The kinds of projects students are asked to engage in are often a surprise because they emerge from the community and local needs. Asked to find an adaptive reuse of the community bullring was a challenge, as was designing a facility for the Monteverde Cloud Forest Preserve that combined ticket selling, boot rental, staff lunchroom, and bird observation. Even the more commonplace idea of working with the local agricultural community and a milk production facility pushed the boundaries of knowledge for our mostly suburban students:

> In America we often solve architectural problems by making things bigger, longer, taller, and wider. Costa Ricans often have the same needs but they fulfill their needs for space by using the spaces allotted to them more creatively and efficiently.

With all of the challenges of working in the cross-cultural setting, it is perhaps ironic that one of the most difficult issues for our students has been the requirement to use local materials and local labor practices. The types of project solutions valued in design studio in their home schools are typically inappropriate and easily dismissed in Monteverde. The assumptions of what constitutes "good" design are significantly challenged—instead of relying on a formal move, a unique form, or a provocative concept, the design of buildings and landscapes have to rely on the structuring of space, accessibility, functionality, sustainability, buildability, and detailing. This doesn't in any way negate the requirement for design quality, but rather expands and deepens a student's understanding of the complexity of design.

## Language and Homestay

One of the most obvious differences in a study abroad program is the challenge of working in a new language. Students frequently comment on how valuable their Spanish lessons are, not only for their coursework, but also for social contact. For students who have often developed elegant and sophisticated ways of interacting and presenting their ideas to suddenly find that they are "inarticulate" is certainly stressful. But it also provides the opportunity to learn new ways of interacting, to clarify and simplify their ideas, and not to rely on a flood of complex words or jargon to camouflage an undeveloped concept. Fortunately, we have found students and community members to be incredibly tolerant of each other's language ability and disabilities, and we have relied on many of the bilingual members of the community. All meetings are bilingual, presentations are given in both languages, and people speak in the language in which they are most comfortable, with translation available. It is a bit of a mini-UN, and before long, the expectation is that multiple languages are used in everyday life.

Placing students in a homestay situation is one of the cornerstone practices of the Monteverde Institute for their longer courses. Without a doubt, it is one of the most scary propositions for students preparing to go, and almost always, is commented on as one of the most valuable experiences of the Sustainable Futures course:

> I never expected to be so welcomed and loved by a family other than my own. These past two weeks have brought much joy, as well as sorrow to this amazing family, and I am humbled and honored to have been a part of their family for this time.

Students consistently find that they have to intensely attend to the world and to the social structure of their lives—something as casual as dinner with your host family is an opportunity to absorb new ways of thinking about family, food, community structures, and so on. The "parents" of their homestay families are often their own age—but are married, have children, jobs, sit on boards, and are functioning as the adults of the community. The material life of most families is sparse, yet they seem content and engaged in their lives:

> My host family . . . was by no means deprived, but they did not have an over abundance of possessions and found a lot of time to spend together. They are a very happy family, in part because they tend to their relationship more than to work and accumulation.

Many students express such sentiments about the lives of their new families even when they, at times, resent the fact that they have to keep their new "mom" informed about when they'll be home for dinner. Learning abroad expands the boundaries of the norm, and students become keen observers of differences and learn to negotiate the tension between their "former" lives and the expectations of life in Monteverde.

## Erasing and Shifting Boundaries

It is fair to ask two questions regarding the specific context in which Sustainable Futures operates. First, how can students from North America achieve anything meaningful in a service-learning experience at a location this culturally and environmentally unfamiliar in just ten weeks? What can students learn and can they actually make a contribution to the community—in other words, is there learning and is there service? Second, given the context for this chapter, what kinds of boundaries or expectations of boundaries are "erased" or eased?

A placemaking-centered immersion study abroad context requires students to consider their role in the community in a much broader context than being a student in a professional program at their home universities. First, they see professional work is less about making things or managing people, and more about placemaking with local and professional knowledge. Secondly, they see how profoundly important their contribution can be to the lives of people in other places, and how the lives of others are a blessing to them. Further, in Monteverde, they continue to be responsible for themselves and their academic requirements, but here they are also representatives of the Institute and the Sustainable Futures program, and they represent their universities and their nation. We have found over the years that, with very few exceptions, students are both willing and able to accept these responsibilities, and to expand the narrow boundary of "student" and "university." This pedagogy, in and of itself, is a profound learning experience.

As anyone who has managed a study abroad and/or service-learning experience with emerging designers and planners knows, these can be profoundly life changing experiences, as is repeatedly expressed during the weekly group sessions, as well as in students' final exams (that asks specifically about the nature of their experience). One of the primary reasons study abroad and service-learning experiences are so important is that they reposition students with respect to their own lives and culture. The boundaries within which they were circumscribed by traditional learning settings are pushed and pulled so that the edges crack or the walls become transparent. It is at this point that students "see through" their social and cultural envelopes and shift the boundaries of what they know:

> I started thinking about all the time I wasted on the computer or on my cell phone. I never got to appreciate the company of my friends until I was totally disconnected from the technology that ran my life in the United States. I realize now that text messages and quick phone calls may be convenient at times but are useless for trying to create a strong relationship.

But are they making a contribution to the Monteverde community? Are we *norteamericanos* actually giving as much as we are receiving from this small rural community in the cloud forest? It may be impossible to answer that question, but it has been clear, over the years, that our work is highly regarded by the Institute and by the local community. There are always more requests for assistance than we can possibly accomplish, and each year we hear a story about a group wanting to undertake a design and planning project and saying, "Let's wait until the Sustainable Futures program arrives."

Each year, ongoing faculty are greeted warmly, as are a whole new cadre of students. If nothing else, at least this suggests we haven't alienated anyone yet! But perhaps the best indicator we have of the quality and reception of our work is that projects are actually built—such as the Institute facility, or the addition to the Friends School library, or the expansion of the EcoBambu cooperative—and our plans, such as the traffic change in Santa Elena, are instituted. Our work on Scenario Planning has contributed to the planning now instituted by the newly formed government, and the Sustainable Futures focus on water is integral for conservation planning in the region. At many levels, we are clearly doing service while we learn.

We have come to believe that, in a sense, the Sustainable Futures study abroad program is a study in boundaries: their existence, construction, reification, and erasure. But perhaps the greatest contribution comes within the concept of "easing" boundaries rather than erasing them—shifting boundaries to be more inclusive and expansive. The program works to make the walls that separate ideas, cultures, professions, and individuals more porous and transparent rather than eliminating them. Boundaries are important as they point to that which connects as well as that which divides—both important aspects of life. Yet, boundaries as identified in this book can be counterproductive and limiting.

Because boundaries will always be constructed, the responsibility of educators is to be sure that they are not invisible—the fish and water situation. What are productive ways to uncover or illuminate boundaries? Our experience suggests that within the framework of a service-learning experience in a study abroad context, students and faculty *have* to address the boundaries of their disciplines and professions and find ways to work together. The Sustainable Futures study abroad program combines an interdisciplinary planning and design studio with service-learning in a study abroad context. The structure of the endeavor itself has sought to redefine student educational expectations through their deep involvement in placemaking far from home and under circumstances very different from their previous life experiences, while, at the same time, contributing to the lives of a small community at the edge of the rainforest.

## CHAPTER 11

# Effecting Change through Humanitarian Design

*Daniel Winterbottom*

## The Program

**S**everal **landscape architecture** programs in the United States, including those at the University of Oregon, University of Massachusetts, University of Illinois at Urbana-Champaign, and Cornell University currently offer design/build courses. Temple University and the University of Washington have established design/build as a required component of their curricula (Tai and Lamba 2003). Faculty in the University of Washington's Department of Landscape Architecture unanimously adopted the design/build teaching model for their bachelor of landscape architecture (BLA) capstone studio in 1995. Each year a community-based design/build project is completed in Seattle and, as opportunities emerge, international service-learning design/build projects are offered to graduate and undergraduate students from diverse disciplines during both the academic year and the Summer quarter. International projects have been built in Mexico, Guatemala, Japan, Bosnia, Herzegovina, and Croatia.

Most landscape architectural programs in the United States currently offer international study, with established programs in Europe and Asia and emerging programs in Central and South America, Africa, and India (See University of Washington Foreign Study website). These experiential immersion programs use field research as a learning model and students use their extended stays to experience another country's culture, study its history, and develop language skills. However, few of these programs offer a service component. The combination of international study with a service-learning design/build experience is rare in landscape architectural programs but offers innovative opportunities as an alternative teaching model.

The University of Washington's Landscape Architecture Design/Build program was initiated in the summer of 1995 when the author approached the university's facilities department with a proposal to involve students in the restoration of a garden destroyed by a water main break. Over the course of six weeks, the author and four students designed and installed a small garden memorializing a former dean of the design college. This was followed by a second project to renovate a vacant lot adjacent to the college's Community Design building to create a demonstration garden for rainwater harvesting, urban edible plantings, and passive cooling to reduce temperatures in the adjacent building. The success of these studio projects led the faculty to establish a capstone design/build studio as part of the BLA curriculum, creating a culminating experience that challenges the students and demonstrates the department's commitment to public service. In 1998, architecture faculty member Sergio Palleroni invited the author to collaborate on a design/build program in Mexico. Students participating in this first international project completed the design and construction of a public *lavandaria* and a water treatment system to filter the gray water and irrigate a community orchard. Five years later, the international design/build studio has completed three projects over a three-year period on a decommissioned dumpsite in Guatemala City. Other recent projects include two gardens for disabled children in Bosnia and Herzegovina and four gardens for high school children in Croatia. As the success of our international work has been recognized through printed articles, presentations, and web documentation, nonprofits in Uganda, Puerto Rico, and Nicaragua have expressed interest in sponsoring projects including a medical clinic and gardens, a community for displaced persons, and gardens for a senior center. In addition to the Seattle-based BLA capstone design/build studio, we currently offer an average of one study abroad design/build studio per year.

## Educational Value

The international service-learning design/build program offers opportunities for learning that lectures and readings can't easily duplicate. The design/build model offers a unique form of experiential learning in which all the many pieces of designing (art) and building (technical) are fully engaged and integrated (Bennet 1998). Subjects that are usually taught in separate courses, such as design, community facilitation, and construction, are integrated in a manner that enables students to understand the iterative and integrative nature of the design process. At the end of the ten-week quarter, as students reflect on their built work, they gain a better sense of the way design incorporates scale, form, and rhythm and a better understanding of the potential uses and expressive characteristics of materials.

Most of the communities we work with are extremely poor, but as the students soon realize, poverty is not stupidity. When the students ask community members to describe their needs, aspirations, and fears, the response is always clear and direct. Our students facilitate a design process that is inclusive and transparent. Sustained community participation and input over the course of the project results in a level of understanding and trust that could not be achieved in a top-down process. Appropriate design is good design, and successful designers must understand and respond to the user's needs. We teach the value of aesthetics, craft, and creativity, but in the end the built work must meet the user's needs.

The process of construction is especially difficult for many students to comprehend until it is experienced as a logical and interdependent sequence of actions from beginning to end. Understanding the building process in this direct way helps students appreciate the relationship between design and construction. An ability to recognize the implications that design can have on the construction process is essential for success in professional design (Carpenter 1997). As Professor Melissa Harris explains, "A design concept cannot be divorced from the reality of construction or from a limited budget or from a need to function. A suggested solution will have to solve several problems simultaneously" (Harris 1997, 121).

The construction process remains vague and disconnected for students and most have difficulty understanding the various steps from layout and excavation to masonry and rough-finish carpentry. When asked to execute their designs during the construction phase, they readily admit it's a mystery where to begin. It is not until the project is close to completion that the parts, sequencing, and integration of trades come together for them. It is at this point that they understand the resource, craft, and economic implications of their designs.

Students participating in the program gain confidence and strengthen fundamental design and building skills. The experience also fosters leadership capacity and development of communication skills as students share design and construction ideas with their community partners. The students confront complex social and environmental problems, which, while disturbing, cannot be dismissed or ignored in the development of their design proposals. The experience can be intimidating and frustrating, but we hold frequent meetings where students can ask questions and voice concerns. Undoubtedly, the most rewarding aspect of the program comes at the completion of our work when the students are able to watch community members using the site. The students are able to reflect on their initial hopes and aspirations and compare them to the built reality. The process of self-reflection and critique is a critical skill for all designers.

## Partners

Our international design/build program depends on reliable, enduring partnerships with local NGOs and community groups. Developing and sustaining relationships requires a considerable time commitment. Typically the NGO partner is responsible for arranging housing, organizing volunteer support, providing translation, raising funds for building materials, and acting as a liaison with the community and governing agencies. The design/build program funds room and board, travel within the country, and faculty salaries. As director of the program, the author works with the NGO partner to oversee site coordination, material acquisition, banking transactions, and compliance with permitting procedures and legal obligations. Lack of familiarity with or insensitivity to local customs and conventions can lead to strained relationships and distrust among the community members. The NGOs have highly developed relationships with community members, government officials, and business partners and can often circumvent or minimize these setbacks.

This relationship with the NGO is an investment that pays increasing dividends each year that it is renewed; local networks expand and working relationships deepen. Prior to project initiation, we evaluate relationships with potential partners to share and understand each other's values, and to clarify our individual and shared responsibilities. While this practice is laudable in its intention, it is often difficult to truly assess partner relationships given the difficulty of arranging face-to-face meetings and the fact that the partners experience frequent staff turnover. While it is our intent to build long-term working relationships through successive projects, this is not always possible. In Guatemala we are entering the sixth year of our partnership and have completed three projects. In other cases, we have not been able to sustain partnerships due to difficulties incurred during the initial project and to leadership changes within the NGO. The long-term partnerships are certainly the most fruitful and fulfilling as we collectively recognize the value of our past efforts and deepen our understanding of the culture and the daily realities of those with whom we are working.

## Course Organization and Student Participation

The international design/build program is structured around four objectives:

1. Student immersion leading to cross-cultural exchange and awareness;
2. Development and facilitation of participatory community design;
3. Investigation of design, craft, and materials through construction;
4. Travel to gain a deeper understanding of the local environment and culture.

Students enrolled in the ten-week course receive a total of twelve to fourteen credits. The credits are distributed among three courses: materials in construction (three credits), design studio (six credits), and sketching or independent research and/or independent study (three credits).

With a growing faculty interest in global perspectives, cross-cultural collaboration, and social justice, student recruitment has become highly competitive. In smaller departments, the student pool may not support a foreign study program and it may be necessary to recruit students from outside the department and/or university. We enroll students from other universities as nonmatriculated students with the agreement to transfer full credit to their home institutions upon successful completion of the course. This relationship requires the agreement of the home institution and department in which the student is matriculated and often depends on the flexibility of institutional and department requirements.

Interest in international design/build service-learning continues to be very high among undergraduate and graduate students. Students from a wide range of programs within the university and from design programs at other institutions have joined the core group of University of Washington landscape architecture students in the design/build program. Interested students complete an application, with an essay explaining their interest in the program along with their knowledge of building, travel experience, and ability to work independently. Students apply for a variety of reasons. All of them express a desire to serve populations in need and to participate in the hands-on building process. Many of the applicants express their desire for an immersion experience that enables them to live in and work with a foreign community. The majority, about 80 percent, are landscape architecture students, but others from anthropology, civil engineering, architecture, industrial design, and general studies have participated successfully in the program. Our intent is to have a cross-section of students with differing backgrounds and a high level of commitment and passion.

A preprogram orientation seminar is held prior to departure to familiarize the students with the country, its history, people, politics, and art. Guest speakers with expertise in indigenous culture, social justice, and politics are invited to respond to students' questions and concerns. Other faculty and specialists from the local Seattle community discuss vernacular building technologies, crafts, and aesthetics and discuss the challenges in negotiating cross-cultural partnerships. The students are instructed in the proper use of tools and given a list of tools they will need to bring with them.

## Case Study: The Children's Garden of Hope, Guatemala City

The problems in Guatemala are complex and, at times, seemingly intractable (O'Kane 2005). Mayan families from agrarian mountain villages fled the thirty-year genocide to find work and safety in Guatemala City. Many are illiterate and the only work they are able to find is the collection, sorting, and reselling of trash to recycle brokers. The transition to urban life is difficult. Domestic abuse is common, the risk of gang recruitment is ever present, and the ingestion of chemicals including glue, gasoline, and industrial solvents is pervasive. Access to nourishing food and medical care is severely limited, and the presence of sewage, toxins, and airborne pollutants from the dump is inescapable.

Our local project partner, Safe Passage, is a nonprofit founded in 1999 to help the poorest of Guatemala's children break out of poverty through education. Their mission is to improve the lives of the children whose families live and work in the Guatemala City garbage dump. Safe Passage has a holistic family-centered approach that includes medical screening, prenatal and medical care, nutritional counseling, gang prevention and intervention, and classroom support (See Safe Passage website). Each child earns assistance, which includes clothing, books, and supplies, by regularly attending school and the daily school reinforcement program. Safe Passage depends on local and foreign volunteers to give the children the individual attention they desperately need.

### The Project

In 2004 Safe Passage was given a small piece of land, a decommissioned section of the existing garbage dump, to expand their program. They were in need of two new school facilities and decided to build a preschool for children three to five years old and a vocational training facility for children eight to seventeen years old on this site. Safe Passage envisioned developing the school grounds as a therapeutic park that would provide outdoor classrooms, recreational facilities, and a safe place for families to gather free from the threats and stress of the surrounding barrio. They named this park the Children's Garden of Hope.

The site is located one block from the entrance to the Guatemala City dump. The largest dump in Central America, it receives domestic, medical, and industrial waste from all over the city. One or both parents of the children participating in the Safe Passage program work in the dump for ten to twelve hours per day. The barrio around the dump is a residential area of metal and tarpaper shacks, some of which have evolved into small concrete-block homes as families are able to purchase building materials. These one- and two-room shacks have very limited space and primitive bathroom and cooking facilities. Most families eat only one or possibly two meals a day. The daily meal that children receive from Safe Passage is their primary source of nutrition.

### The Master Plan

In 2004 the author worked with Safe Passage teachers and administrators, a local landscape architect, and community members to prepare a master plan for the site. The plan proposed improvements that would complement the educational programs, providing outdoor classrooms, environments for play therapy, community gardens, sensory gardens, and recreational areas for physical and social development.

The site includes the two school buildings, and the landscape master plan divides the remaining area on the site into five activity zones. The first zone is an entry sequence that links the two buildings and serves as the formal gateway into the park. The second zone is an adventure play area located within the preschool. This play area is designed to encourage activities that address a range of social, physical, and cognitive developmental and educational goals. A modest raised soccer field, the third of the five zones, lies in the center of the park. An exploratory path weaves around the field and through gardens, trees, and graded grass mounds connecting the remaining zones. The fourth zone is the community garden with raised beds where mothers and children can grow vegetables to supplement their diets without the threat of toxic contamination. The fifth zone is an outdoor garden classroom that incorporates a gathering pavilion, passive play elements, and ethnobotanical gardens.

Focus group involving local Guatemalan mothers and university students, 2007. *Photo by Daniel Winterbottom*

## Project Start-Up and Student Arrival

When construction of the school buildings began in 2006, the University of Washington landscape architecture design/build program formed a partnership with Safe Passage to bring students to Guatemala to design and build four primary components of the park in five successive phases. The project teams ranged from eleven to nineteen students primarily from the University of Washington's Department of Landscape Architecture. The program has been led by a full-time faculty member and one or two teaching assistants with support from Safe Passage volunteer coordinators and staff. Students and faculty have been housed with local families in Antigua during the ten-week quarter and have commuted forty-five minutes Monday through Friday on a local "chicken bus" to work at the site in Guatemala City. Antigua, the old capital city, a world heritage site with walkable streets and tourist amenities, provides a retreat from the congestion of Guatemala City.

The first week was devoted to immersion exercises, community meetings, and site analysis. The students developed a community design process to encourage the participation of park users and invited parents, children, teachers, and care providers to a community workshop. At the workshop, the students facilitated small group focus sessions that enabled participants to share their needs and suggest ideas for the park. The students conducted photo surveys and prepared drawings to illustrate potential park activities so that community members would be better able to discuss and share their preferences. A student scribe documented the process and tabulated the results. Through the workshops, the students gained a deeper understanding of community needs and desires as well as the site constraints. The community participants developed a growing sense of ownership that promoted stewardship of the project within the community.

Over the ensuing two weeks, the students focused on conceptual design, design development, and community design review. Working in groups of three to five, they developed conceptual plans, which were presented and reviewed by a committee made up of administrators, teachers, and parents. Following the review, student representatives from each of the concept teams prepared a design proposal that integrated the preferred strategies and design elements. This design proposal was then presented to the committee for review. Once approved, the students spent the fourth week in design development and construction documentation. The following five weeks were devoted to construction, while the final week was reserved for guided travel to significant cultural and ecological sites.

### Construction

The construction day began at seven o'clock in the morning when the students caught the "chicken bus" in Antigua. Arriving in Guatemala City approximately an hour later, they began the work day with a group meeting to discuss the day's activities, explain construction methods, provide schedule and budget updates, and discuss emerging issues. The activities changed each day depending on the tasks to be accomplished. Students volunteered to lead the various tasks, and over the five weeks each student was responsible for a number of tasks. Students also volunteered for special jobs such as budget management, material selection, development of shop drawings for specialty fabrication, and development of instructional sessions for the Safe Passage students working with us. Periodic meetings were held with the Safe Passage project managers to discuss the progress and address issues needing attention.

We have typically worked with local materials and tend to limit the variety of construction materials used so that students can develop some sense of competence with them. In each case, the selection of materials was based on the site program. In 2006 the entry plaza was constructed using unit paving, concrete, and wood timbers. Wood, earth sculpting, and mosaic paving were chosen for the children's play area built in 2007, and in 2009 the students worked with concrete masonry units, stone, wood, and steel. Planting and soil improvements were addressed in each project. The students carried out most of the construction, including footings, masonry

Teaching assistant Malcolm Dole supervising students as they stake out columns for the adventure play structure constructed in 2007. *Photo by Daniel Winterbottom*

walls, tile installation, rebar work, wood framing, finish work, grading, and planting. Occasionally, we have had elements fabricated when we didn't have the tools or shop to do the work.

The location of the park on a decommissioned dump required that we take steps to mitigate the risk of health problems that could result from contamination in the soil and air. During construction, the students always wore protective clothing wherever contaminants were found. Most of the park was capped with either imported clay, soil, or paving material, and drainage systems were installed to reduce flooding.[1] Extensive tree plantings are being established to absorb soil toxins through phytoremediation, and hedgerows serve as catchments for migrating airborne particulates. The soils have been tested within the park and initial tests indicate that there are no significant levels of toxicity.

## Outcomes

Phase One, completed in the summer of 2006, includes a small soccer field, gathering area, entry structure, children's garden, and sensory gardens. Phase Two, an adventure play space at the elementary school, was built in Fall

2007, and Phase Three, a series of outdoor classrooms, was completed in Fall 2009. Rotary International has been the primary project funder, with additional help from private donors and foundations.

The transformation of the site, from a trash- and rubble-strewn vacant land into lush and verdant gardens that attract a diverse range of birds and insects, has brought a new sense of hope and pride to the community. The gardens provide a safe and calming refuge for the community and create a unique learning environment for the students. Many of the students who worked with us on site construction have entered the Safe Passage carpentry program at the vocational school, while other students provide site maintenance as part of their vocational training.

The students in the service-learning course gain immeasurable skills and have transformative life experiences. Few have ever experienced the level of poverty, desperation, and marginalization found in the barrio. Overwhelmed by the scale of the poverty, many struggle to develop design proposals that respond adequately to the community needs and agonize over the choices they must make. In the process of translating design proposals into built projects, the students develop a deeper understanding and appreciation for the design and documentation process. However, the most significant outcome is the students' journey from the project start-up, as they face a seemingly impossible task, to project completion, when they are able to reflect on their collective accomplishments. The students experience great satisfaction as community members embrace and enjoy their completed work.

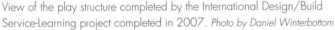

View of the play structure completed by the International Design/Build Service-Learning project completed in 2007. *Photo by Daniel Winterbottom*

## Reflections

It requires one and a half to two years to prepare for a foreign study project. In addition to the project selection and partnership development, faculty need to promote the course, recruit students, develop seminars, and administer the project. Once abroad, student contact averages ten to twelve hours per day, five days a week, with an additional two hours per day required for paperwork and administration. Projects in the developing world present challenges not typically encountered in conventional studios. In Guatemala, material acquisition and timely delivery, community politics, and governmental tampering all had an impact on project scheduling and completion. Because of the long-term commitment to our community partners, we accept these difficulties and work through them, building stronger relationships with community members, local material providers, and politicians.

### Student Support

Student health and safety is a paramount and daily concern. The risk of physical injury weighs on the faculty in charge, the departmental chairs, the college dean, and the university provosts. The university's Offices of International Programs and Risk Management address these concerns through a required orientation session and written guidelines intended to minimize risk (See University of Washington Office of Risk Management website). They stress the importance of wearing appropriate safety equipment, providing instructions on tool use, maintaining equipment, and monitoring safety on the construction site. The design/build program attends very closely to safety protocol; maintaining a safe environment is our foremost concern. However, we know that the risk from inexperience and distraction is always present, especially when working to complete a project on schedule. We typically have up to six teams working simultaneously on various tasks, with one faculty and a teaching assistant to monitor their work. Over many years of teaching design/build studios, I have had only one serious injury requiring hospitalization and recovery.

When the students arrive in Guatemala, Safe Passage provides further guidance for the students. Appropriate clothing, both for construction and modesty, is required. To avoid drawing unnecessary attention to our group, Safe Passage arranges transportation to and from the project site on a chicken bus. Students are asked to travel in pairs or in groups for safety. After dark we request that they take cabs and/or buses. In Guatemala, crime is increasing and, while caution is the best practice (US Department of State website), we have had our share of nerve-racking experiences despite being prudent about our behavior and travel patterns.

Our students can experience emotional strains as they work with families who are war refugees with visible effects of trauma. Many children suffer from abusive family situations and bear witness to horrific events in their homes and neighborhoods. As our students hear the stories and observe behavior resulting from these difficult circumstances, they are curious to learn more about the underlying problems. Many have difficulty comprehending and condoning behavior that appears to have tacit acceptance within the community. The students are in the difficult position of growing fond of the mothers and children, while feeling powerless to alleviate their troubled lives. To help the students work through these problems, we hold discussion sessions with social workers and counselors from Safe Passage. These counselors offer their insights and provide assurances that the Safe Passage programs and the students' contributions are effectively alleviating some of the problems facing the community.

### Engaging the Other, or Compassionate Design

The international design/build program places students in communities of which they have only a superficial understanding. As students confront the reality of the Guatemala City barrio, they are forced to acknowledge the privilege of their own lives. Students with little experience traveling in the third world find it hard to comprehend the prevalence and depth of poverty, violence, corruption, and the lack of social services. For many this is an uncomfortable and profound experience. As the students initiate the participatory design process, they often experience a level of community reticence and distrust. Students can find this disturbing; they are challenged as they work to facilitate collaboration and build trust. We encourage an ongoing process of self-reflection to help students uncover stereotypes and recognize preconceptions. We ask them to consider how their perspectives influence their day-to-day experience and we challenge them to think about their experience from a different cultural perspective. With the passage of time, barriers begin to break down. The intimacy of working together, eating meals together, sharing the successes of the day, the week, and the months creates a camaraderie through which cultural misunderstandings are revealed and negotiated.

Compassionate design evolves through student collaboration with community members during the design and construction process. Through informal conversation, community visits, and classroom discussion, the students come to understand community values, traditions, and needs. The students quickly recognize the community's seemingly intractable problems and special needs and begin to work through design studies to find ways that environmental design can reduce stress, support learning, and foster a healthier lifestyle. The students quickly reached out to the Mayan children, the innocent victims of poverty and marginalization, but it was not as easy for them to find compassion for rough teenagers who had developed delinquent behavior after years of gang membership. However, working side by side with the teens on the construction site, students began to understand the complexity of their lives and the challenges of their home and work situations. Through their participation in the project, the teenagers learned skills, developed a work ethic, and improved social skills as they communicated with those from a radically different culture and class. Empathy for those we are serving is woven throughout our process.

## The Student Experience

Students come to the international service-learning design/build program with differing expectations, skills, and life experiences. Over the last decade, we have seen more students embrace service as a critical, instructive component of their education. Our program views design as an act of compassion and believes that the privilege of education comes with the responsibility to improve the lives of others. Students who immerse themselves in the design/build program witness the difficulties and the aspirations of their

University of Washington student working with Safe Passage students to build a bench swing in 2006. *Photo by Daniel Winterbottom*

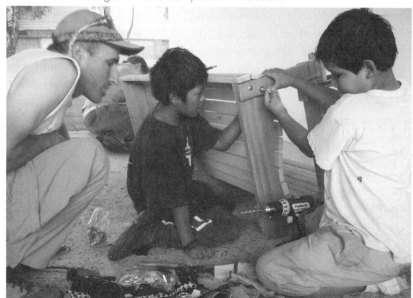

community partners and the inequity that exists in parts of the world. After a decade of working with students and marginalized populations, I find that most, though not all, have gained a deeper sense of compassionate service. For a few, roughly 10 to 20 percent, the experience directly influences their professional career decisions.

Nearly all of the students learn more about themselves and their relationships with others. The design students apply and validate their training as they solve complex problems, provide constructive peer critiques, and carry design studies forward through construction. Graduate students with previous travel experience adjust to cultural differences and commit eagerly to the demanding work schedule. The undergraduate students tend to be less intellectually rigorous in their approach to the program, but more open and relaxed with the many new aspects of experiential learning. The students return with an increased sense of self-confidence and independence. Alumni recall that the experience changed their perspectives of landscape architecture and that they came to recognize the potential of the profession to address issues of environmental and social justice. Many have described the service-learning course as one of their most memorable academic experiences.

## Institutional Impact and Support

Service-learning brings welcome recognition to institutions of higher learning. For a state university, these projects underscore the community benefits and "good deeds" that tax payers are in part supporting. The accomplishments of our projects, the human drama and laudable goals, make our story noteworthy. Our program has received numerous national awards and the university paper regularly publishes articles about our projects. Clearly the public relations value of the international service-learning design/build program is a benefit to the college; yet the College of Built Environments provides little funding. Funding is necessary for scholarship aid, outreach, project development, and equipment maintenance. The International Study Programs Office provides small grants ranging from $2,500 to $3,000 to encourage and expand international educational opportunities. However, as increasing numbers of students participate in international studies, these limited funds make it difficult to offset operating costs and keep program fees low. Faculty time spent to secure funding limits the time that is available to spend on instructional development, scholarly research, and publishing. The lack of funding support by the college mirrors the lack of scholarly recognition given to this work during the tenure and promotion process.

## Conclusion

The success of our service work is tied to strong partner relationships and to the open and responsive nature of our design/build process. Our long-term relationship with Safe Passage has given us the unique opportunity to reevaluate and adjust the master plan in response to emerging issues and staff insights. There are limitations to what we can accomplish given the complexity and scale of the problems, the limitations of time and resources, and the range of skills among the students. However, it is our hope that through our partnership, the community will gain the confidence and initiative to carry on change long after we leave. Community empowerment is the guiding principle of our work.

The challenges facing the families of the Guatemala City garbage dump are monumental. Our small team works at a modest scale. For our community partners, the results are transformative, but given the thousands of families in need, a relatively small number are engaged by our service. We believe that our service-learning design/build program can serve as a model for others. The organization and the process are transferable and replicable. NGOs working with similar populations in Nicaragua, Panama, and Cuba have visited our project sites and are using our template and applying it with modifications to meet their specific goals.

The benefits of small projects can be surprisingly profound. For the children living in the barrio, the gardens are a verdant oasis. Plantings weave along the paths, through the plazas, and around the play equipment, providing shade under the arbors. Children and mothers are transported to a place that seems far away, safe, and nurturing. For these families, the plants and protected areas in the park offer a therapeutic counterpoint to the stresses they confront on a daily basis.

Landscape architects offer pro bono services to create designs for schools, community centers, and gardens, but few offer such services in other countries. As an alternative learning model, the international service-learning design/build program introduces students to a different culture, facilitates their participation in meaningful service, and introduces an alternative practice. Students acquire expertise in participatory community design, the ability to evaluate the appropriateness of design from different cultural perspectives, and the capacity to participate in compassionate design. Some of the most important transformations are invisible and perhaps only indirectly related to practice. And yet, if we seek to prepare future practitioners who are compassionate designers and committed world citizens, these inner changes matter greatly.

# PART FOUR

# Confronting Academic Boundaries

## Editor's Introduction

**A** **cademic frameworks and** boundaries—institutional, curricular, and pedagogical—impact and often hinder the ability of faculty to embrace and adopt service-learning. Disciplinary boundaries put educators in separate silos that limit the ability to address complex real-world problems that are not neatly organized into separate boxes. The curricular and institutional structures of universities are often lagging in their ability to foster theories and practices of collaboration, collective problem solving, and relationship building. Specialized courses in design and planning can neglect the need to integrate knowledge and experience. And the hierarchies of administrators and educators within universities may limit the extent to which university resources can be coordinated and maximized.

Service-learning courses are not structured around a particular discipline but are typically based on a community-identified problem that is often ill defined, open-ended, complex, and messy. Even with thoughtful planning on the part of faculty and community partners, it is impossible to foresee all the practical and pedagogical problems that might arise when the space of learning shifts to a community context. This requires a more open and flexible approach to curricula and more flexible institutions.

The chapters in this section suggest how to deal constructively with academic boundaries. They show how experiences involving community service are prodding faculty, departments, and academic units to adjust, adapt, and change their academic programs so that the full transformative value of service-learning can be achieved.

There is a need to recognize and transform the academic boundaries and structures—many of them self-imposed—that restrict the dynamic relations and knowledge exchange sought by service-learning. So suggest the team of University of Michigan authors, *Pat Crawford, Zenia Kotval,* and *Patricia Machemer,* who argue that disciplinary autonomy, reinforced in professional curricula, pedagogy, and departmental structures, is one of the major limiting factors in professional design and planning education. Often missing from education are the synergistic exchanges one needs to understand and address complex contemporary community and environmental problems. In their paper, these authors show how the "boundaries model" of education constrains and hinders dialogue and cooperative action.

The Commonwealth Avenue Studio Project at Virginia Tech's Washington Alexandria Architecture Center, described in the paper by *Paul Kelsch* and *Joseph Schilling,* focuses on bridging disciplines, balancing student abilities, furthering educational objectives, and addressing community needs. Their story chronicles how they improvised and adapted their respective disciplinary approaches, course objectives, and working modes to address the complex set of issues and problems facing a diverse group of neighborhoods along an historic road corridor.

In their senior year, landscape architecture students at the University of Maryland enroll in a capstone studio working with underserved neighborhoods. The studio's prominence in the undergraduate curriculum reflects the university's institutional support for the scholarship of engagement. *Jack Sullivan* shows how the capstone project emphasizes participatory community design to accomplish one of its core learning goals—engagement.

*Linda Corkery* and *Ann Quinlan* close the chapter by demonstrating how the FBEOutThere! program at the University of New South Wales (UNSW) in Australia facilitates and administers a scholarship of engagement within the Faculty of the Built Environment's six professional disciplines. The program is an established institution within the university that helps legitimize community engagement. It helps to deepen the pedagogy of engagement, advance built environment research through inquiry-based design projects, and facilitate interdisciplinary collaboration.

## Prescriptions for Change: Crossing Academic Boundaries

Disciplinary knowledge alone—of urban planning, architecture, and landscape architecture—will not adequately prepare students for life and work after college. Practitioners must have the capacity to understand and distinguish broad societal contexts, be responsive and receptive to the needs of others, collaborate and collectively problem solve, connect cause and effect, and realize the limits and potential for taking action.

Rooted in living worlds and situated problems, not disciplines, service-learning stimulates cooperative action across communities, disciplines, and subject areas. As an agent for collaboration and relationship building, the educator can be a vital force behind alternative models based on integration and synergy instead of separation and division. Only by understanding and questioning boundaries will designers and planners overcome the barriers arising from pedagogy, professional education, disciplinary autonomy, and academic curricula. With the priority now placed on sustainability, the design and planning professions are rediscovering holistic, cross-disciplinary approaches. But institutional obstacles and disciplinary and pedagogical boundaries can make these approaches difficult and cumbersome to undertake.

Unlike the typical on-campus studio course, community-based service-learning demands a deliberate, incremental approach involving ongoing revisions, negotiations, and adjustments. This arises as a function of the complex relationships among all players—academic and community alike. Success requires a continuous and methodical effort to link theory and practice. Integrated reflection and evaluation practices underscore and emphasize the importance and value of this link.

## CHAPTER 12

# From Boundaries to Synergies of Knowledge and Expertise

*Using Pedagogy as a Driving Force for Change*

*Pat Crawford, Zenia Kotval, and Patricia Machemer*

## Introduction

**This chapter attempts** to address the question of how we can overcome boundaries created by our current academic curricula, pedagogical strategies, and professional education practices in order to better serve communities through academic service-learning. We draw upon our experiences confronting the boundaries separating our own disciplines of landscape architecture, urban planning, and architecture, and we call for more cross-disciplinary service-learning activities and community-based research and practice.

Unearthing and understanding both the boundaries and potential synergies created by our professional education practices and institutional settings is the first step toward answering this central question. Too often, the current institutional climate (which encompasses physical classroom accommodations, semester time constraints, and even faculty promotion and tenure requirements) supports and reinforces professional and educational boundaries through academic curricula, a focus on disciplinary autonomy, and pedagogical strategies.

This chapter examines existing scholarship on service-learning and then discusses the potential synergies of, as well as barriers to, interdisciplinary service-learning within the academic setting. We conclude by presenting a visual model of the boundaries showing how traditional professional education reinforces boundaries, followed by a synergies model in which pedagogical strategies, especially service-learning, act as the driving force to create synergies that better support interdisciplinary service to communities.

## Previous Scholarship on Cross-Disciplinary Experiential Learning

Professional programs benefit from applied, field-based research and practice. One form of practice is service-based learning, which we value not only as a teaching tool but also for the social good it creates. We believe that professional programs such as urban planning, community development, and landscape architecture ought to embrace service-learning, which, grounded as it is in holistic service to the community, is by its nature cross-disciplinary.

An initial search for scholarly articles on fieldwork, experiential learning, service-based learning, or applied learning indicates much interest in this service-based pedagogy across subject areas (Gibbs 1992; Harland 1998; Kolb 1994). While service-learning is almost mandatory in our fields of study (landscape architecture, urban planning, and architecture), it is also present in other disciplines, such as biology, engineering, and economics. While the structure and value of courses built around service-learning vary by disciplines, most educators agree that it is a valid teaching technique that enhances student learning and experience. The *Journal of Planning Education and Research* (special issue 1998) dedicated an entire volume to university and community partnerships. Scholars have addressed effective delivery of field courses and the importance of transferable skills such as the ability to communicate and present material, time management, problem solving, and negotiation (Chapman 2000; Crawford and Machemer 2008; Fink 2003; Kotval 2003; Marsick and Watkins 2001).

The professional disciplines of planning and design are built on experience and learning by doing (Wagner and Gansemer-Topf 2005). Through experiential immersion, students learn how to take the complex disciplinary components of the profession and integrate them into practice (Educating LAs 1998).

These approaches aim to educate the whole student (Camp 1996) by providing a venue in which students can expand their professional practice knowledge and skills, develop lifelong-learning skills, and enhance interpersonal skills. Service-learning, which is one type of experiential learning, provides students with an "experience component that ... adds a whole new dimension of quality to their learning" (Fink 2003, 21). Learn and Serve America, a program of the Corporation of National and Community Service (a federal agency), defines service-learning as "a teaching and learning strategy that integrates meaningful community service with instruction and reflection to enrich the learning experience, teach civic responsibility, and strengthen communities" (Seifer and Connors 2007, 4).

Students who participate in service-learning take responsibility for their learning and become active participants in the learning process. Advocates claim that service-learning also fosters increased personal development, a sense of social responsibility, commitment to service, ability to apply learning to real-world situations, problem analysis, critical thinking, and student satisfaction (Eyler et al. 2001). Addressing student learning and motivation, McAleavey (1996, 2) comments that "service-learning provides a vehicle to effect change because it readily engages the emotions and spirit, which is … deeply motivating." Expressed or implied in descriptions of service-learning is a constructivist view of knowledge, as is clear from the fact that the professor is not a "sage on stage" but a facilitator and coach for the learning experience.

## Barriers and Synergies

In spite of the fact that professional fields as varied as health sciences, human resources, urban planning, management, public administration, engineering, information technology, and even economics, geography, and biology have a need for cross-disciplinary and service-based learning (Kotval 2003), cross-disciplinary teaching and coursework is still not a part of the mainstream curriculum. And yet, the fields of urban planning, landscape architecture, and design benefit enormously from cross-disciplinary and service-based learning when it is available. Service-learning for these fields mainly involves communities, and community development is interdisciplinary in nature. Working in communities requires many skills. One cannot approach it from a planning perspective alone, for example, because it also has sociopolitical ramifications. But neither can one approach it from the angle of social work alone, because community development is also concerned with improving the physical condition of place and space. But it is also more than architecture and design, because one has to understand the broader urban and regional context (Deitrick and Soska 2008). To be truly effective, those in the fields of urban planning, landscape architecture, and architecture need to partner with people in public affairs and social work, business and law, public policy and administration, and political science.

We do this in professional practice. Any consulting team working on a community project brings professionals from different disciplines to form a team. So why is it so difficult in academia? We can find all these disciplines on a single university campus, so why not at the same table? Shaffer and Marcouiller (2006) suggest that holistic and multidimensional approaches to solving community problems are just too big and messy to operationalize. And perhaps, in academia, there is no incentive to deal with the additional challenge. Academics seem more comfortable with scientific research, academic freedom, and disciplinary rigor than the muddy reality of community-based problems. Furthermore, the career path of an academic, even in professional programs, has little to do with community engagement and service-learning. Promotion and tenure rely heavily on grants and publications in scholarly journals. This is true even at land-grant universities, where community service and outreach is a mandate.

For the purposes of our work, we define barriers as the real or understood limitations that hinder explorations outside our disciplinary boundaries. We define synergy, on the other hand, as a cooperative action that crosses disciplines and strengthens the overall result. Synergies act as catalysts to bring seemingly disparate parts together to create a holistic solution. In this paper, we address the barriers and synergies to multidisciplinary work within our academic setting in three areas: pedagogy, academic curriculum, and disciplinary autonomy.

### Pedagogy—Service-Learning

**Synergies.** If we accept service-learning as valuable pedagogy, we must realize the need to work across our disciplines. One cannot work in the community and remain barricaded behind disciplinary boundaries: community development problems are transdisciplinary and involve multiple stakeholders. Service-learning may be the perfect place to start working across disciplinary boundaries. Our professional fields share a common goal—improving the quality of life of people. The value of service-learning for our students is discussed in many scholarly articles. The value of incidental learning, developing transferable life skills, interacting collaboratively, and learning to compromise within teams has been explored and discussed. As such, the synergies seem quite clear.

Service-learning in planning and design fields involves multiple stakeholders (professionals, community members, legislators, etc.). Often these stakeholders are intimately connected with the project and perceive the interconnectedness of their real-world issues. To work with the clients, the class must address issues that appear to be outside their disciplinary bounds. Instructors and students often take off their disciplinary lenses in an attempt to see the planning project in the same light as their clients. They move out of their comfort zones in order to be sensitive to the clients and to comprehend real-world issues. Willingness to accept the discomfort creates an environment for synergies to flourish as participants seek out collaborators.

**Barriers.** It may be that our faculty have insufficient interdisciplinary knowledge. We teach our courses within our programs and sometimes invite colleagues to give guest lectures or seminars, but we do not profess to be experts in one another's fields. We are comfortable with that model.

What would happen in an interdisciplinary course where multiple professors have equal roles and students bring their disparate disciplinary ideals with them? The expression of alternate, often differing, ideas can create a messy teaching and learning environment. The concept of not having full control over your class, of losing autonomy, of making concessions on the course without agreeing adds an additional layer to an already complicated studio environment. Not all faculty are comfortable in this environment.

From a student perspective, the traditional model of "listen and absorb" is shattered. The entire dynamic of learning is changed. You are not being taught by a single professor or expert, you are being subjected to different ideas, different perceptions. If the professors do not agree on one "right" way, how do you follow? Students in this environment are expected to think, participate, evaluate, and adjust their ideas based on multiple viewpoints. This teaching and learning environment might call for a more mature student, someone comfortable with ambiguity and complexity (Greening 1998). Students have to have a level of critical thinking that is beyond the dualist or multiplicity mode, as described by Perry (1999).

This endeavor requires not only able and willing students but also able and willing instructors. It takes far more effort on the part of both faculty and student to contribute in this multidisciplinary environment. It requires additional management and skills, and it induces stress and frustration that affect collegiality and reduce autonomy. One might well ask, why bother? If it's not an absolute requirement and the academic setting does not provide enough incentive or recognition to warrant the extra effort and commitment, is it worth our time and effort to accept greater risk, manage an uncertain project, deal with messy interruptions, and work in an uncontrolled, nonspecified environment?

## Academic Curriculum

**Synergies.** We are dealing with professional disciplines. We train our students to go out into the community and practice in their fields. We understand and accept that our field is multifaceted. Our professional responsibility, then, is to encourage and facilitate an interdisciplinary curriculum, at minimum, or better still, the loftier goal of an integrated curriculum. One curricular approach that recognizes the transdisciplinary nature of landscape architecture, urban planning, and architecture is the cross-referencing of classes offered. This starts to frame an interdisciplinary curriculum. When classes and curricula are developed around the problem and not the discipline, integrated learning can be achieved (Beane 1997; Huber and Hutchings 2004).

Today's educators are faced with the millennium generation, those students who were born after 1992. These individuals have never known a world without computer technology, cell phones, and nearly instantaneous communication. This has given them skills in multitasking, social decision making, and tackling real-life issues that makes them receptive to integrated learning (Tucker 2006; Tyler 2007). The integrated curriculum is congruent with their social approach to problem solving.

Curricula influence pedagogical choices and degree of flexibility. A curriculum can allow for a variety of pedagogical experiences within the students' academic career. For landscape architects, planners, and architects, for example, Beaux Arts studio experiences can be complemented by large-classroom experiences. A curriculum built around a studio environment permits continuous feedback opportunities among students and instructors. Additionally, students are allowed to fail without failing. A curriculum built around large classrooms also has advantages. Such classes provide economies of scale and allow for a diversity of students from different disciplines within a course. At institutions of higher education, where there is a wide diversity of disciplines, these large classrooms allow students to meet and interact with others outside their own specialty. This environment promotes metacognitive-level questioning as students bring their own areas of interest and knowledge to bear.

**Barriers.** We operate within our individual academic curricular environments. Our disciplines have separate philosophies, accreditation boards, preconceived opinions, skill requirements, codes of ethics, and stakeholders driving curriculum development. In many instances, our disciplines are housed in multiple colleges and even in different buildings. These physical barriers sustain an individualistic work environment. We cannot assume we even know one another's faculty or curricula.

Our accrediting bodies often specify the number of credits needed for graduation, along with the key subject areas that need to be taught. Given the time and cost of graduate education, we often try to streamline our curricula to the bare necessities. Our curricula do not mandate or even encourage interdisciplinary education. Furthermore, our unfamiliarity with curricula and faculty outside our own disciplines makes cross-disciplinary collaboration very difficult. While collaborating outside our disciplines is encouraged by upper administration, the reality remains that one is evaluated within one's own department or program, and the expectation is that one's focus will be on furthering program missions. Tight curriculum structures and lack of incentives for collaborating mean that neither faculty nor students are encouraged to go the extra step.

### Disciplinary Autonomy

**Synergies.** An appreciation of excellence is a common denominator across disciplines, and the presence of excellence is often a precursor to collaboration and interdisciplinary projects. Appreciation of excellence leads to respect, a required element for erasing boundaries. Because we are autonomous, we have the freedom to engage others to achieve quality planning and design projects. And because these projects are always complex and multifaceted, we must, in fact, engage other experts during all phases of the project. Our disciplines will remain specialized because "generalization never matches the results achieved by effective collaboration between skilled specialists" (Spence, Macmillan, and Kirby 2001, xi).

It is our autonomy that allows us to work collaboratively. Spence, Macmillan, and Kirby (2001) propose that collaboration depends on:

- Excellence in our own fields;
- Understanding the concerns of fellow participants;
- An inclusive and shared approach to the task;
- Ability to listen;
- Communication of our enthusiasm and passion.

Because of our autonomy, it is possible to achieve the above elements, and these elements allow a strong individual to foster collaborative excellence.

**Barriers.** There are a number of barriers to the integration of landscape architecture, planning, and architecture that emanate from disciplinary autonomy. The methods and approaches used in both research and education are often different. For example, planning programs accept qualitative research methods, such as using surveys, while architecture may view quantitative analysis as the only acceptable method. This difference may be a result of different foci of study or the age and evolution of the discipline. Each discipline has its own history, and too often the histories are used to highlight the chasm between disciplines rather than to find the overlap. Related to this is the lack of theory and theory development both within and across the disciplines. Without a theoretical foundation, it is difficult for the disciplines to even begin the conversation, much less articulate points of a common theory.

The disciplines also have different social norms and ways of doing things. The studio mentality in landscape architecture and architecture may be unfamiliar and uncomfortable to planning students and their professors. The disciplines tend to use their own languages, so that even when there is a common approach, the language used prevents the participants from recognizing the sameness. For example, planning students are familiar with SWOT (strengths, weaknesses, opportunities, and threats) analysis, while students in landscape architecture speak in terms of site opportunities and constraints. In both cases, the students are analyzing a site or situation and identifying both positive and negative elements, but the language can be a barrier.

Disciplinary autonomy often tacitly discourages questioning of disciplinary assumptions. The nature of disciplines is to hold fast to the assumptions that identify the discipline. It is difficult for the disciplines to erase the boundaries between them if they are unwilling to question their own disciplinary assumptions.

The academic career paths of professors in the various disciplines both emphasize and reinforce disciplinary autonomy and at the same time act as barriers to interdisciplinary cooperation. Professional practice in search of real-world solutions requires team building and multifaceted organizations. It is common to see a professional firm with architects, planners, and landscape architects working alongside one another. In academia, professors often begin their careers in post-secondary education, then continue on to graduate school and land a faculty position without ever working in the profession. Departments frequently use their own discipline as a filter for hiring faculty. The role of practice and cross-disciplinary work is too often relegated to professionals acting as adjunct faculty.

## The Models

The following visual models show the interaction between the synergies and boundaries of pedagogy, academic curricula, and disciplinary autonomy in professional education in the disciplines under consideration.

### The Boundaries Model

For our work, a boundary is defined as the real or understood line marking a limit. In the boundaries model, professional education operates as a closed system. This strengthens disciplinary silos and pushes the disciplines of architecture, landscape architecture, and urban planning apart.

The primary force maintaining boundaries is professional education practices and each discipline's desire to "claim a slice of the pie." Faculty and students populate each slice to foster and maintain the parochial disciplinary cultures. Traditionally, each discipline competes individually for research funding, student seat counts, and physical space. In the boundaries model, professional education is located at the circumference, and the disciplines are graphically demarcated by dashed lines, which represent real, understood, and, in some cases, self-imposed boundaries. Pedagogical strategies, academic curricula, and disciplinary autonomy are present inside each slice and as internal drivers of boundaries. Each is diagrammed as a separate box because they too can operate in isolation. For example, professional program

Boundaries model.
*Illustration by Pat Crawford*

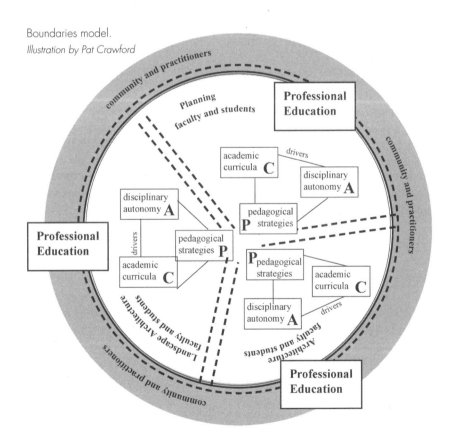

accreditation can be used to reinforce disciplinary autonomy through curriculum design. Autonomy at the individual faculty level can be so strong in an institutional mind-set that the academic curriculum is fragmented.

Communities and practitioners orbit the outer perimeter with limited direct or meaningful engagement. Outsiders must access each discipline separately through multiple contacts to create a full planning, landscape architectural, and architectural picture. Community engagement is allowed along the narrow pathway into the center. Once at the center, a community must select a discipline to engage.

Pedagogical strategies for each discipline are intentionally diagrammed closer to the center of the circle. Service-learning, often enacted as community-based planning and design, is a common pedagogical strategy. While the service-learning pedagogy creates an entry point for communities, the professional-education barriers are so strong and the overall institutional context is so unsupportive that it is difficult for service-learning to become a catalyst for interdisciplinary engagement.

Within the boundaries model, the central location of pedagogical strategies positions this aspect of professional education as a potential driving force for change.

## From a Boundaries Model to a Synergies Model

Given all these individual and institutional barriers, how do we begin to erase the boundaries amongst our disciplines? How can we change the culture so that taking risks and trying something different is acceptable, uncertain learning outcomes are acceptable, and thorny problems with no systematic solution may be introduced?

There is a new generation of practice-based scholars who see the need for service-learning across disciplines. We are teaching a generation of students who are exposed to collaboration and multitasking and encouraged to think and question authority. Given the professional and practice-oriented nature of our disciplines, we need to chart a new trajectory within academia.

We do have a common purpose; we do have courses within our curriculum that lend themselves to interdisciplinary activities. We can collaborate on applied research. We can be deliberative scholars who reflect on the relevance of our teaching and how it affects the well-being of our professions. Toward this goal, we offer a model that can help move from boundaries to synergies of knowledge and expertise, using pedagogy as a driving force for change.

### The Synergies Model

Synergy is at the heart of community design and planning that requires many components. The service-learning approach is a natural fit for community engagement in planning and design processes and can operate as the primary synergistic force to bring about change. This pedagogy, with its emphasis on learning through action, applied research, and experience, can help erase the boundaries separating the community planning and design disciplines.

In the synergies model, pedagogical strategies are moved to the circumference and professional education takes up the full center. (In the boundaries model, the center was empty space, representing a dead or neutral zone.) The disciplines still maintain an identifiable core and professional identity,

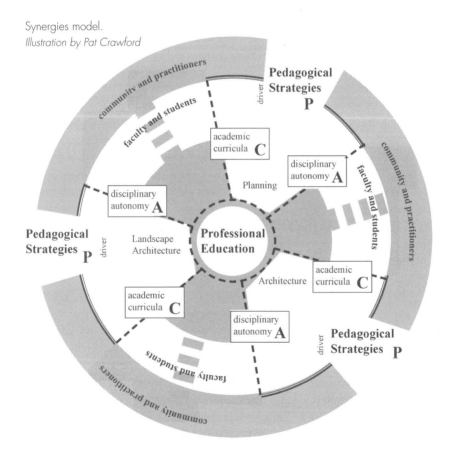

Synergies model.
*Illustration by Pat Crawford*

but disciplinary autonomy and academic curricula are allowed to break the boundary edges when appropriate. Faculty and students create a broadened human zone, creating a connective flow between community and practitioners within the professional education arena.

The synergies model addresses the seven issue areas identified by Gelmon (Gelmon et al. 2001). They frame the institutional movement from teaching to learning with seven key issue areas: knowledge, focus, instruction, student learning, curriculum definition, design, and continued change. With a service-learning pedagogical strategy as the synergistic force, passive knowledge acquisition bounded by professional discipline gives way to an active learning experience within communities and across disciplines. The educational focus moves from the individual faculty or student, with a banking instructional approach, to a team and community endeavor with a collective approach. Communities and students can help define the curriculum, and learning sequences can be designed to help remove barriers. A virtuous cycle of continuous improvement can be established as collective learning occurs.

## Interpretation

Universities are steeped in tradition. They pride themselves on excellence and a successful track record. Universities are responsible for making the scientific and technological discoveries that will guide future generations. They are institutions of higher learning. The world of practice, for its part, requires a patchwork of skills, degrees of compromise, and political acuteness. Practice is more about solving today's problems, being understanding and equitable.

Professionals in the field see universities as lofty institutions isolated from real life. Conversely, many academics think of practitioners as anti-intellectuals. This conflict between academic theory and professional practice has been documented and argued for generations.

In professions such as ours, professional organizations attempt to bridge the gap between the university on one side and the cross-disciplinary issues facing professionals in the field today on the other. While the academy labors to change, professional organizations are creating their own training programs. Continuing education programs are being offered by the American Planning Association, the Urban Institute, International City/County Management Association, International Economic Development Council, the US Green Building Council, and the International Downtown Association (Deitrick and Soska 2008). State governments are developing and adopting tool kits to help understand the multiple facets of sustainability, healthy communities, green design, and infrastructure. Even the federal government sponsors programs, including the Development Training Institute, NeighborWorks, local-initiative programs, and faith-based efforts.

Even research universities are creating centers or institutes that engage faculty and students in interdisciplinary projects. The Center for Economic Development at the University of Massachusetts, the Global Urban Studies Program and Land Policy Institute at Michigan State, and the Center for Urban and Regional Policy at Northeastern are just a few examples of the rapid proliferation of cross-disciplinary activities. These nonacademic units do not suffer from a need to protect disciplinary autonomy; they can work across different academic programs to create a holistic project greater than any single discipline. In other words, they create synergies. Furthermore, these centers and institutes are able to explore multiple funding options, reach broader audiences, create hybrid solutions, and chart new territory. Perhaps this proliferation of centers and programs ought to serve as a wake-up call to academic units about their lack of coordination and the limits of their current curriculum design.

Service-learning undertaken within a university environment where engaged scholarship is recognized and valued will dismantle the professional education silos that have all too long acted as barriers to integration. University structure must transition to a holistic approach that not only encourages transdisciplinary teaching, research, and outreach, but also requires disciplines, such as landscape architecture and planning, to collaborate.

If we are to move from dialogue to action, both top-down and bottom-up approaches are needed. From the top, academic institutions—particularly academic administrations—need to recognize and give merit to transdisciplinary research and service-learning as scholarship. Simultaneously, faculty need to transition from a focus on the community service and active learning aspects of service-learning to see service-learning as the scholarship of engagement.

We need to connect our passions with our scholarship. With a milieu of scholarship as discovery, integration, application, and teaching (Boyer 1990; Glassick, Huber, and Maeroff 1997), we can tackle our boundaries and encourage the synergies that lead to positive change.

## CHAPTER 13

# Integrating Disciplines, Practices, and Perspectives in the Commonwealth Avenue Project

*Paul Kelsch and Joseph Schilling*

**In late 2005** the Del Ray Citizen Association approached the Washington Alexandria Architecture Center (Alexandria Center), a twenty-five-year-old urban extension of Virginia Tech's College of Architecture and Urban Studies, seeking assistance in designing traffic-calming measures and safer street crossings in their neighborhood's section of Commonwealth Avenue. Commonwealth Avenue runs for two and a half miles through Alexandria, Virginia, following the route of the first trolley line leading from Washington, DC, into Virginia. Today it travels through three distinct communities—Rosemont, Del Ray, and Arlandria—and functions as an especially busy corridor for local residents and commuters on their way to and from Old Town Alexandria.

While the city of Alexandria touts its park character and role, Commonwealth Avenue currently falls short of being a linear park for the neighborhoods it serves. In some places, Commonwealth Avenue has a wide median shaded by beautiful mature oaks and providing ample room for sidewalks, bike paths, and parking. Yet, often the street narrows, the median disappears, and pedestrians are forced to walk in the street while dodging bicycles and cars. Though used by pedestrians and bicyclists, commuters are the Avenue's primary users especially during the morning and evening rush hours. Situated in a slight valley crossing a local watershed boundary, Commonwealth Avenue's culverted streams and storm sewers are particularly vulnerable to flooding and in need of stormwater management.

## Community Context

Commonwealth Avenue and the communities it traverses cover a large geographical area with diverse neighborhoods, physical attributes, functions, activities, and patterns influencing its community character, identity, and impact. The avenue's three distinct communities include Rosemont at the south end, an almost exclusively residential area, and due to its metro access, the priciest place to live. At Rosemont's southern end, the avenue includes a wide median with diverse vegetation and a couple of adjacent, remnant landscapes being used as neighborhood parks. Del Ray, the middle neighborhood, maintains a strong sense of identity due to its small but lively arts community and thriving, eclectic commercial districts on Mount Vernon and Commonwealth Avenues. The local library branch, a community center, and an elementary school and schoolyard are all found in the Del Ray section of the avenue. At the avenue's north end, Arlandria is the most economically and socially diverse section with more than 50 percent of its residents being non-white and living in rental housing units (US Census 2000). It has sizeable Latino and African American populations and a mix of commercial, residential, and institutional uses both along and adjacent to the avenue. The Arlandria neighborhood feels quite divided from Del Ray and Rosemont socially, topographically, economically, and visually.[1] Crime, safety, and vandalism pose a major concern to long-standing Arlandria residents.

A significant physical barrier to the neighborhood is the intersection of Commonwealth Avenue and Mount Vernon Avenue, which also divides Arlandria and Del Ray. The intersection is complicated to cross, and the dramatic change in its physical character makes it feel like two distinct places. On the Arlandria side of the intersection, Commonwealth Avenue runs downhill toward Four Mile Run, where flooding and stormwater problems frequently impact the schoolyard and park at the northern end. A narrow median planted with small ornamental trees—not the tall oaks of Del Ray and Rosemont—leads to the street's final stretch, which narrows even further before terminating in a little used cul-de-sac adjacent to Four Mile Run.

## Studio Overview

Del Ray residents perceived their interests were being overlooked by city leaders and hoped that by working with Virginia Tech, they could gain a voice in determining Commonwealth Avenue's future. While touring Del Ray with urban planning and landscape architecture faculty, Jim Snyder from the Del Ray Citizens Association repeatedly emphasized the avenue's bigger issues including inconsistent sidewalks and bike lanes, declining vegetation, increasing traffic, and especially its fragmented character as it passes through communities. The initial goal of traffic calming quickly gave way to expressing a greater need directed at creating a coherent vision for transforming Commonwealth Avenue into a park-like landscape. A joint planning and landscape architecture studio was immediately conceived to assist Del Ray and its neighboring communities with identifying ways to make Commonwealth Avenue serve their open space needs. Such an approach synced with the city's current Open Space Plan and the fact that Alexandria's fully developed urban landscape provides few opportunities for new parks (City of Alexandria 2002, 44). The Del Ray Citizens Association raised roughly $3,500 from its annual home tour, allowing Virginia Tech to cover direct studio costs and preparation of the final studio report. It agreed to help organize and attend meetings and focus groups and link students and faculty to community partners.

Three graduate-level Alexandria Center classes joined forces to undertake what became known as the Commonwealth Avenue Studio Project. Professor Joseph Schilling led a planning studio, Professor Paul Kelsch, a landscape architecture studio, and Schilling and adjunct Professor Kathryn McCarty co-led a community involvement course. It was decided that students in the community involvement class would identify community concerns and collect resident feedback—thereby providing a link between the community and the planning and design studios that were tasked to conceive design and planning alternatives. As in any community-based planning and development effort, decisions involve a myriad of diverse parties, often with competing and conflicting interests. A well-designed community involvement process helps participants constructively share their concerns and, it is hoped, build consensus around a set of solutions representing their common interests and goals (Innes 1996).

This was the Alexandria Center's first joint studio of this type and logistics proved challenging from the outset. The planning and landscape architecture studios met at different times and had different credit hours; the community involvement students were not enrolled in the studios or vice versa; Schilling and Kelsch were assigned to the project and had never met one another; Kelsch was brand new to the Center; Schilling had not taught a studio before; and neither was very familiar with the other's discipline. However, Schilling and McCarty each had significant experience designing and facilitating public meetings in planning processes; Kelsch had worked with communities in Baltimore in previous design studios; and all three were excited about the opportunities that the project held for both the academic and community partners.

In spite of a lack of familiarity between disciplines and pedagogy, the faculty and, subsequently, the students quickly found that their complementary styles and shared emphasis on open-ended, intuitive learning provided a common ground. To proceed, the collaborating faculty agreed that the project process needed to stay open to flexibility and improvisation. The group agreed it was not necessary to preplan the whole semester and worked together to initiate first steps; then, let the process unfold, guided by a desire to develop and hone—through the service-learning project—the students' planning and design capabilities, their facilitation and public engagement skills, and their ability to benefit from collaboration and cross-disciplinary exchange. Furthermore, all agreed that finding a balance between three key factors would ensure a greater likelihood of success: the abilities of the students, the educational objectives of the course(s), and the desires of the community. Equilibrium in these three areas reinforces the transformative nature of service-learning: students (and professors) grow and learn in important and valuable ways; they make a substantial contribution to the community; and the community grows and sees opportunities that they had not previously imagined (Forsyth, Lu, and McGirr 2000). Without such a balance, students may not develop important insights and may feel overwhelmed, while community partners may feel they did not receive the outcomes or products they expected. Our hypothesis is somewhat similar to the analysis of Forsyth, Lu, and McGirr (2000); they contend that good service-learning for planning and design education must concentrate on the respective roles of students, faculty, and the outside community.

## Balancing Student Abilities

All participating students from the three courses were graduate level but significant differences in educational background, work experience, and degree status distinguished them. Many planning students were returning to study after working in the field, but the landscape architecture students were only in their second year of study toward their three-year first professional degree. The Commonwealth Avenue Project offered a rare opportunity to bridge disciplinary boundaries between planners and landscape architects. Instructors encouraged students to view their abilities and knowledge as complementary and to work collaboratively with one another. In today's design, development, and planning fields, especially in light of the priority being placed on sustainability, greater value is being placed on holistic, cross-disciplinary approaches. These emerging trends will require students entering the professional practice world to have broader perspectives.[2]

It was decided that students should begin by developing individual perspectives and giving voice to insights unique to their respective discipline's point of view. For their initial exercise, each student in the landscape and planning studios was assigned a random intersection on Commonwealth Avenue and asked to represent it graphically. Since this exercise played to the graphic strengths of the landscape architecture students, observation, rather than graphic quality, was stressed. Collective discussion of the representations allowed both planners and landscape architects to gain familiarity with one another personally and professionally. Through the exercise, students discovered differences in perspective, in disciplinary vocabulary, and in expertise. When a planning student referred to a closed-off street as a "street vacation," landscape architecture students, who had never heard the term before, imagined the street laying on a beach in Florida. The ensuing laughter over interpretation provided a learning opportunity related to becoming aware of the terminologies and meanings of each other's discipline.

Following the individual projects, instructors developed specific assignments to promote disciplinary contributions and co-learning. The planning students, in keeping with their discipline, were charged with identifying a particular issue and using it to develop an analytic map representing the entirety of Commonwealth Avenue. For example, Scott Rowe compiled a map of the city of Alexandria's other planning initiatives for areas adjoining Commonwealth Avenue. His analysis revealed how Commonwealth Avenue intersects the Mount Vernon Avenue Urban Overlay Zone, an area defined by the Mount Vernon Avenue Business Area Plan.[3] This is the Avenue's busiest and most problematic intersection, dividing Arlandria and Del Ray. Rowe's map confirmed the residents' sense that Commonwealth Avenue is being overshadowed by other city planning initiatives and, at the same time, provided residents with knowledge of how they might leverage the Mount Vernon Avenue Business Area Plan to affect change to Commonwealth Avenue.

Turning to a more local scale, the landscape architecture students began by investigating one of six avenue segments. They then expanded outward to encompass the larger Commonwealth Avenue context, thereby bridging multiple scales and maintaining the immediacy of each specific site. Their drawings generally represented Commonwealth Avenue at multiple scales with a particular viewpoint as the focus of their segment. For example, Daria Hutchinson identified and documented a concentration of churches and schools in her avenue segment and revealed how they interact with bike paths and the boulevard median to comprise a "civic landscape." Irene Mills discovered the upper reaches of Hooff's Run buried beneath her section and used historical maps to chart its location and impact at various scales from block to street to Potomac River watershed to Chesapeake Bay. The six landscape architecture students investigated and represented aspects of the Avenue differently, but their drawings shared a given scale so they could be linked together to create a composite representation of the avenue.

While the design and planning students were investigating the avenue and learning to represent it graphically, the community involvement students were learning fundamental engagement strategies and testing their public meeting facilitation skills. During an initial three-week module students learned the fundamentals of interest-based negotiations, participated in four negotiation exercises (i.e., role plays) and conducted a stakeholder analysis for a simulated Brownfields redevelopment project. Student teams were then assigned to each of the three Commonwealth neighborhoods as they worked with the planning studio students to inventory neighborhood organizations and contact community leaders. Their first step involved completing a "stakeholder assessment" by identifying and interviewing the relevant parties and agencies potentially involved in the decision related to Commonwealth Avenue. This was followed by writing student assessments documenting the different civic capacity of the groups and organizations engaged in each of the three Commonwealth Avenue neighborhoods. Such a synthesizing process is crucial for a facilitator working with stakeholders and aiming to identify areas for mutual understanding and agreement (Susskind, McKearnan, and Thomas-Larmer 1999).

After the stakeholder assessments, Professors Schilling and McCarty met with all of the teams to offer feedback, evaluate the most relevant community involvement tools, and prepare agendas and logistics for an upcoming series of neighborhood focus groups. Several of the community involvement students had prior meeting facilitation experience, while others were naturally gifted public speakers. A few of the more reserved and quiet students initially struggled with the simulations and role plays—they could think on their feet but found it hard to take command. For facilitating both the in-class simulations and neighborhood focus groups, students operated as teams with more experienced students acting as lead facilitators and others providing support in transcribing notes and flip charts. Each student was also given a speaking part in the meeting. By the end of the term, every student could design a public involvement process and facilitate a public meeting.

Following their disciplinary assignments, a major turning point occurred when students joined together in temporary, interdisciplinary teams (based on personalities, perspectives, and working styles) for a brief in-class charrette. Even though this was the first time the students from each studio had shared their work with one another, each team worked well and decided to remain together for the rest of the semester. Each team was charged with developing an overall Commonwealth Avenue master plan as well as detailed designs and planning guidelines to help implement it. Typical of most design studios, each team was encouraged to develop its own way of working. It was through such team interactions that most of the students fully learned about each other's way of approaching the project.

Professor Schilling led the coordination between the Community Involvement class and the Planning and Landscape Architecture Studios. Schilling and McCarty were excited about providing their students with an opportunity to test and hone their facilitation skills with members of the public. They hoped that student-led facilitation of internal planning meetings between the landscape and planning students would also support greater cross-disciplinary exchange and understanding. One of Schilling and McCarty's former students was called on to act as a graduate assistant helping to coordinate the community involvement and studio students.

Student team discusses design ideas with Commonwealth Avenue residents. *Photo by Joseph Schilling*

## Meeting Educational Objectives

The Commonwealth Studio highlights four important educational objectives: bridging disciplines, facilitating inventive thinking, increasing sensitivity to communities' needs, and testing community facilitation skills.

**Bridging disciplines.** As a way to bridge the disciplinary boundaries between planning and landscape architecture and to develop complementary bodies of knowledge, planning and design students worked in cross-disciplinary teams of two landscape architects and two planners. Teams were formed on the basis of the abilities, interests, and sensibilities of the students as they emerged in the first portion of the course. Each team developed a collaborative master plan for the entire avenue, while the landscape students created site-specific design proposals and the planning students proposed planning changes (e.g., zoning ordinances, development incentives, etc.) and project ideas. In this way, they relied upon each other's disciplinary knowledge to develop the master plan into a workable scheme. This process placed different demands on the students within each team. Planning students had to work in a less familiar milieu, and landscape architecture students had to learn about planning from their teammates, since the initial readings and exercises in the course had been weighted in the direction of landscape architecture.

**Facilitating inventive thinking.** Merely working on a real project does not ensure a good educational experience, a point that required reinforcing in discussions with the project partner Del Ray Citizens Association. In order to provide a good educational experience, a good "problem" needs to be imbedded into the project—one that has the potential to generate a range of conceptual approaches, subvert preconceptions, and stimulate imagination. Consistent with design studio education, one important educational objective was to evoke innovative thinking and imaginative proposals for the project.[4] By its nature, Commonwealth Avenue bridges typologies acting at once as "street" and "park." By subverting preconceptions of what a street or a park typically is, students were directed toward greater invention. The street/park ambiguity was reinforced by eschewing conventional terms like "greenway" and "parkway" in favor of phrases like "a hybrid street/park landscape." While it may not dance lightly off the tongue, this phrase seemed to allow the freedom needed to explore ideas without bias.

One team's bold vision illustrates the importance of student inventiveness. Their plan adapted the European "Living Street" model to the two-and-a-half-mile stretch of Commonwealth Avenue by relocating through traffic to just one side of the street and designing its remaining side as a local, slow-speed, combined pedestrian and vehicular street and linear park, or *woonerf*—a Dutch concept for pedestrian urban streets. The proposal would substitute off-street parking for on-street parking, eliminate some intersections, and reduce the total paving by nearly half. Living Street team member Mary Ellis proposed a formal rose garden in the Rosemont section as a symbol of Rosemont and the gateway to Commonwealth Avenue.

**Increasing sensitivity to communities' needs.** Although quite imaginative and considered "crazy enough that it just might work," it would be unfair to claim that the Living Street concept met the communities' desires. Another team's proposal, "Connecting Communities," demonstrates the educational goal of increasing sensitivity to communities' needs. This scheme, albeit modest, emphasizes using sidewalks and bike lanes to create continuity and join the community. The Connecting Communities proposal responds to the community by acknowledging and studying the existing gaps that limit use and access and then modifying parking and adjacent topography to create continuity along the avenue's entire length. They also propose continuous stormwater infiltration channels uniting communities with shared hydrology and visible water flows. Gina Benincasa's design proposes changes to the Commonwealth / Mount Vernon intersection as part of the larger Connecting Communities proposal. At this key meeting point for both streets, she proposes a semi-circular town green to unite them, handle traffic flows, and stimulate community gathering and events.

**Testing community facilitation skills.** The Commonwealth Avenue project provided Community Involvement course participants with firsthand experience related to conducting public meetings and using negotiation and facilitation skills. Designing and facilitating a public meeting demands an ability to draw upon both intuition and skills. For the most part, students were encouraged to select appropriate facilitation techniques suiting both their abilities and the goals of the focus groups. Students were encouraged to be sensitive to diverse neighborhood demographics and styles in their focus group design. Students quickly discovered scheduling difficulties arising from working with busy neighborhood groups and communication gaps related to the Del Ray Citizens Association's involvement in leading the project. An added demand involved coordinating their efforts with the ongoing activities of students in the planning and landscape architecture studios. The Del Ray focus group meeting occurred early enough in the process to enable information gathering, brainstorming, and solicitation of ideas. Design and planning students attended and acted as observers—not active participants. The Arlandria meeting, on the other hand, required scheduling later in the semester after master plans and design schemes were already underway. For this meeting, teams convened a series of roundtable discussions between community members and students representing each of the planning and design teams. This approach promised to be more interactive; however, when only two community residents attended the Arlandria focus group, student facilitators were forced to adapt their agenda and experienced a valuable lesson related to gauging turnout and participation in public meetings. At debriefing sessions following each community meeting, Professors Schilling and McCarty led students in discussing and evaluating such things as neighborhood outreach techniques while reflecting on incidents and experiences that can't be easily "taught" or learned in a classroom.

## Integrating Community Desires and Needs

Projects similar in scale to Commonwealth Avenue are particularly challenging when it comes to assessing and responding to a community's desires and managing community relationships and expectations (Forsyth, Lu, and McGirr 2000). Often the unpredictable dynamics of neighborhood politics and differing community goals make project design and development challenging to organize. Local government planning and development processes are often alien to professors and students, and universities lack sufficient strategies for effectively understanding and negotiating complex and competing interests and processes.

Engaging a separate Community Involvement course in the Commonwealth Avenue Studio Project had distinct advantages and one significant drawback. The separate course allowed for development of a careful process for community engagement, which increased the likelihood of getting representative input from each of the three diverse neighborhoods along the Avenue. At the same time, it was difficult to synchronize the activities of all three courses.

Given the separation of the studios from the Community Involvement class, there was relatively little direct correspondence between the outcomes of the community meetings and an online survey and the students' proposed plans and designs. This was mostly due to the difficulty in coordinating feedback from neighborhood meetings with the quicker pace of the design teams. For example, by the time the community involvement students had identified important neighborhood groups and sent them information about the studio, the design teams were well on their way to assessing existing conditions along the avenue and had deadlines to submit preliminary ideas. This is not to suggest that the communities' voices were not heard or that the students did not give them due consideration. Collectively, there was a

Students and community members discuss design ideas at a community open house. *Photo by Joseph Schilling*

flow of ideas and understanding among the students in all the classes that informed the work. Furthermore, students in the design and planning studios gained understanding from informal conversations with people using the Avenue and through their own on-site observations and experiences with such realities as discontinuous sidewalks.

**Commonwealth open house.** At semester's end, the three classes hosted an open house in the local branch of the public library. Posters and fliers helped to draw sixty residents, more than half from the Del Ray neighborhood, to the event. The enthusiasm for the work was infectious: community members received it as professional work and perceived it as real, leading many to wonder when the city might break ground. It became apparent that the master plan proposals uncovered aspects of the Avenue that many residents had not initially perceived. The plans also targeted issues that both city officials and residents had overlooked, for example the physical and psychological barrier of the Commonwealth and Mount Vernon Avenue intersection. On the whole, student proposals addressed the community goal of creating more usable park space, as well as offering provocative and imaginary ideas to consider in the redesign of Commonwealth Avenue.

**Final studio report.** A final report representing the project findings and proposals was generated to help advance the community's efforts in relationship to Commonwealth Avenue. The report is meant to serve as a catalyst for community discussion and dialogue with the City of Alexandria, not merely a menu of design options. It includes five segments beginning with

"A Tour of the Avenue" overviewing the Avenue's everyday character and the opportunities, problems, and conditions of each of its discrete segments. The second section presents such issues as hydrology, pedestrian and bicycle transportation, history, local planning initiatives, etc. Proposed master plans and area designs are presented in the third section, while the fourth section focuses on four theme areas addressed by the participants: ecology, connectivity, history, and sense of place. By organizing the different master plans by theme, the student work is seen as raising issues for community discussion, not solving problems. A final section, "Conclusions and Next Steps," suggests specific short-term and longer-range actions that the communities can take to advance the dialogue (Final Studio Report 2006).[5]

**Community briefings (Del Ray and city council).** Following the report completion, Professors Kelsch and Schilling presented the product of their students' efforts at an April 2007 meeting of the Del Ray Citizens Association. Many of the sixty residents attending had taken part in the previous year's focus group and open house. When the report was later presented to the mayor and city council at a May 2007 workshop, its ideas were highly praised but its potential budget and fiscal impacts criticized. One of the best ways of realizing aspects of the proposed master plans may lie with the Parks and Recreation Commission as it identifies available open space and oversee implementing the city's Open Space and Urban Forestry plans. Early in 2008, the city's Parks and Open Space Department acquired the largest vacant lot along Commonwealth Avenue and began park planning with area residents. While they are proceeding on this parcel without an overall vision in mind, it seems likely that the Commonwealth Avenue Studio played a part in helping to generate interest and action related to transforming Commonwealth Avenue into a successful boulevard urban park.

## Conclusion—Studio Reflections and Service-Learning Insights

The experience of the Commonwealth Avenue Studio resulted in important learning and insights for everyone involved.

**Community scale of the studio.** It proved critical, from the perspective of good landscape design and effective land use planning, to work on the entire Commonwealth Avenue to overcome its perception as being fragmented and disjointed. Expanding to this comprehensive scale, while limiting the amount of direct contact with community residents, enabled student participants to adopt a role of visionaries and catalysts generating imaginative and substantive proposals for change. Such an approach uncovered relevant issues and led to identifying unseen opportunities for the Avenue. Through the

Commonwealth Avenue Studio, Del Ray, Rosemont, and Arlandria became equipped with new knowledge to inform their dialogue, with one another and with city officials, related to transforming a neglected and fragmented community asset into a cohesive and dynamic public green space.

**Type of community served.** Many service-learning endeavors focus on underserved, distressed, and disadvantaged communities (Forsyth, Lu, and McGirr 2000). The Arlandria neighborhood would qualify as such but the demographics of Del Ray and Rosemont would not. Given the keen competition for local government budgets and philanthropic resources, providing assistance to community-based organizations in middle-income neighborhoods for a modest studio fee seems appropriate. Moreover, working on a project that involved public space furthered service-learning goals and helped advance partnerships between Virginia Tech and its neighbors.

**Challenges in connecting with city planners.** Tension and conflict are inherent in any community-university partnership, yet they can also promote learning and growth (Prins 2005). The goal of a less fragmented and more park-like Commonwealth Avenue was initially neither at the forefront of community concerns nor high on the city's priority list. Yet the studio helped to identify and highlight an unarticulated critical issue while providing the Del Ray Citizens Association with the necessary knowledge to approach the City of Alexandria. As the community engagement process unfolded, city planning staff were contacted and pulled into the process. Later, after the studio's completion, a few city staff shared their frustrations about not being highly involved in providing what they felt was a needed "reality check" related to redeveloping Commonwealth Avenue. They were likely responding to residents' rising expectations being generated by the Virginia Tech studio. While informing and reaching out to the city might have been approached differently, their involvement might have imposed a serious limitation on the studio's creative climate and jeopardized the Del Ray Citizens Association's ability to challenge the approaches and strategies originating in city hall.

**Preparing and managing the studio.** In spite of only one month spent preparing their first joint planning/landscape architecture studio, the participating faculty wholeheartedly embraced the opportunity for community engagement and service-learning. In the future, preplanning is needed to enable dialogue between instructors and neighborhood and city partners to clarify roles, manage expectations, set realistic educational objectives, and prepare the teaching and service-learning approach. Cross-disciplinary service-learning requires greater university support in the form of resources and time devoted to collaboration, adjusting teaching loads, and/or integrating research expectations (Loveridge 2002).

The second challenge was coordinating the goals, schedules, and coursework of the three courses. Conventional design studio structure made it difficult for integrating lectures and readings on planning principles and methods. With Kelsch co-leading the planning studio, the planning students received a good orientation to design principles within the park context, but there was more emphasis placed on design rather than planning. Ultimately the landscape students did gain some planning insights by working in the cross-disciplinary teams; however, the ideal cross-disciplinary studio would include the design and planning students in a collaborative learning environment.

It was important to synchronize the two studio classes while coordinating the community outreach and the studio work through the community involvement. Fragmented schedules required out-of-class meetings, and timing between the studios and the Community Involvement course was always a bit off because of the different educational goals and student abilities for each of the courses. As the design students were finishing their preliminary concepts, the community involvement students were just completing their stakeholder assessments and beginning to schedule focus groups. Also, course meeting times need to be coordinated and graduate assistants are needed to help manage and prepare for the various classes. Unfortunately, there were neither academic nor community resources available to support a graduate assistant.

**Respective roles of designers and planners.** While urban planning and landscape architecture evolved from similar disciplinary roots, the different perspectives of planners and landscape architects continued surfacing throughout our studio. By forming cross-disciplinary teams, the studio structure bridged this inherent divide. Careful selection of students with compatible working styles and attributes balanced their relative strengths, skills, planning, and design experience. Most of the planning students viewed the challenges of Commonwealth Avenue through the lens of city plans and policies that govern the development, land uses, and structures of its built environment and its surrounding spaces. The planner's role is essentially to translate community desires and needs into development projects, maps, diagrams, ordinances, and guidelines through a series of informal and formal public involvement processes. Landscape architects are more likely to play a visionary role, and these students were more comfortable proposing bolder changes to the avenue. As the studio progressed, their challenge was to make their visions for the Avenue realistic within the limits of the communities and the existing conditions of the landscape.

**Student reflection.** As newcomers to community engagement, we failed to heed service-learning literature's reflection emphasis and only came to understand the impact of the project on the students primarily from anecdotal conversations, course evaluations, and community involvement student journals. Evidence from these sources suggests that the interdisciplinary aspects of the project and the engagement with the community were valuable. While a solid 80 percent of the students from the three courses rated the overall experience high, it is hard to speculate on their individual motivations. Did they like their classmates? Did Commonwealth Avenue pose a unique challenge? Did they enjoy the professors? A few written comments offer some insights. For example, a minority of students (mainly the planning students who craved structure) were frustrated by the flexible structure of the course—that each week did not follow a written syllabus. Having a cohesive syllabus from the first day would have better managed these expectations, mitigated student confusion, and minimized professor frustrations (Roakes and Norris-Tirrell 2000). Many students were excited about working on a real project with the hope that somehow their work might result in changes. Only a handful of the planning students reflected about the inherent tensions and benefit of having a joint studio; perhaps these students will transfer this lesson learned to other areas of their academic and professional work.

The most reflective insights came from the community involvement students. As part of the course, students were required to keep an e-mail journal during the semester. After each internal meeting or outreach activity, they wrote a few pages of things they observed, felt, and did from the vantage point of a neutral facilitator. For the final paper, the students were to compile and synthesize these e-mail entries into a reflective essay about their Commonwealth Avenue Studio experiences. The community involvement students very much valued the opportunity to facilitate meetings among their peers and with the community. They also recognized the importance of having internal planning meetings to plan the outreach activities. Several students noted that it was difficult to keep the studio students (planning and landscape) informed and up to date about the results of the external outreach meetings—the time frame of trying to plan these community outreach activities within the scope of one semester was a constant challenge. Beyond the tactical insights, several students acknowledged the importance of flexibility when you design and execute any public involvement strategy as events and dynamics are always changing and evolving—a fundamental premise of good facilitation.

Several students shared their insights into the differences between planners and designers, but one landscape student enrolled in the Community Involvement class made this telling observation:

> In preparation for the March 1st meeting with the Del Ray Civic Association we met with Planning and Landscape Architecture students to find out what sort of information they would like us to get from the community and what would be helpful to their design process. What we found was that the landscape architecture students didn't seem to want a lot of detail because they wanted freedom to be imaginative with their designs. The planning students on the other hand were interested in getting as much detail as possible to help them get a better understanding of exactly what the community is interested in and how to write up these interests. I have heard planning students express frustration regarding this difference in interest and their concern that the ideas of the landscape architecture students are too unrealistic. I think the way landscape architects and planners are taught to approach projects are very different. This Commonwealth Avenue project is an excellent opportunity to combine talents and to learn from each other. In the limited time this semester we were not able to dedicate much time to working through these differences of opinion, but possibly if this is done in the future there could be a group designated to internal facilitation and really trying to help these groups work together. I think it is so important to work together in an educational setting so that after we finish school we can continue to collaborate and work together to enhance projects.

**Service-learning beyond the studio.** Studio projects often take on a "life of their own" well beyond the end of the term. At the outset of the studio, faculty should establish clear boundaries about the end of their involvement with the client. For the Commonwealth Avenue Studio the project required significant ongoing efforts by Kelsch and Schilling including hiring, with community funds, a landscape architecture student to compile the student proposals and to collaborate with the faculty to write, format, layout, and publish the final studio report.

Having funded the project, the community had expectations of a tangible product, and the university had expectations of some sort of professional recognition or publication. For example, the final studio report was critical for the Del Ray Citizens Association in their advocacy with city officials to garner political support for funding the revitalization of Commonwealth

Avenue. Moreover, these extra efforts were consistent with the university's combined educational, scholarly, and service missions.

Another important service-learning opportunity is showcasing studio results and sharing lessons learned with other service-learning professors and students. With support from the planning and landscape programs, during the summer of 2006, landscape architecture student Irene Mills and Jim Snyder from the Del Ray Citizens Association joined the faculty at Virginia Tech's first Annual Engagement Conference. Professors and students from Virginia and other mid-Atlantic states shared dozens of different outreach and engagement projects, with the Commonwealth Avenue Studio being one of the few focused on design and planning. Mills also presented the work at a university-wide symposium on environmental work entitled, "The Deans' Forum on the Environment," and was awarded the top award in the student category for work in the built environment. The document was acknowledged with a Communication Award by the Potomac Chapter of the American Society of Landscape Architects.

**Impacts on the respective departments.** The Commonwealth Avenue Studio's impact on the Alexandria Center exists more in planning than in landscape architecture. It led to an expansion of the number and type of studios in the Urban Affairs and Planning Program and directed Professor Schilling toward four consecutive semesters teaching an Environmental Planning Studio charged with formulating an Eco-City Charter and Action Plan for the city of Alexandria. The Planning Program's two new "professors in practice" with urban design and planning expertise have enabled the program to offer two to three studios per semester.

Since the Commonwealth Avenue Studio, another collaborative endeavor has failed to occur in large part because of difficulties created by course scheduling and divergent curriculum goals. Unspoken barriers include a lack of academic incentives to cross-disciplinary boundaries, differing perspectives on the roles of design and planning studios, and competition with other academic pressures and commitments. Still, pressures from outside academia continue to drive our respective professions towards collaboration. Issues such as social justice, climate change, ecological infrastructure, health, transportation, and renewable energy summon us to develop multidisciplinary solutions through environmental design and policy planning. Collaborations like the Commonwealth Avenue Studio Project are needed to help future planners and designers test and develop their knowledge while acknowledging the value of how their different contributions and perspectives work together to address the pressing problems our communities face.

## CHAPTER 14

# Forging Lasting Community Impacts and Linkages through the Capstone Community Design Studio

*Jack Sullivan*[1]

## Introduction

**When a community** is underserved due to limited monetary resources and a lack of political clout, landscape architects—in the profession and in the academy—have an opportunity to use design and community participation as catalysts for much-needed transformation of the urban environment. The cooperative design process can establish insightful analysis, sensible design thinking, integration of community opinions and perceptions, and strategies for physical improvements. With the help of design students and professionals, residents see their community in a new light, one where it is possible to build upon its strengths, overcome its weaknesses, and begin a cycle of positive change. Success occurs when citizens, public officials, and designers work together to forge a vision that is based on goals that respond to identified needs and are broadly supported within the community.

The Community Design Studio at the University of Maryland's professionally accredited four-year Bachelor of Landscape Architecture (BLA) Program partners faculty and students with local communities in participatory design and planning projects. Landscape architects must consider social, economic, and environmental issues related to the character and stability of the community. In this studio, students learn to be present, pay attention, and learn from their community partners. Working closely with local citizens on projects of local importance, the students continue to develop technical skills in planning and design as they are introduced to new skills of facilitation and communication.

The studio learning and discovery process includes investigations into the role of the landscape architect as an advocate for justice and an agent for change. The studio seeks to uncover the designer's biases and to consider how these can be checked in the design process. It attempts to reveal how the landscape architect can most effectively collect information, document community values and perceptions, collect and analyze community data, and accurately describe the character of an established community. It embraces the challenge of translating community dialogue into design propositions that reflect the vision of a diverse population. The studio-community engagement gives students the opportunity to explore communication strategies as they explain design ideas to a lay audience that is unfamiliar with the language of planning and design.

Acting as both communicators and visionaries, landscape architecture students help community residents recognize and articulate opportunities and challenges, understand the potential to address these through physical design change, and develop strategies to implement design proposals. Thoughtful synthesis and clear communication are key factors in the participatory process. Once the community has developed and established consensus around a vision, the process continues as students and citizens search for ways to accomplish the vision by identifying tangible interventions that can be accomplished with limited resources. The success of this studio design process is evident in the significant funding that partnering communities have received using student reports as the basis for grant applications. Yet, the skills and the quality of the experience that students and the community have developed together are immeasurable.

## The Studio in the Context of Scholarship and Service-Learning

During the 1990s, Ernest L. Boyer, then president of the Carnegie Foundation for the Advancement of Teaching, introduced a new and integrative vision for academic scholarship that he referred to as the "scholarship of engagement." He recognized the potential of this scholarship to connect "the rich resources of the university to our most pressing social, civic, and ethical problems to our children, to our schools, to our teachers, and to our cities" (Boyer 1996, 21). Boyer's work illustrated the potential of scholarship in higher education to build "connections across the disciplines, placing the specialties in a larger context, illuminating data in a revealing way, and often educating non-specialists, too" (Eisman 2005). He encouraged the academic community to expand their traditional definitions of scholarship to include applied and integrative activities. Boyer's writing stimulated a renewed interest in the public aspects of academic scholarship, including the potential of service-learning in higher education; however, it was clear that the success of engaged scholarship and service-learning would depend on the institutional support and backing of university and college administrators.

The literature on service-learning and community engagement has been well documented by Derek Barker, a research assistant for the Kettering Foundation. He states that scholars "are finding creative ways to communicate to public audiences, work for the public good, and generate knowledge with public participation. Like advocates of service-learning, engaged scholars share the concern to reconnect American higher education with its sense of civic mission." Barker (2004) identifies the important contributions by scholars who "are trying to make the case in the clearest possible terms that their scholarship is at least as rigorous as traditional academic work."

The Landscape Architecture Program at Maryland is fortunate to have many advocates within the university community who support community scholarship and service-learning. For the past fifteen years, the Community Design Studio at the University of Maryland has received institutional and departmental support that has enabled faculty and students in this service-learning studio to work with community residents, government representatives, and technical specialists to find the best solutions for neighborhood preservation and improvement.

The Office of Community Service-Learning Document 17 promotes connections among "students, faculty, staff and community partners to encourage community service-learning that is mutually beneficial to the university and our local community" (www.csl.umd.edu/). The University of Maryland recognizes the value of service-learning and public scholarship as well as the need for leadership to promote service-learning, and it encourages student involvement in this service-learning across the curriculum. The Academy for Excellence in Teaching and Learning, "a community of scholars committed to fostering a culture of excellence," has been a strong proponent for academic recognition of service-learning programs that will benefit tenure and promotion (www.aetl.umd.edu/).

The University of Maryland's support for service-learning and the scholarship of engagement was tested in the promotion and tenure proceedings for three faculty members in the Landscape Architecture Program. All three—Margarita M. Hill in 1999, David Myers in 2005, and Shenglin E. Chang in 2005—had significant portfolios of integrated scholarship and service-learning projects, well documented in respected peer-reviewed publications that reflected the quality and contribution of their work in this field. All three were promoted with tenure.

## The Studio in the Context of the BLA Curriculum

The undergraduate degree at the University of Maryland requires 120 credits; in addition to the BLA requirements, the program includes electives and core requirements in the arts and humanities, social and behavioral sciences, social and political history, and physical sciences and mathematical reasoning. Because the core BLA studio sequence must be completed in a prescribed order, scheduling is challenging, especially for the nontraditional transfers who make up 75 percent of the program and contribute to its diverse student body.

The professional degree curriculum balances coursework in hand-drawing, digital graphics, and design studios with lecture-and-lab courses in horticultural science, plant identification, soil science, site engineering, landscape structures and materials, and environmental resources. Landscape history and theory courses prepare students for demanding research investigations that require development of methodologies and rigorous research that lead toward grounded findings. Advanced design studios build on this background, emphasizing critical thinking and articulating communication in all media—graphics, writing, and oral presentation. In the third year, the Site Planning and Design Studio gives students the ability to decipher and organize complex programs, address challenging site conditions, and synthesize the myriad options for creating sustainable landscapes. In the following semester, the Regional Design Studio familiarizes students with the Geographic Information System (GIS), which provides social, political, economic, and environmental community data. The Urban Design Studio builds student confidence for making decisions regarding comprehensive urban planning and detailed design development. By the time they have completed this studio sequence, students have a well-grounded skill set and valuable learning experiences.

The Community Design Studio is currently the "capstone" of the four-year Bachelor of Landscape Architecture Program curriculum. As the culmination of academic accomplishments in a major field of inquiry, the capstone is defined by its requirements for independent research, collaboration with peers, and written and oral dissemination to the university community. The studio offers students the opportunity to further develop design skills and to explore a different method of design thinking and process. Each student establishes goals that will most fully enrich his or her design studio experience. The studio serves the students well as a final entry in the academic portfolio, enabling them to explore new directions and develop new insights, thought processes, and methods of graphic and verbal communication.

The Community Design Studio was initially introduced in 1993 as a third-year studio by Margarita M. Hill. The course provided valuable assistance to local communities and was popular with the students. However, third-year students had yet to complete courses in construction technology and urban design; faculty in the Landscape Architecture Program concluded that fourth-year students would have more expertise to offer the community. Following a strategic planning process, the faculty reassessed and revised the curriculum in 2001. To better integrate the BLA courses and provide greater technical expertise for the students prior to the community design studio, the faculty decided to place this studio in the final semester, making it the capstone experience. Since that time, four different faculty members have taught the Community Design Studio. Each of them has brought a unique perspective, personal experience, scholarly interest, and set of skills to the evolution of the course. The course instructors have inspired students, citizens, and community leaders to establish collaborative, synergetic, and productive working partnerships.

## The Studio Partners

Landscape architecture professionals are well regarded for their leadership in collaborative practice. To this end, the Community Design Studio nurtures cooperative work environments within the academy and throughout the community. It encourages the development of strong partnerships with local residents, experts in related fields of inquiry, and government officials. As instigators of this collaborative process, landscape architects—and students of the profession—serve as agents of physical and social change. As both communicators and visionaries, they enable their community partners to recognize community constraints and to embrace community opportunities. They help the community understand the potential and rationale for possible design interventions, the consequences of these actions, and the means by which design proposals can be implemented. Since 1993, the studio has worked with local citizens in neighboring Prince George's County to create beautiful, safe, and sustainable neighborhoods.

The studio's success over the years is due in large part to the resources and commitment of the program's many partners. Outstanding among these is the Neighborhood Design Center (NDC), a nonprofit organization established in Baltimore in 1968 to support the development of livable neighborhoods by coordinating local professional pro bono design services that assist with community-sponsored design and planning initiatives. The NDC strives to strengthen community participation, to educate the public about the value of good design and planning, and to serve as a catalyst for increased investment in neighborhood development (www.ndc-md.org/). Strong academic/community partnerships require commitments from both partners. Many studio instructors have established relationships beyond the studio. Margarita Hill was instrumental in making the initial contact with NDC; in 1996 she was appointed to its board of directors, a position in which she served for five years. Shenglin Chang, another faculty member in the Community Design Studio, also served on the NDC Prince George's County Advisory Board. Jan Townshend, an alumna of the Maryland BLA Program, is the NDC program manager in the Prince George's County office, where she works tirelessly with the students and faculty on a variety of projects. In addition to nonprofit organizations, the studio has worked with foundations, county planning offices, and both state and federal agencies/departments.

Within the University of Maryland, the Community Design Studio has developed partnerships with the Center for Environmental Science, the Department of Environmental Science and Technology, the School of Architecture, Planning and Preservation, and scientists in the Department of Plant Science and Landscape Architecture. These cross-campus and in-house collaborations have brought students and faculty together to share varied expertise within the university, reveal complementary lines of scholarship, and build collaborative partnerships through interdisciplinary exchange.

Most importantly, however, the success of the studio has resulted from the commitment and contributions of local citizen participants. Community activists, concerned residents, property owners, business investors, shop owners, teachers, students, police officers, religious leaders, and government officials have given their time and energy to fill out surveys, participate in workshops, advise students, lead walking tours, rally others to the cause, and become lasting friends of the Landscape Architecture Program. Their willingness to share local knowledge, insights, and experience has been critical to the service-learning process.

## Community Design Methodology

The studio semester is divided into four parts: (1) Community Investigations, (2) Design Framework, (3) Community Design Exploration, and

(4) Revision and Translation. Community Investigations, which include inventory and analysis, community surveys and workshops, and literature research, take up most of the first half of the semester, approximately seven weeks. The Design Framework and Design Explorations are established over a four- to five-week period, and the final documentation, report editing, in-house presentation and review, and final public presentation occur throughout the final four weeks of the semester.

### Part 1: Community Investigations

This studio begins with literature research and the gathering of citizen input that guides and informs the community inventory and analysis. Students discuss the required readings and use these as the basis for understanding the theory and practice of participatory design. At the same time, students collect and assess information about the community from a number of perspectives and sources, including questionnaires and surveys, individual interviews with key community leaders, the county census, historic archives, GIS data, and personal observations. The students learn a great deal about the community's physical, social, cultural, and economic environment through these activities. Upon completion of the site and community analysis, each student establishes a framework plan that identifies his or her research focus and a design strategy to further explore land use issues. Students examine the site's development potential from this perspective using traditional and innovative methods to map the community in a manner that integrates the community perspective. Students summarize their findings from this initial investigation and present them to the community for review, confirmation (or correction), and refinement. Each student is responsible for documenting his or her particular community research investigation using written text and illustrative drawings.

**Literature research.** During the first three weeks of the course, students read selected articles and book chapters pertaining to community design. Each week, a two-person team is assigned to lead a discussion on these readings covering topics of community design theory and the various approaches to the inclusive design process.

The literature review is an important first step for the students, grounding them in the history, context, and practices of community design. The readings begin with the writings of Jane Jacobs and her defense of her West Village neighborhood during the 1960s when New York planners proposed large-scale highway schemes. Her book, *The Death and Life of Great American Cities* (1961), describes her threatened West Village community as wonderfully diverse, economically viable, visually attractive, and mutually supportive. She wrote about the value of neighborhood preservation and self-determination, inspiring others to take control of their destiny through active participation and political involvement. As a result of her work, scholars, planners, and observers of urban life now recognize the relationships connecting community structure, scale, traditions, and community spirit. Citizens have since learned how important it is to get involved in their communities, to understand development options available to them, and to strengthen their voice in decisions about their neighborhoods.

Readings of the literature by design professionals are also important. Randy Hester was one of the first landscape architecture and planning scholars to define the term "community design" and illustrate the importance of user participation in the design of public landscapes. Hester (1974) recognized the need for face-to face dialogue between community members and designers to set goals, resolve conflicts, and evaluate the benefits of various design alternatives.[2] His writings encouraged designers to consider their role as community advocates in the design and planning process. Hester's work demonstrates ways that the traditional design process can be modified to include community residents so that designers are able to gain a better understanding of local knowledge, practices, and values. This understanding can then be applied to develop design proposals that respond to local needs and values.

The students critically review current writings and case studies of inclusive decision making in the design of public open space. An understanding of the literature on democratic process, participatory design, and issues of social justice guides the students' inquiry and design process. Selected readings include excerpts from *The American City: What Works and What Doesn't*, by Alexander Garvin (1996); *Design for Ecological Democracy*, by Randolph Hester (2006); *Everyday Urbanism*, edited by John Chase, Margaret Crawford, and John Kaliski (1999); *Smart Communities: How Citizens and Local Leaders Can Use Strategic Thinking to Build a Better Future*, by Suzanne W. Morse (2001); *Community Participation Methods in Design and Planning*, by Henry Sanoff (2000); and *Theory in Landscape Architecture: A Reader*, edited by Simon Swaffield (2002).

**Site and community inventory and analysis.** Students collaborate to collect environmental and demographic information about their community. They divide the workload and accumulate significant data from a variety of sources including Geographic Information Systems (GIS). Current data is made available to the University of Maryland by Prince George's County Planning Department. Physical characteristics of topography, hy-

Student Molline Smith presents analysis and research findings to citizens of the Port Towns of the Anacostia River. *Photo by Jack Sullivan*

drology, and vegetation can be readily documented in a series of overlay maps. Soil data and interpretation are available through the USDA Natural Resource Conservation Service. Soil information is collected and analyzed for potential environmental and developmental problems and opportunities. Information about family size and income, school locations, community centers, and places of worship, all of which are available through GIS, contributes to a comprehensive understanding of the community. Google Earth has also become a favorite means of acquiring a visual overview of the built and natural environment, including transportation access, park and open space connections (existing and potential), and land use conflicts. Nevertheless, nothing beats the advantage of experiencing the site through reconnaissance, and students are encouraged to visit often, photograph the site, and talk with the citizens.

**Surveys and workshops.** During the initial period of investigation, students also get to know the community in well-organized "town hall" meetings and workshops. The instructor, the Neighborhood Design Center, and community leaders coordinate to organize at least two workshops in the first half of the semester. These gatherings are scheduled to optimize community attendance and include a broad representation that reflects the community's diversity. Designed by the students, these sessions are strategically located and thoughtfully prepared to assure that they are well-attended, productive gatherings. Elementary school-age children are most accessible during school hours, whereas many middle school and high school students might be more readily available immediately after classes in the mid-afternoon. The best time to attract working adults with children is often immediately following religious services. Saturdays, when many families are busy with sports events, shopping trips, and household chores, are avoided due to low turnout. Evening meetings can attract a representative community cross-section, but it doesn't hurt to sweeten the invitation with the promise of food and beverages. All meetings take place within the community to maintain a level of familiarity and create a comfortable setting conducive to sharing ideas.

To attract a broad spectrum of participants, the workshops are advertised through a variety of media, including community e-mail and websites, announcements distributed to school children, and posted fliers at grocery stores, laundromats, recreation centers, and church halls. If more than one language is spoken in the community, announcements should be translated and local citizens may need to be recruited to serve as interpreters at the workshops.

The first workshop follows the student's initial interviews with community leaders. The students have a sense of the major concerns in the com-

University of Maryland student Joshua Twardowski facilitates a workshop with students at Fairmont Heights High School. *Photo by Brian Kane*

munity and the workshop confirms and builds on this understanding. At the second workshop, the students collect more detailed information through surveys and activities that facilitate in-depth consideration of existing conditions, concerns, and desired change. Confidential questionnaires allow the citizens to voice their personal interests without fear of reprisal, criticism, or scorn; assurance of privacy is particularly important when engaging teenagers. Young children often respond most effectively through drawings rather than written responses. Adults often need a little friendly coaxing, and it never hurts to offer a self-effacing sense of humor to break the ice, while the presence of food and social interaction helps to put participants at ease. The workshop activities vary and results often depend on the nature and number of the participants. More often than not, the citizens are pleased to be asked for their opinions and soon become willing team players.

After the workshops, students work in teams to document the community input and compile the results of their individual and collaborative investigations in graphic presentations and written accounts for public dissemination. Following the student presentations, the community responds to the data and interpretations in verbal and written comments that clarify, confirm, and revise the findings.

## Part 2: Design Framework

Following the community workshops, the students synthesize the workshop findings and physical inventory to identify potential areas for further study. Each student identifies a key issue or problem that he or she wishes to address and develops a research proposal that outlines a framework for this design study. The written proposal clarifies the connection between the proposed project and the evidence drawn from the research, community investigations, and analysis. Students often have good ideas for a project early in the semester, but the clarification of a framework from which they will work can be a challenging task. The instructor reviews these proposals during the spring break and returns them to the students with comments upon their return. With guidance from the instructor, the students proceed further into the design process.

## Part 3: Community Design Exploration

Once the instructor has approved the framework plans, students develop a design strategy to explore their identified land use issues. Students examine the issues at regional, local, and neighborhood scales, develop full design solutions, propose specific design details, and identify relevant precedents that support the validity of their proposals in a similar setting. The students promote visions for a healthy and sustainable community, establish goals for the community's renewal, and propose design interventions that address the community's shortcomings and capitalize on its best features.

Projects have ranged from streetscape studies and building infill projects to the design of interpretive historic trails, community parks, and environmental education/community centers. Students study the spatial organization and site layout and illustrate the spatial character of their design proposals using sketches and computer simulations. They also provide a timeline for phased implementation and develop details that will enable the community to advance the project.

The students present their findings to the community in a public meeting at the end of the semester. During this presentation, they provide examples of professional projects that have addressed similar issues and discuss the relevance of current practice and theory to their design proposals. For example, a student proposing a series of pedestrian improvements may offer examples of low-cost, low-impact streetscape solutions that have been implemented successfully elsewhere. The instructors encourage students to be fully conversant in any technical and engineering matters that they propose and to be prepared to respond to questions that may arise from the community. Final design products often include conceptual building studies, site plans, preliminary feasibility studies and cost estimates, neighborhood master plans, and community development guidelines.

## Part 4: Revision and Translation

All findings are compiled in a summary document that records the entire semester experience. This document integrates the initial inventory and analysis, the community profiles, and the collective design solutions. One student in the class prepares a document template that the entire studio follows as they prepare their submittals. Students document initial group work including the inventory, analysis, and community assessment materials. Each student compiles his or her research investigation and design study. Student editors work with the instructor to compile, review, and edit all documents. This step is repeated a second time by an alternate team of editors to assure accuracy in spelling, grammar, and format compliance before the final publication. A limited print edition of the report is distributed to the community, and a PDF version is posted online at www.larc.umd.edu and distributed on a CD.

The report disseminates the process, findings, and recommendations of the studio experience, making information available to the community and providing material for future funding requests. The preparation of materials for the publication strengthens students' technical writing skills and promotes better communication between the studio members and their lay community partners. Over the years, the reports have been used to secure project funding for neighborhood revitalization from organizations and agencies including: Prince George's County Neighborhood Improvement Grant Program, Maryland Department of Housing and Community Development, Maryland Community Development Block Grant Program, Maryland Sustainable Communities Initiative, Maryland Parks & People's Community Greening Mini-Grants and Social Enterprise Programs, US Department of Transportation T-21 Highway Enhancement Program, and the Morris & Gwendolyn Cafritz Foundation Community Services Grants Program.

## Assessment: What the Studio Achieves; What Could be Better

Students benefit from their experience in the service-learning studio by identifying and designing key projects that promote increased health, safety, and sustainability in neighborhoods. The participatory process provides the opportunity to engage in work that meets the needs and desires of an established community. The students learn by helping community residents envision changes in their physical environment that can lead to a better future. Community participants benefit by participating in the community analysis. Their voices are heard and recorded, contributing to the students' understanding of the community. They contribute to the development of design proposals that they may someday use as templates for projects that will transform their communities. Most significantly, the citizens are empowered to guide change and receive tools that they can use to implement the change that they have envisioned.

Course evaluations, senior exit interviews, and anecdotal feedback from BLA alumni have identified the Community Design Studio as the most highly regarded design studio in the curriculum. Students appreciate the well-organized course materials, meeting schedules, and studio process, and they have often remarked on the value of working directly with a community. They recognize that this course, as the "capstone" of their learning experience, is intended to draw on the many skills they have developed over the years. As the final presentation takes shape in the last weeks of the semester, the students, having worked with the community to explore options for its improvement, find that they are genuinely excited to have had the opportunity to serve the community through the profession they love. Addressing the public audience during their final presentations, the students discover the community's excitement and appreciation. Words of gratitude, support, and praise from all of the participants leave a lasting impression on the hearts and minds of everyone involved. Yet, it is long after they have completed the course that they realize what they have accomplished.

The Community Design Studio involves students and faculty in a full range of scholarly and applied activity. This service-learning model promotes awareness, acceptance, and affirmation of the cultural diversity that is particularly rich in the gateway communities of Prince George's County. The anecdotal evidence in post-course interviews with students and collaborating partners indicates that the experience allowed participants to make great strides toward dispelling unfounded stereotypes (of the community and of the students), prompting students and citizens to develop friendships, establish trust, and address questions of societal inequality.

The Community Design Studio's long-standing, highly regarded reputation and reliable follow-through have established many trusted relationships and long-term partnerships. Fifteen years of experience has also brought insight that has allowed us to refine our teaching methods and to set realistic goals for educational processes, environmental improvements, and economic stimuli. The studio enables students to see themselves as integral members of a team rather than lone artists or designers and to imagine their future professional careers from a new perspective. Community members participating in the design and planning process can envision a better future and recognize their potential to contribute to change in their community.

## CHAPTER 15

# Toward a Scholarship of Engagement

*A Model from Australia*

*Linda Corkery and Ann Quinlan*

## Introduction

**While the context** of the higher education landscape in Australia is different from that of the United States, there is commonality in the aspirations of educational programs preparing students to contribute to the built environment professions and their practice in a complex global environment. This chapter introduces the context of service-learning and community engagement in universities in Australia, with a particular focus on the Faculty of the Built Environment at the research-intensive University of New South Wales, Sydney, where a unique organizational unit was established to facilitate these activities. Two case studies are presented to illustrate the structure and operation of the unit, and a discussion follows on the potential for such a unit to complement the customary modes of preparing students for entry into built environment professional domains.

## The Australian University Context for Community Engagement

As a starting point, it is relevant to have an understanding of the university context in Australia, a geographically large country with a total population of about twenty-one million. Australia has thirty-nine universities, thirty-seven of which are public institutions. All public universities are funded for teaching and research, primarily by the federal government. Students are charged tuition fees on a sliding scale, according to degree program and student citizenship status. Broadly speaking, all universities engage in the three streams of research, teaching, and service. Eight universities (known as the Group of Eight, or the Go8)[1] form an alliance of research-intensive institutions, of which the University of New South Wales (UNSW) is a member. Each Go8 university has a student population of 30,000 to 40,000 students.

Although they are federally funded, public universities were originally founded as corporations under state parliament legislation with the expectation that they would carry out their activities in the best interests of the people of the state in which they are located (Meek and Hayden 2005). While teaching and research activities are broadly agreed upon and publicly and nationally scrutinized, how and whether universities interpret the "third stream"—service—in regard to "community engagement" varies in meaning and practice from one institution to another relative to each university's constituency, context, and institutional and pedagogical ethos.

In Australian universities, there is acceptance of the idea of community engagement. It is, however, variously interpreted, and institutions have varying levels of commitment to the idea and its practice. The differing stances and perspectives are evident in universities' strategic plans and mission statements. Several of the Go8 universities have been explicit about how community engagement is to be implemented in their institutions. In some cases, the senior executive team includes a position responsible for this; for example, the University of Adelaide has a director of community engagement. The University of Melbourne has adopted a "knowledge transfer" approach, which rewards "initiatives that achieve the goal of a two-way relationship and uptake of ideas between the University and the broader community" (www.knowledgetransfer.unimelb.edu.au/). In Brisbane, the University of Queensland's Boilerhouse Community Engagement Centre is active in linking community engagement with innovative research undertakings (www.uq.edu.au/).

UNSW's strategic vision document outlines a corporate model of community engagement that aims for interactions with communities comprising of alumni and potential industry partners. The university's strategic vision speaks of community engagement in the context of "being recognised as a key source of expertise" and developing "reciprocal relationships with alumni and former staff," rather than engagement for the purpose of working mutually with communities to address social issues or needs (University of New South Wales 2007).

Australian academics seeking to establish and advance the nexus between community engagement and service-learning have been assisted by the work of the Australian University Community Engagement Alliance (AUCEA). This organization supports universities that wish to incorporate community engagement in students' educational experiences. Since its inauguration in 2002, the thirty-one-member AUCEA has helped define modes of engagement, practices, and scholarship as they relate to service-learning and community engagement; AUCEA has also advanced the scholarship of community engagement in the Australian context through regular symposia, conferences, and publications and recognized the various modes of engagement as demonstrated by their impact in local and regional communities (Winter and Muirhead 2006).

As a result, community engagement

is now better defined as a two-way relationship leading to productive partnerships that yield mutually beneficial outcomes. It is thus much more than community participation, community consultation, community service and community development . . . Community engagement is a scholarly activity in which a university's teaching and learning are integrated with research activities that involve the community as genuine partners. (Willis 2006, 2)

This affirmation of community engagement as a *scholarly* activity has significantly strengthened the argument for service-learning as an activator of connections linking student learning, teaching, and research. In research-intensive universities such as UNSW, which gives priority to research productivity that is often disconnected from student learning, this is a welcome and affirming stance for those academics who aspire to actualize the mutuality linking student learning, teaching, and research with community needs.

The Faculty of the Built Environment (FBE) has a history of community outreach and engagement activities that until recently have not been conceptualized or organized in a coherent manner. The foundation and operation of a faculty-based engagement unit has brought a strategic and pedagogically cogent approach to FBE's activities that frames community engagement as a form of scholarship rather than as a mode of outreach; that is, it endeavors to actualize the links connecting learning, teaching, and research in a manner that is mutually beneficial for all participants.

## Context and Framework for Service-Learning in the FBE

The FBE is one of the largest and most diverse faculties of its kind in Australia, offering six professional degree programs in architecture, interior architecture, landscape architecture, industrial design, planning and urban development, and building construction project management. Since its inception, FBE has enjoyed strong links with professional practice as well as strong relationships with numerous communities in the Sydney metropolitan region and throughout the state of New South Wales (NSW). For example, since the mid-1980s, several architecture studios have addressed the needs of indigenous people, migrants, and public housing tenants in inner Sydney. Groups of students have traveled to regional towns in the state to consult, design, and build projects with communities, while others have been involved with projects including a sustainable schools program and, in collaboration with UNSW's School of Social Work and the NSW State Department of Housing, a long-running community development project.

These activities would now be recognized as aligning with the intent and pedagogical approach of service-learning, but at the time they were not undertaken within that framework. As a result, these individual projects were not consolidated as a "body of knowledge." There was little or no documentation of their approach, educational goals, administration, relationship to various curricula, management of relationships with community partners, participants' reflections on their experiences, and so on. Furthermore, the unique educational approach that distinguished these teaching and learning experiences was not well conceptualized, published, or appreciated beyond the scope of those immediately involved in the projects. To consolidate and coordinate these activities, to provide an administrative structure, and to heighten their legitimacy at both the academic and community levels, a resource unit was established in the faculty. It was known as FBEOutThere! (FBEOT).

## Role, Structure, and Operation of FBEOutThere!

FBEOutThere! sits in a unique position within the faculty, operating independently of the degree programs but interacting with them as project opportunities arise. Its strategic direction and operation are overseen by a reference group that includes three academics who meet regularly with the unit's manager and other project officers. FBEOT is resourced independently by the faculty, as well as being funded by external project and/or research grant income.

Community groups contact the FBEOT in various ways—through the FBE website, letters to the dean, phone calls to individual academics, word-of-mouth recommendations from colleagues in other faculties of the university, and so on. Acting as a clearinghouse and project broker, FBEOT responds to communications from prospective client groups, evaluating proposed projects and negotiating engagement activities that align with the educational resources and research initiatives of the faculty and the university.

This liaison role provides potential community partners with an introduction to the university and orients them to FBEOT's purpose and operations. Through these initial discussions, proposals can be considered within the philosophical and educational framework of the faculty's approach to community engagement and service-learning activities, ensuring an optimum fit between community aspirations and FBE's educational aims. Examples of this process will be demonstrated in the case studies.

When the FBEOT manager and reference group assess the suitability of potential projects, preference is given to groups that are considered marginalized in some way or not otherwise able to access design assistance. Projects and partners that are likely to generate a long-term relationship rather than a one-off interaction are preferred, but FBEOT projects do not involve construction with or for the client. To date, projects have occurred mostly within NSW and have been conducted within the time frame of the university semester. FBEOT staff are not directly responsible for leading courses; rather, they act as a liaison, a resource, a "critical friend" and point of contact for students, course leaders, and community partners throughout the various phases of the projects.

FBEOT facilitates the development of community engagement/service-learning projects in several modes. For example, it can:

- Offer the course as a credit-bearing faculty elective;
- Co-convene a course in association with an individual program, such as architecture or planning, as a core subject or an elective in that degree curriculum;
- Identify projects that one or more students undertake independently as a research project with a nominated academic supervisor;
- Act as a resource to academics for course development and delivery—for example, delivering workshops on sustainable development and group dynamics and interviewing community members.

## Pedagogical Framework

The pedagogy for service-learning and community engagement that underpins FBEOT has been inspired by conceptual and practice frameworks that focus on preparing students of built environment design for active citizenship. These include the work of Paulo Freire, whose work in Brazil sought to empower communities to exercise active citizenship and decision-making governance in matters that affected their lives (1985). The pedagogy also draws on the work of social psychologist Kurt Lewin, whose contributions relative to service-learning include establishing a link between behavior and physical environment, developing a model for participation that sensitively addresses attitudes of cultural and racial prejudice, and making a link between action research and social change (Kember and Kelly 1993).

These ideas have been well integrated into built environment disciplines, as exemplified by the teaching and practice of Henry Sanoff and others committed to advancing participatory planning and design processes (Sanoff 2007; Hester 2006). Sanoff's model of engagement is collaborative, empowering all participants to share their expertise so that "the outcome . . . [is more] insightful and powerful than the sum of individual perspectives." He reminds us that "participation is not only for the purposes of achieving agreement. It is also to engage people in meaningful and purposive adaptation and change to their daily environment" (Sanoff 2007, 213).

In the academic arena, Ernest Boyer's seminal scholarship model also gives prominence to principles of active citizenship and participation, repositioning the relevance and commitment of higher education to contemporary society by linking disciplinary knowledge with social issues through engaged practice. Service-learning and the notion of "engaged scholarship" clearly resonate with Boyer's scholarship of application, while interdisciplinary learning and teaching relates to his scholarship of integration (Boyer 1990).

These pedagogical principles have given rise to the following guidelines for curriculum design in FBEOT-related courses. These guidelines were reviewed and adopted by FBE's Education Committee for use in developing future service-learning engagement courses.

- **FBEOT courses should take an inquiry-based design approach.** FBEOT projects are generally undertaken in a studio format, including a significant component of research and background reading so that students can develop a full understanding of the issues and a basis for interrogating the design brief and initiating their speculations.

- **FBEOT courses should prepare students for interacting with communities.** Working in mutuality with communities requires students to be both sensitive and confident in managing their involvement with client groups in the consultation process. Course activities prepare them for participation in group and individual interviews and workshops processes, and include debriefing sessions after consultations and client interactions.

- **FBEOT courses should include reflective practice.** Reflective practice occurs throughout the course rather than as an evaluative exercise at the end.

- **FBEOT courses should facilitate interdisciplinary learning.**
  FBEOT studios aim to attract a mixed student cohort from across
  the faculty's programs. They should take an interdisciplinary approach as the starting point for responding to complex social issues
  and generating design speculations.
- **FBEOT courses should focus on continuity and capacity building.** Capacity building for all participants is an explicit aim of the
  projects, and community clients are asked to nominate a "project
  champion" to represent the group and take charge of the project during and after the students' work has been completed.
- **FBEOT courses should include feedback and evaluation.** For institutional validation and for continual improvement of the courses,
  a formal third-party evaluation of each course is undertaken following its completion. This allows for anonymous feedback and reflection from all participants—students, academics, and community
  members.
- **FBEOT courses should include opportunities for public presentation and exhibition of projects.** Students present and discuss
  their project work with community participants in the setting of the
  community. The project work is exhibited for a period of time in
  the community locale for comment and discussion, which is communicated to the students. Student projects are also exhibited in the
  faculty.
- **FBEOT courses should include opportunities for publication and
  dissemination of projects.** This occurs within the university, in
  journals, and at symposia and conferences.

## FBEOT in Practice

In built environment disciplines, designers engage simultaneously and dia-
lectically with imagined possibilities and with material realities. In student
design learning, the ability to translate creative ideas into material reality
is nurtured through project-based learning. Typically, built environment
design studio projects are set for students by their tutor and involve projects on hypothetical sites with imaginary briefs and clients. The projects
are designed to focus student learning on issues particular to the discipline.

In contrast, service-learning experiences allow students to

> participate in an organized service activity that meets identified com-
> munity needs and reflect on the service activity in such a way as to gain
> further understanding of course content, a broader appreciation of the

discipline, and an enhanced sense of civic responsibility. *(Bringle and Hatcher 1996, 222)*

Four key components are central to this concept of service-learning, clarifying its relationship to community engagement:

- The community identifies and defines the need, issue, or agenda to be addressed;

- Community partners are active participants in developing the projects and contributing to the studio activities along with students and academics;

- Service-learning principles are intentionally integrated into the curriculum of the degree programs;

- Students are co-learners with their teachers and community partners in "discovery-based learning experiences" (Subotzky 1999), which engender the connections linking research, learning, and teaching.

Thus, when design studio projects are conceptualized as service-learning experiences, students are necessarily connected to specific sites, places, or contexts, with real clients who have pressing social needs. In the service-learning approach, students must connect what they *think* they know in their disciplinary field with what *they actually need to know* to address and engage with clients' lived realities. This approach encourages students to develop the values, attitudes, and behaviors expected of the built environment professional as an active citizen in service to the community (Quinlan, Corkery, and Roche 2008).

Two case studies of recent FBEOT projects are described below, offering examples of how the unit facilitates service-learning and community engagement within the faculty, with reference to the pedagogic principles and guidelines outlined above. Both projects dealt with issues related to providing safe, community-based services for people with mental and physical disabilities.

## Case Study: Wollongong Clubhouse Project

The Wollongong Clubhouse Project is an example of how FBEOT acted as a resource in the development and delivery of an interdisciplinary studio design elective and facilitated structured course evaluation by, and feedback from, all the participants in the project.

Wollongong is a city on the east coast of Australia, fifty miles south of Sydney, with a population of about 280,000. The Wollongong Clubhouse, an initiative of the Lord Mayor's Light & Hope Mental Health Projects, is supported by a civic committee that generates support for the construction and management of the new facility. The Wollongong Clubhouse program is associated with the International Centre for Clubhouse Development (ICCD), which promotes programs and services that give people living with mental illness access to friendship, housing, education, and employment. To date, there has been no permanent location for this program.

A project committee member approached FBEOT with the idea of involving students in designing the new facility. The viability of the project was assessed through a series of discussions between FBEOT and the client representative, highlighting the opportunity it presented to engage students with the social issue of mental health and local resourcing of critical social services. Once the project was confirmed, the course structure and content were developed collaboratively by academics from landscape architecture, planning, and architecture. The class was conducted in a studio format and met once a week for four hours over a fourteen-week session. Eighteen undergraduate students representing four of the faculty's undergraduate programs—architecture (7), interior architecture (9), planning (1), and landscape architecture (1)—were enrolled in the elective course.

In preparation for working effectively and sensitively with the client group, the first three weeks of the semester were devoted to gaining an understanding of the complex issues related to mental health, particularly the difficulties of delivering community-based services in under-resourced circumstances. FBEOT assisted the studio teacher in planning these first class sessions and provided a resource for students on systems thinking and sustainable building approaches. The students researched issues related to mental health and heard presentations from representatives of the NSW Schizophrenia Fellowship and the Clubhouse program in preparation for a half-day workshop in Wollongong with Council representatives, the Clubhouse program proponents, and the "carers and consumers." This provided a face-to-face introduction with the future users of the Clubhouse, a confronting interaction for some of the students but invaluable for putting faces and personal aspirations to the project they were about to undertake. In addition, the students were inducted into the mundane professional realities of producing a project proposal that met the Council's planning expectations.

Following this introduction, the students worked in three groups of mixed disciplines. Each group developed a separate design proposal for a building and for site development that met the standard requirements of both the international Clubhouse and the City of Wollongong.

At mid-semester, three concepts were presented to the client group at another workshop in Wollongong. After receiving feedback on the schemes from the consumers and carers, the preferred concepts were consolidated into one proposal. For the final half of the semester, the entire group worked together to develop one design concept—along with preparing the supporting documentation required for the development application process. The students presented their final scheme to the Lord Mayor, the Light & Hope Committee, and the carers and consumers. The ideas were appreciatively and enthusiastically received, as the comments below illustrate:

> I am impressed with how well the students and teams have understood the Clubhouse principles . . . This is going to be a world class project . . . This will set the benchmark . . . It represents 100 percent of the Lord Mayor's vision . . . Will lead the way for the world. It is also a great blow for social justice . . . for people with mental illness who usually get the back end of a church hall for their activities. *(Committee member)*

> I can imagine many hours of fun times, this will be a great asset for the community. *(Service consumer)*

The design pays a compliment to the users and anticipates that there will be great international interest in what has been achieved here.

A committee member, who admitted he was dubious about involving students in the design project and advised against it, felt the results had proven him wrong.

At the conclusion of the studio, FBEOT's project officer created an online e-mail survey to gather feedback on the Clubhouse project from the students, participating academics, and community/client stakeholders. The officer also carried out an independent project evaluation. The survey consisted of open-ended questions asking the participants to reflect on their individual experiences of the project. All the responding students affirmed that working on the project had significantly increased their understanding of a major health issue and their empathy for those who live with that issue, partly because they had to analyze the hitherto unmet design needs of people living with mental illness. It also increased their understanding of the gaps in community services and facilities for those with schizophrenia and those who care for them and widened their understanding of the ramifications and social impacts of mental health issues, while also making clear the importance of government services and community support.

Two architecture students expanded on how the project challenged them to research appropriate designs for mental health sufferers and to explore the healing powers of good buildings and landscapes. The students had discovered very few context-relevant precedents in Australia, but this studio project took them into a new territory of learning:

> What I learnt from this course was the healing potential that architecture and landscape had. From the readings we were provided with and the first research assignment, my perspective of mental illness and architecture shifted dramatically.

> This course definitely raised awareness of the true nature of a subject that a lot of people are prejudiced about.

Comments from the course teacher and community-based stakeholders verified the effectiveness of the project as an innovative means of developing a community-specific design for the facility and also of involving future Clubhouse members in its design, thus heightening their "buy-in" and prospects of using the facility in the future:

> That students would . . . experience and learn extremely valuable skills that they were not able to learn in an academic/studio-only environment . . . [and] would deliver a workable, intelligent, sensitive design, in the given time frame, which reflected the briefing of the relevant parties . . . That bridges and contacts [would be] formed between UNSW and the greater community . . . Students would engage meaningfully in a project that had ethical, social and cultural implications, and learn important life skills by doing so. (Course teacher)

We also asked community participants about their "expectations for the project outcomes in working with the students from UNSW." They responded:

> I suppose I thought we would get some concept sketches. I did not expect such a thorough consultation process.

> I believed, from the outset, that this would be an innovative, well-resourced and thoughtful project . . . that would culminate in a series of detailed presentations of a clubhouse design sufficient for presentation to Council's planners. We hoped that the final design would reflect the community's desire to take some leadership on the mental issues.

As these comments confirm from the community participants' point of view, there was a genuine mutual benefit for all involved, validating FBEOT's role as the initial "point of contact" in project formulation, as "critical friend" throughout the process, and in assisting the interpretation of participants' feedback.

### Case Study: Rural Community Well-Being Enhanced through Design

The Rural Community Well-Being Enhanced through Design project demonstrates the role FBEOT played as an intermediary with the community partner, supporting an ongoing, iterative, and phased community engagement and facilitating productive interactions that led to community group capacity building. This case study also provides an example of how service-learning can advance built environment research through inquiry-based design projects.

This project connected students with Lambing Flat Enterprises (LFE), a rural community service group in Young, which is a prosperous and progressive regional city in central western NSW. Nearly a four hour drive southwest from Sydney, Young is located in an agricultural region that is susceptible to drought and experiences extreme seasonal temperature changes. LFE was established in 1972 and operates according to a social enterprise model, with a mission to

> provide training, support and advocacy to individuals with challenged ability, enabling individuals to fulfil their greatest potential. In every aspect of service delivery, LFE is always focused upon the needs and choices of the individual.

LFE meets its commitment to rural people with challenged abilities in western NSW by providing a range of services and innovative, supported employment enterprises. With over one hundred children and adults and their families in the community of Young, its district and region benefit from these activities.

The project was initiated in 1979 when LFE decided to build a residential complex where rural people with intellectual and physical disabilities could live independently while learning and practicing life skills and training for employment in the workplace. LFE approached the UNSW School of Architecture for assistance, and the school responded by arranging for third-year students to develop design proposals for a short-term accommodation residential complex, reported to be the first of its kind in Australia.

Twenty-seven years later, LFE again approached the FBE seeking assistance in the form of student-design proposals for residential accommodation to meet the needs of LFE community members as they aged. The idea was to allow members to live independently in the community, receiving quality support in a familiar environment without fear of having to move prematurely into institutional care for the aged. After a letter from LFE to the faculty dean, FBEOT initiated a consultation with executive members of LFE about the needs of their community service users. FBEOT prepared a briefing report based on wide-ranging community consultation and identified the following guidelines to take the project framework through a phased design approach:

- An emphasis on enhancing the well-being and quality of life of the service users should guide the design of affordable, independent living accommodation responsive to the specificity of the service users' daily lives;

- Student design proposals should incorporate environmentally and socially sustainable best-practice design to enhance individual and collective service-user health and well-being;

- The project's learning experiences should include opportunities for reciprocal learning—with intentional reflection—among socially and culturally diverse students, community workers, and people with challenging mental and physical disabilities;

- The project should acknowledge LFE's aspiration to provide an integrated community service on a consolidated site, facilitated by the phased design, development, and construction of a master-planned campus of affordable and sustainable homes, a community center, and respite care facilities.

Mindful of LFE's long-term goal and recognizing the comprehensive requirements of the project, FBEOT planned a phased service-learning experience over two academic semesters. The plan involved architecture students in the first phase, and architecture and landscape architecture students working together in teams during the second phase. FBEOT sought and gained agreement from the heads of the degree programs to offer the project as a service-learning community engagement design project within the core curricula of their respective degree programs.

In the first phase, the architecture program offered the project as one of several design project options to fourth-year bachelor of architecture and first-year master of architecture students. In early 2007, sixteen students elected to undertake the fourteen-week design project, which meant that the architecture program considered this studio program educationally appropriate and financially viable. A full-time academic, conversant with service-learning, elected to lead the project and worked mutually with FBEOT and LFE to design an action research approach to the educational program for the project so as to activate FBEOT pedagogical principles.

Staff and students focused on meeting LFE's desire to enhance the well-being and quality of life of the service users through attention to issues of domestic spatiality. Also, the following key points guided the students' design endeavors in their approach to social themes such as quality of life, well-being, universal design, flexibility, affordability, and sustainability:

- Consideration of appropriate models of disability, in particular the social model, which seeks to affirm and empower people with impairments;
- Analysis of conventional design interaction with and for people with disabilities;
- Basic understanding of aging in contemporary society;
- An awareness of the need of all people for "home-like" domestic environments;
- An awareness of the specific needs of rural and regional people with disabilities;
- An awareness of the complicated nature of real community engagement.

Students working in groups were encouraged to take a collaborative and consultative inquiry, evidence-based design approach rather than one driven by their personal intuitive needs as designers. In teams, they consulted with the service users and staff, and visited service users' existing homes to understand and document their specific spatial needs and experiences. Drawing upon these shared resources, students developed affordable designs that provided privacy and autonomy, room for personalization, and connection to external spaces. The progress of their designs was discussed with community members in studio.

In addition, students kept ongoing reflective journals, which assisted them in thinking about the research findings, their interaction with the service users and their needs, and how these impacted on their design approach to the project in its responsive resolution and communication. Some students found the disabilities of the service users confronting, whereas others, attuned to the medical model of disability, were challenged by the focus on well-being. Still others, comfortable with intuitively-driven design practices, reacted to the discipline of an inquiry-based, action research approach to architectural design. For these students, FBEOT assistants were particularly important resources. They acted as "critical friends" for discussing the project, facilitating the overall endeavor but remaining independent of the day-to-day studio operations. Equally important was the FBEOT staff role of "critical friend" to the course leader and to LFE, through participation in progressive design reviews of student projects.

The completed student designs were exhibited in the town to allow for community and student feedback and to advance community discussion about project approaches that best met their needs. In her project reflections, the general manager of LFE commented:

> The students were absolutely invaluable in helping progress LFE's own thinking and appreciation of what is needed in this project. The whole program could not have got off the ground had the students not embraced the total project with such empathy and understanding of the needs of the people involved.

As with the Wollongong Clubhouse Project, at the conclusion of the studio, FBEOT's project officer created an online e-mail survey to gather feedback on the effectiveness of the project from the students, participating academics, and community/client stakeholders. This survey complemented the reflective journals kept by the students. A strong theme that emerged from student reflections related to the responsibility, "weight," or gravity of producing a meaningful outcome for the service users of the LFE community:

> This design studio was able to narrow the gap between architect–user interaction and understanding. It was very useful and inspiring to be able to communicate closely with a community group. Instead of always designing in an idealistic manner, we are forced to design creatively to balance out between the ideal and the reality.
>
> . . . to work on an option which honestly attended to the issues we faced. This sense of responsibility meant that to the best of my ability I searched for a solution that was backed through research, and not just one I assumed would work.

This additional layer of accountability pushed many of the students beyond their normal boundaries. Many, upon reflection, noted the transformative quality of their learning upon their design practice. (For more information about the students' design proposals and the knowledge generated by their research, see Quinlan, Corkery, and Roche 2008.)

### Participant Reflections on Service-Learning and Engagement Outcomes

It is evident from participants' reflections that FBEOT projects not only resulted in real and beneficial design project outcomes for the partners but also facilitated rich student learning experiences and community capacity building in both of the project contexts. From these reflections, several themes emerge.

**Sense of ownership and responsibility.** Working on a real project, as distinct from a theoretical design studio project, generated a particular sense of ownership, which students believed motivated them and generated improved performance:

> The idea that it is a real project, and we had real clients and a real site was great; [it] made the design approach and process quite different . . . Also the level of interaction with many people and various professionals involved in the project provided quite a diverse range of expertise and views on the project.

For the future service users of the Wollongong Clubhouse and the LFE residential units, active contribution to the design process with the students heightened their sense of belonging to the outcomes. As the project champion for the Wollongong project noted:

> [Users] of the facility (consumers and carers) [were] involved with young, enthusiastic students . . . [and took] great pride in being able to communicate with the community that they were fully involved in their "second home." (Wollongong Clubhouse committee member)

**The ability to deal with ambiguity inherent in design projects.** The challenges associated with the uncertainty and mutuality of real-world projects were perceived to be highly beneficial to the students as emerging architects. Students' responses to formal university course evaluations affirmed this perception in relation to several key indicators. For example, students generally perceived that FBEOT courses were "challenging and interesting," and the numerical evaluation scores were substantiated with written comments:

> It was difficult as the brief was not clearly defined as the studio proceeded. However . . . this kind of situation is likely to happen in real practice.

Considering this increased capability, one student described the learning outcome as preparing them for practice "in a way a theoretical course cannot." Another student felt the experience "could help us [as designers] to make more considered design decisions and provide more liveable environments."

**The capacity for self-directed learning.** Students perceived that these community-based design projects encouraged them to be "self-directed in their learning" and stimulated their "curiosity and independence":

> Although I understand that there was a lot to be discovered as we went along . . . as students we weren't able to cope so well with this, which just highlights our inability to be more self-direct(ed) in our education, which is something that is hard but necessary to learn.

**Benefits of interdisciplinary learning and practice.** In the online feedback and in their reflective diaries, students reported that the FBEOT project courses delivered a range of significant benefits related to interdisciplinary practice not previously experienced during discipline-specific design studios. Students perceived these benefits to include teamwork, pooling of individual expertise in the collaborative nature of the design process, and sharing of knowledge and ideas. Teamwork provided the opportunity for students to extend themselves beyond the conceptual limitations of their discipline to explore new concepts and practice approaches. As such, students commented that they gained a holistic understanding of factors likely to be involved in undertaking genuine design projects:

> The diversity of students gives you a greater range of expertise, so the work is more complete in a sense. The teamwork also allowed for a lot of cross communication and critical analysis of ideas, and working collaboratively for the best final outcome, compared to a more introspective analysis in a studio.

Overall, students agreed that their education would benefit from:

> . . . more integrated courses or experiences which encourage a multidisciplinary approach to design projects, so that architecture students could understand and consider other areas of design for a more holistic and well-rounded design approach.

These four key themes—feeling responsibility, dealing with ambiguity, gaining a capacity for self-direction, and working in interdisciplinary modes—all bring to mind Ronald Barnett's writings on the need for curriculum to be responsive to "super-complexity" and for higher education to prepare students to operate in a global context "where nothing can be taken for granted . . . a world in which we are conceptually challenged, and continually so" (Barnett 2000, 257). The service-learning framework introduces students to approaching projects in practice-type situations where they must not only perform the designer's familiar tasks of analysis, synthesis, and communication of ideas, but must also acquire the capacity to be flexible, adaptable, self-reliant, and responsive in situations where "communication is made both more problematic and more urgent" (Barnett 2000, 258).

With the predisposition for practice-based learning that exists within built environment programs, there is great potential for generating new knowledge through the teaching and learning associated with community-based design projects and for the action research paradigms that can emanate from these projects. This demonstrates Michael Gibbons's (2007) notion of Mode 2 knowledge, where knowledge that originates in academia (Mode 1) is called upon to solve problems in the world, resulting in innovations or new understandings that in turn constitute a new intellectual field (Mode 2). Barnett refers to this as a "slide in the epistemology of knowledge fields" (Barnett 2000, 261).

Built environment professional degree programs in architecture and landscape architecture are responsive to the requirements of their national accrediting bodies.[2] Consequently, within these programs students are increasingly expected to demonstrate professionally relevant "core skills"; hence the focus on written, oral, and graphic communication skills, the ability to work in project groups, and so on. In service-learning projects, such as the two case studies described herein, these skills have certainly been tested and demonstrated, but another dimension of learning is also demonstrated—what Barnett describes as "self-monitoring," and that Schön identifies as the "reflective practitioner" (Barnett 2000; Schön 1987).

As the case studies reveal, the courses facilitated by FBEOT have introduced an approach to learning and teaching that prepares built environment students for professional practice in a way that requires much more than just disciplinary knowledge. They must have a broad understanding of the world and the specific context in which they are working, an understanding of themselves as individuals with unique worldviews and values, and a sense of self-confidence and security to act in an open and receptive way so as to hear and respond to the needs of others (Barnett 2000, 257).

## Conclusions

The positive outcomes generated in the two case studies presented in this paper can be linked to FBEOT's involvement throughout the development and implementation of the projects. Being situated between the administrative and academic units of the faculty has afforded the unit considerable flexibility and enabled it to be proactive in facilitating engagement, advancing best-practice approaches to university teaching, and learning guided by a service-learning framework that informs and enriches customary built environment education.

Importantly, as a resource unit within a built environment faculty, FBEOT demonstrates a contextual organizational approach that validates the scholarship of engagement in a research-intensive university. For faculties keen to activate the agency and practice contributions of their disciplines and to encourage continual improvement in learning, teaching, and research, such a unit also presents an effective vehicle for achieving goals in these areas. These results are consistent with the potentially positive impacts community engagement can have for an institution working for mutual benefits with community partners (Holland 2005, 15). Above all, for a faculty with the "core business" of preparing students to enter professional built environment domains, FBEOT presents a unique and perhaps essential model for leading scholarship practice that connects student learning, teaching, research, and service in engaged and contextualized modes to mutually benefit communities.

# Endnotes

## Introduction

1. Leading the fields were the Pratt Institute, Community Based Projects at Ball State, Arch 2001 at Carnegie Mellon, the Community Development Group at North Carolina State, and the Carl Small Town Center at Mississippi State.

## Chapter 1

1. The author wishes to thank her excellent project colleagues: Diana Nicholas, Juris Milestone, Jim Kise, and Harris Steinberg; the Shared Prosperity Steering Committee, especially Lily Yeh, Reverend Donna Jones, Brian Kelly, and John Ballard; Temple University and the students in the Urban Workshop Studio: Ron Ammen, Mary Lou Bailey, Mike Kitchen, Sita Ng, Ansel Radway, Nichole Rivest, Ryan Solimeo, Stephanie Saile, Justin Tocci, Jerry Varman, and Alex Will.

2. Lily Yeh, interview with the author, June 10, 2008.

## Chapter 2

1. Many arguments have been made regarding the relationship between power and space. See, for example, Lefebvre 1974; Harvey 1996; and Massey 2005.

2. I use 'post-critical' here in the sociological, nonliterary sense to describe what has followed a twentieth-century feminist and cultural critique of domination, and which assumes that we have arrived in a neutral society and are thus relieved of the need to question motives.

3. For a discussion outlining recognition theory, see Young 1990. For a critique of recognition theory, see Fraser 1997.

4. Examples of texts used in the course: Anderson 1999; Castells 1983; Swanstrom, Dreier, and Mollenkopf 2004; Frug 1999; Chase, Crawford, and Kaliski 1999; and Harvey 2000.

## Chapter 3

1. The author would like to thank Joyce Pisnanont, Alan Lee, Guihui Yuan, and members of the WILD program for making the partnership a productive and rewarding learning experience. The project was made possible through the Internationalizing UW's Under-

graduate Curriculum Course Development Grant from the Undergraduate Academic Affairs, International Program and Exchange, and the Curriculum Transformation Project at the University of Washington.

2. Student feedback on the course was solicited through the standard student evaluation required by the university and an additional questionnaire with questions specific to the studio experience developed by the instructor. A separate questionnaire was distributed to the WILD participants at the end of the program.

3. The author was the instructor for the studio.

4. Former Secretary of Housing and Urban Development Henry Cisneros (1995) more directly argues that universities have self-interest to work with their neighboring distressed communities to reduce crime, poverty, and economic stagnation.

5. The transformation parallels a shift in community organization theory in the recent decades from the confrontational approach to a consensus-building model (Hutchinson and Loukaitou-Sideris 2001).

6. For more information on WILD and IDHA, see www.apialliance.org.

7. The students, in turn, receive service-learning credits required for high school completion. However, many students have stayed involved after the completion of their service-learning hours and even participated for the second or third time.

8. For more information, see www.caup.washington.edu/larch/.

9. These community service-learning initiatives were highlighted in the first of a case study series put together by the University of Washington's Educational Partnerships and Learning Technologies (Symes 2003).

10. The author was subsequently invited to join the board of the International District Housing Alliance. His board membership has further strengthened the collaboration between the two programs.

11. For more information on the Children's Park studio, see courses.washington.edu/.

12. National Night Out is a crime/drug-prevention program that encourages neighborhoods around North America to organize against crimes. See www.natw.org/.

13. The studio was taught by the author and funded through a mini-grant from the university that supported the field trip to Richmond, BC, and the construction of the installations. The program involved fifteen UW students (including one exchange student from China) and thirteen WILD students from various high schools in Seattle. More information on the studio is available at courses.washington.edu/nightmkt/.

14. There was also a significant difference in the racial and ethnic makeup of the UW students versus the WILD youths. With the exception of one exchange student from China, all UW students were Caucasian, reflecting the general student population in landscape architecture. The WILD youths include new immigrant students and second-generation students from China, South Korea, Taiwan, Thailand, and Vietnam.

15. In retrospect, another approach would be to reverse the roles. However, the process would be more challenging and time-consuming.

16. All the installations were assembled and put on display during a review to which community members were invited. However, due to limited space and technical challenges, only one installation was assembled on site for the night market in 2007. The plan was to have the different installations put up on a rotating basis.

17. While recognition often needs to come first, the strategies or steps described here need not be entirely linear or sequential. For example, negotiation is an important task that must take place throughout the collaborative process.

## Chapter 4

1.  In order to be consistent, this paper uses the term "community-engaged design studios"; however, this term has direct associations with service-learning studios and the associated literature.

2.  Race is understood as a socially constructed classification system intended to maintain social, economic, and other distinctions (Foner and Frederickson 2004).

3.  The ESLARP website (www.eslarp.illinois.edu) includes demographic data, data collected from resident surveys and meetings, historic texts, oral histories, reports, and past student design proposals.

4.  Scales include the Psychosocial Cost of Racism to Whites Scale to measure whites' experiences of negative consequences of societal racism (Spanierman and Heppner 2004); the Color-Blind Racial Attitudes Scale to assess if participants minimize or distort the existence of racism in the US (Neville et al. 2000); the Modern Racism Scale to assess participants' attitudes toward racial minorities (McConahay 1986); and the Miville-Guzman Universality Diversity Short Scale to assess participants' orientation to diversity (Fuertes et al. 2000). Due to the small number of participants, the scales provide descriptive rather than quantitative data. The studio instructor was not present during recruitment or data collection sessions and was not given results until after grades were submitted. Focus group data was not included in this article to avoid conflict with education psychology research protocol but will be published by Dr. Spanierman as part of her ongoing research on student perceptions of race. The process was overseen by two trained graduate students (i.e., the third and fourth authors of this paper).

5.  Specific information about the students' socioeconomic and ethnic status was not collected; however, departmental demographics for that year indicated that of the 125 undergraduates, 91 percent were white and 97 percent were from the state of Illinois. Most UIUC undergraduates in that year came from suburban counties around Chicago.

## Chapter 6

1.  Student names have been changed to maintain the confidentiality of their journal entries, but the gender and ethnicity of the students are suggested by the new names. We attempted to contact each of the site supervisors for their input on an earlier version of this paper. We thank those who offered their additional insights and comments, which we incorporated into the final draft.

## Chapter 7 ·

1.  Portions of this chapter were developed earlier. See Rios 2004; Bowns and Rios 2005.

## Chapter 9

1.  While these suggested links cannot be construed as causal, taken together responses in these two parts of the study suggest links that should be examined in future studies using more statistically rigorous techniques.

2.  Chi-square analyses performed on the study data show that the college major of respondents did not significantly influence the responses to this series of questions.

## Chapter 10

1.  "Tico" is a common term for anyone or anything native to Costa Rica; unlike many other colloquial names for local populations, the term Tico underscores a very positive national identity.

2.  The four life zones found in Monteverde are home to more than 100 species of mammals, 400 species of birds, 500 species of butterflies, 120 reptile and amphibian species,

2,500 plant species (among them 420 different types of orchids and 200 fern species), 500 species of trees, and thousands of insect species (Centro Científico Tropical, 2005).

3.  One of the indicator species, the three-wattled bellbird, has attracted attention around the world because of its dependence on fragile ecological conditions that are disappearing (Strap 2000; Costa Rican Conservation Foundation 2004). By tracking the birds, George Powell, Deb Deroiser, and other scientists identified key gaps in habitat and found many of these areas to be privately held lands. Using aerial photographs, extensive field reconnaissance, and GIS, Sustainable Futures has been able to propose new or expanded biocorridors to reconnect isolated fragments of forest, a classic application of the principals of landscape ecology (Dramstad, Olsen, and Forman 1997).

## Chapter 11

1.  Ed Mahoney, interview with the author, 2007.

## Chapter 13

1.  According to the 2000 US Census, the residents of Del Ray and Rosemont were more than 50 percent white.

2.  We see increasing numbers of students seeking cross-disciplinary educational experiences and dual degrees, such as architecture or landscape architecture students getting planning degrees and planning students getting degrees in natural resources and sustainability. Several students in the Commonwealth Studio (e.g., four architecture /landscape architecture students) were enrolled in the Planning Studio or the Community Involvement class.

3.  Mount Vernon Avenue Business Area Plan became part of the Potomac West Small Area Plan in March 2005; for more information, see www.alexandriava.gov/planning/info /default.aspx?id=7032&terms=Potomac+West+Small+Area+Plan.

4.  Although planning education does not typically promote innovation in the same way, the emphasis on creative design imposed on the landscape studio students encouraged the planning students to also consider new and bold planning approaches within each team's master plans.

5.  Examples of the interviews and survey questionnaire are available in the 2007 Fairmount Heights Community Report.

## Chapter 14

1.  Brian Kane, American Society of Landscape Architects, made significant contributions to the content of this article.

2.  This article was a precursor to Hester's book, *Neighborhood Space: User Needs and Design Responsibilities* (1975).

## Chapter 15

1.  Group of Eight members are the University of Western Australia, University of Adelaide, University of Melbourne, Monash University, Australian National University, University of Sydney, University of New South Wales, and the University of Queensland. With the exception of the Australian National University, located in Canberra, the national capital, all are major state universities located in capital cities.

2.  In Australia, these accreditation bodies include the Australian Institute of Landscape Architects, Architects Accreditation Council of Australia, and respective state and territory registration boards recognized by the Australian Institute of Architects.

# References

Alsop, D. n.d. *National Turnaround in Public Transportation*. Washington, DC: American Public Transportation Association.

American Institute of Architects (AIA). n.d. *AIA Grassroots Advocacy: Why Architects Need to Get Involved*. aiawebdev2.aia.org/adv_whyarchitectsneedtogetinvolved.

Andersen, S. M. 1998. "Service-Learning: A National Strategy for Youth Development." Washington, DC: Education Policy Task Force, Institute for Communitarian Policy Studies.

Anderson, E. 1999. *Code of the Street*. New York: W. W. Norton.

Angotti, T. 2008. *New York for Sale: Community Planning Confronts Global Real Estate*. Cambridge, MA: MIT Press.

Arnold, R., B. Burke, C. James, D. A. Martin, and B. Thomas. 1991. *Educating for a Change*. Toronto: Between the Lines Press.

Association of African American Professionals. n.d. "California Elder Care Initiative."

Avin, U. P., and J. L. Dembner. 2001. "Getting Scenario-Building Right." *Planning*, no. 57: 22–27.

Bachim, R. 2003. "Cultivating Unity: The Changing Role of Parks in Urban America." *Places* 23 (2): 12–17.

Barker, D. 2004. "From Service Learning to the Scholarship of Engagement: A Taxonomy of Civic Renewal in American Higher Education." Paper presented at the annual meeting of the *American Political Science Association*, Hilton Chicago and the Palmer House Hilton, Chicago, IL, September 2. Online on June 28, 2008. www.allacademic.com/meta/p59505_index.html.

Barkey, M. 2000. "Models of Effective Compassion: Dr. John Perkins and the 'Three Rs of Community Development.'" *Journal of the Acton Institute for the Study of Religion and Liberty*, June 29. Accessed December 2010. www.acton.org/commentary/commentary_19.php.

Barnett, R. 2000. "Supercomplexity and the Curriculum." *Studies in Higher Education* 25 (3): 255–65.

Barrows, H. S., and R. W. Tamblyn. 1980. *Problem-Based Learning: An Approach to Medical Education*. New York: Springer.

Baum, H. 2000. "Fantasies and Realities of University-Community Partnerships." *Journal of Planning Education and Research* 20 (2): 234–46.

Beane, J. A. 1997. *Curriculum Integration: Designing the Core of Democratic Education*. New York: Teachers College Press.

Beauregard, R. 2003. "Democracy, Storytelling, and the Sustainable City." In *Story and Sustainability: Planning, Practice, and Possibility for American Cities*, edited by B. Eckstein and J. A. Throgmorton. Cambridge, MA: MIT Press.

Behar, R. 1996. *The Vulnerable Observer: Anthropology that Breaks Your Heart*. Boston: Beacon Press.

Bell, B., ed. 2004. *Good Deeds, Good Design: Community Service through Architecture*. New York: Princeton Architectural Press.

Bennett, P. 1998. "Approaching It Hands-On." *Landscape Architecture* 88 (4) April: 46–51.

Benson, L., I. Harkavy, and J. Puckett. 2007. *Dewey's Dream: Universities and Democracies in an Age of Education Reform*. Philadelphia: Temple University Press.

Bernard, B. 2007. "The Hope of Prevention: Individual, Family, and Community Resilience." In *Prevention is Primary: Strategies for Community Well-Being*, edited by L. Cohen, V. Chavez, and S. Chehimi. New York: John Wiley & Sons.

Beveridge, C. E. 1986. *Toward a Definition of Olmstedian Principles of Design*. National Association for Olmsted Parks.

Billigs, S. 2000. "Research on K–12 School-Based Service Learning: The Evidence Builds." *Phi Delta Kappan* 81 (9): 658–64.

Birge, J. 2005. "The Aesthetical Basis for Service-Learning Practice." In *Service Learning in Higher Education: Critical Issues and Directions*, edited by D. Butin. New York: Palgrave Macmillan.

Bonilla-Silva, E. 2001. *White Supremacy and Racism in the Post-Civil Rights Era*. Boulder: Lynne Rienner.

Bosselman, F. 1972. *The Quiet Revolution in Land Use Control*. Washington, DC: Government Printing Office.

Bowns, C., and M. Rios. 2005. "Reflection in Action: A Case Study of Service Learning in Design Education." *Proceedings of the 5th Annual US-Brazil Higher Education Consortia Meeting*, Howard University, Washington, DC.

Boyer, E. L. 1990. *Scholarship Reconsidered: Priorities of the Professoriate*. Princeton: Carnegie Foundation for the Advancement of Teaching.

————. 1996. "The Scholarship of Engagement." *Journal of Public Service & Outreach* 1 (1), Spring: 11–21.

Boyer, E. L., and L. D. Mitgang. 1996. *Building Community: A New Future for Architecture Education and Practice*. Princeton: Carnegie Foundation for the Advancement of Teaching.

Bransford, J. D., and N. J. Vye. 1989. "A Perspective on Cognitive Research and Its Implications for Instruction." In *Toward the Thinking Curriculum: Current Cognitive Research*, edited by L. B. Resnick and L. E. Klopfer. Alexandria, VA: Association for Supervision and Curriculum Development.

Bringle, R. G., and J. Hatcher. 1996. "Implementing Service Learning in Higher Education." *Journal of Higher Education* 67 (2): 221–39.

_____. 2002. "Campus-Community Partnerships: The Terms of Engagement." *Journal of Social Issues* 58 (3): 503–16.

Brouwer, R. 2002. "Service-Learning for First-Year Engineering Students." In *Commitment & Connection: Service-Learning and Christian Higher Education*, edited by G. G. Heffner and C. D. Beversluis. Lanham, MD: University Press of America.

Burnett, J. A., D. Hamel, and L. L. Long. 2004. "Service Learning in Graduate Counselor Education: Developing Multicultural Competency." *Journal of Multicultural Counseling and Development*, no. 32: 180–91.

Burton, J., L. Kaplan, J. Mohraz, L. Munns, and C. Weinberg. 2002. "Liberal Arts College Faculty Reflect on Service-Learning: Steps on a Transformative Journey." In *Learning to Serve: Promoting Civil Society through Service Learning*, edited by M. E. Kenny, L. A. K. Simon, K. Kiley-Brabeck, and R. M. Lerner. Boston: Kluwer Academic Publishers.

Cameron, M., A. Forsyth, W. A. Green, H. Lu, P. McGirr, P. E. Owens, and R. Stoltz. 2001. "Learning through Service." *College Teaching* 49 (33): 105–14.

Camp, G. 1996. "Problem-Based Learning: A Paradigm Shift or a Passing Fad?" *Medical Education Online* 1 (2). Accessed December 2010. www.med-ed-online.org/f0000003.htm.

Carnegie Foundation for the Advancement of Teaching. 2006. *Community Engagement Classification*. Palo Alto, CA: Carnegie Foundation for the Advancement of Teaching.

Carpenter, W. 1997. *Learning by Building: Design and Construction in Architectural Education*. New York: John Wiley & Sons.

Carr, W., and S. Kemmis. 1986. *Becoming Critical: Education, Knowledge and Action Research*. London: Falmer Press.

Carson, C., ed. 1998. *The Autobiography of Dr. Martin Luther King, Jr.* New York: Warner Books.

Cary, J., ed. 2000. *ACSA Sourcebook of Community Design Programs at Schools of Architecture in North America*. Washington, DC: Association of Collegiate Schools of Architecture.

Castells, M. 1983. *The City and the Grassroots: Cross-Cultural Theory of Urban Social Movements*. New York: Hodder Arnold.

Centro Cientifico Tropical / Tropical Science Center. 2005. *Biological Diversity*. Monteverde, Puntarenas, Costa Rica. www.cct.or.cr/english/reserva_monteverde/reserva_monteverde2.php.

Chapman, D. W. 2000. "Designing Problems for Motivation and Engagement in the PBL Classroom." *Journal on Excellence in College Teaching* 11 (2–3): 73–82.

Chase, J., M. Crawford, and J. Kaliski, eds. 1999. *Everyday Urbanism*. New York: Monacelli Press.

Chin, D. 2001. *Seattle's International District: The Making of a Pan-Asian American Community*. Seattle: International Examiner Press.

Chrysler, C. G. 1995. "Critical Pedagogy and Architectural Education." *Journal of Architectural Education* 48 (4): 208–17.

Cisneros, H. G. 1995. *The University and Urban Challenge*. Washington, DC: US Department of Housing and Urban Development.

City of Alexandria, Virginia. 2002. "Open Space Master Plan." City of Alexandria, Virginia. Accessed August 10, 2008. alexandriava.gov/uploadedfiles/recreation/info/OpenSpacePlan.pdf.

_____. 2003. "Park Planning, Design + Capital Projects." City of Alexandria, Virginia. Accessed December 2010. alexandriava.gov/recreation/info/default.aspx?id=18078.

Coalition for Utah's Future. 2007. *Newsletter*, Spring. Salt Lake City, UT. www.envisionutah.org/.

____. 2008. *Envision Utah: How We Grow Matters*. Salt Lake City, UT: Coalition for Utah's Future. www.envisionutah.org/resourcesfiles/49/EU%20brochure%20web.pdf.

____. n.d. *The History of Envision Utah*. Salt Lake City, UT. www.envisionutah.org/.

Coles, R. 1993. *The Call of Service: A Witness to Idealism*. New York: Houghton Mifflin.

College of Architecture & Planning, University of Utah. 2008a. *ARCH Course Descriptions*. www.acs.utah.edu/GenCatalog/crsdesc/arch.html.

____. 2008b. *URBPL Course Descriptions*. www.acs.utah.edu/GenCatalog/crsdesc/urbpl .html.

Community Redevelopment Agency of the City of Los Angeles. n.d. "About Us." www .crala.org/internet-site/About/index.cfm.

Conrad, D., and D. Hedin. 1991. "School-Based Community Service: What We Know from Research and Theory." *Phi Delta Kappan* 72 (10): 743–49.

Costa Rican Conservation Foundation. 2004. "Bellbird Conservation Project." Santa Elena, Puntarenas, Costa Rica. Accessed December 2010. www.fccmonteverde.org/bbcp.html.

Cranz, G., and M. Boland. 2004. "Defining the Sustainable Park: A Fifth Model." *Landscape Journal* 23 (2): 102–20.

Crawford, M. 1999. "Blurring the Boundaries: Public Space and Private Life." In *Everyday Urbanism*, edited by J. Chase, M. Crawford, and J. Kaliski. New York: Monacelli Press.

Crawford, P., and P. Machemer. 2008. "Measuring Incidental Learning in a PBL Environment." *Journal of Faculty Development* 2 (2): 104–11.

Cruz, N. I., and D. Giles. 2000. "Where's the Community in Service-Learning Research?" Special Issue. *Michigan Journal of Community Service Learning*, Fall: 28–34.

Danko, S., J. Meneely, and M. Portillo. 2006. "Humanizing Design through Narrative Inquiry." *Journal of Interior Design* 31 (2): 10–28.

Davidoff, P. 1965. "Advocacy and Pluralism in Planning." *Journal of the American Institute of Planners* 31 (4): 331–338.

Davis, M. 1992. *City of Quartz: Excavating the Future in Los Angeles*. New York: Vintage Books.

Davis, N. J. 1992. "Teaching About Inequality: Student Resistance, Paralysis, and Rage." *Teaching Sociology*, no. 20: 232–38.

de Certeau, M. 1977. *Culture in the Plural*. Minneapolis: University of Minnesota Press.

____. 1984. *The Practice of Everyday Life*. Berkeley: University of California Press.

De Lissovoy, N. 2008. *Power, Crisis and Education for Liberation: Rethinking Critical Pedagogy*. New York: Palgrave MacMillan.

Dean, A. O., and T. Hursley. 2002. *Rural Studio: Samuel Mockbee and the Architecture of Decency*. New York: Princeton Architectural Press.

Deitrick, S., and T. Soska. 2008. "Economic and Community Development Workforce Initiative." Unpublished paper.

Deleuze, G. 1994. *Difference and Repetition*. Translated by P. Patton. New York: Columbia University Press.

Depoe, S., and J. W. Delicath. 2004. "Introduction." In *Communication and Public Participation in Environmental Decision Making*, edited by S. P. Depoe, J. W. Delicath, and M. A. Elsenbeer. Albany, NY: State University of New York Press.

Dewar, M. E., and C. B. Isaac. 1998. "Learning from Difference: The Potentially Transforming Experience of Community-University Collaboration." *Journal of Planning Education and Research*, no. 17: 334–47.

Dewey, J. 1897. "My Pedagogic Creed." University of Chicago. www.rjgeib.com/biography /credo/dewey.html.

_____. 1916. *Democracy and Education: An Introduction to the Philosophy of Education*. New York: The Macmillan Company.

_____. 1938. *Experience and Education*. The Kappa Delta Pi Lecture Series. New York: The Macmillan Company.

Dramstad, W., J. Olsen, and R. Forman. 1997. *Landscape Ecology Principles in Landscape Architecture and Land-Use Planning*. Washington, DC: Island Press.

Dutton, T. A. 1991. "Cultural Politics and Education." *Journal of Architectural Education*, 44 (2): 67–68.

Dutton, T. A., and L. H. Mann. 1996. "Introduction: Modernism, Postmodernism, and Architecture's Social Project." In *Reconstructing Architecture: Critical Discourses and Social Practices*, edited by T. A. Dutton and L. H. Mann. Minneapolis: University of Minnesota Press.

East St. Louis Action Research Project. n.d. "Mission Statement." East St. Louis Action Research Project. Accessed December 2010. www.eslarp.uiuc.edu/view/mission-statement .aspx.

_____. "The Way We Work." East St. Louis Action Research Project. Accessed December 2010. www.eslarp.uiuc.edu/view/what-is-eslarp_1.aspx.

Eckstein, B. 2003. "Making Space: Stories in the Practice of Planning." In *Story and Sustainability: Planning, Practice, and Possibility for American Cities*, edited by B. Eckstein and J. A. Throgmorton. Cambridge, MA: MIT Press.

Educating LAs. 1998. *Landscape Architecture* 88 (10): 100–45.

Eisman, G. 2005. "Boyer, Engaged Scholarship, and New Models of RTP (Retention, Tenure and Promotion)." Lecture presented at Sonoma State University, April 28. www .calstate.edu/cce/resource_center/documents/boyer_rtp_sonoma.pdf.

Ewing, R., K. Bartholomew, S. Winkelman, J. Walters, and D. Chen. 2008. *Growing Cooler: The Evidence on Urban Development and Climate Change*. Washington, DC: Urban Land Institute.

Eyler, J., and D. E. Giles. 1999. "Identifying the Learning Outcomes of Service." In *Where's the Learning in Service-Learning?* edited by J. Eyler and D. E. Giles. San Francisco: Jossey-Bass.

Eyler, J., D. E. Giles, C. M. Stenson, and C. J. Gray. 2001. *At a Glance: What We Know about the Effects of Service-Learning on College Students, Faculty, Institutions and Communities, 1993–2000*. 3rd ed. Washington, DC: Corporation for National Service.

Final Studio Report. 2006. "Commonwealth Avenue—Love Me, Love Me Not." The Washington Alexandria Architecture Center. Accessed August 10, 2008. www.nvc.vt.edu /uap/research/commonwealth_avenue.html.

Fincher, R., and K. Iveson. 2008. *Planning and Diversity in the City: Redistribution, Recognition and Encounter*. New York: Palgrave Macmillan.

Fink, L. D. 2003. *Creating Significant Learning Experiences: An Integrated Approach to Designing College Courses*. San Francisco: Jossey-Bass.

Finnegan, R. 1998. *Tales of the City: A Study of Narrative and Urban Life*. Cambridge, UK: Cambridge University Press.

Foner, N., and G. M. Frederickson, eds. 2004. *Not Just Black and White: Historical and Contemporary Perspective on Immigration, Race, and Ethnicity in the United States*. New York: Russell Sage Foundation.

Foppiano, A. 2005. "Rural Studio: Taboo Landscape." *Abitare*, November: 150–59.

Forester, J. 1989. *Planning in the Face of Power*. Berkeley: University of California Press.

_____. 1999. *The Deliberative Practitioner: Encouraging Participatory Planning Process.* Cambridge, MA: MIT Press.

Forsyth, A. 1995. "Diversity Issues in a Professional Curriculum: Four Stories and Some Suggestions for Change." *Journal of Planning Education and Research* 15 (1): 58–63.

_____. 1996. "Feminist Theory and Planning Theory: The Epistemological Linkages." In *Readings in Planning Theory,* edited by S. Campbell and S. Feinstein, 471–474. Oxford: Blackwell Publishing.

Forsyth, A, H. Lu, and P. McGirr. 1999. "Inside the Service Learning Studio in Urban Design." *Landscape Journal* 18 (2): 166–78.

_____. 2000. "Service Learning in an Urban Context: Implications for Planning and Design Education." *Journal of Architectural and Planning Research* 17 (3), Autumn: 236–59.

Francis, M. 1999. "Proactive Practice: Visionary Thought and Participatory Action in Environmental Design." *Places* 12 (2): 60–68.

Franck, K. A., and Q. Stevens. 2006. *Loose Space: Possibility and Diversity in Urban Life.* London: Routledge.

Fraser, N. 1997. *Justice Interruptus.* New York: Routledge.

Freire, P. 1970. *Pedagogy of the Oppressed.* Translated by M. B. Ramos, 1997. New York: Continuum.

_____. 1973. *Education for Critical Consciousness.* New York: Continuum.

_____. 1985. *The Politics of Education.* New York: Bergin and Garvey.

_____. 2001. *Pedagogy of Freedom: Ethics, Democracy and Civic Courage.* New York: Roman & Littlefield.

Friedmann, J. 1987. *Planning in the Public Domain.* Princeton: Princeton University Press.

Frug, G. E. 1999. *City Making: Building Communities without Building Walls.* Princeton: Princeton University Press.

Fuertes, J. N., M. L. Miville, J. J. Mohr, W. E. Sedlacek, and D. Gretchen. 2000. "Factor Structure and Short Form of the Miville–Guzman Universality-Diversity Scale." *Measurement and Evaluation in Counseling and Development,* no. 33: 157–69.

Furco, A. 2001. "Advancing Service Learning at Research Universities." *New Directions for Higher Education,* no. 114: 67–77.

Gadotti, M. 1994. *Reading Paulo Freire: His Life and Work.* New York: State University of New York Press.

Garvin, A. 1996. *The American City: What Works and What Doesn't.* New York: McGraw-Hill.

Garvin, A., and G. Berens. 1997. *Urban Parks and Open Space.* Washington, DC: Urban Land Institute.

Gelmon, S. B., B. A. Holland, A. Driscoll, A. Spring, and S. Kerrigan. 2001. *Assessing Service-Learning and Civic Engagement: Principles and Techniques.* Providence, RI: Campus Compact.

Gergen, M., and K. J. Gergen. 2000. "Qualitative Inquiry: Tensions and Transformations." In *Handbook of Qualitative Research,* edited by N. Denzin and Y. S. Lincoln. Thousand Oaks, CA: SAGE Publications.

Gibbons, M. 2007. "Engagement as a Core Value in a Mode 2 Society." In *Proceedings of the Community Engagement in Higher Education Conference.* Capetown: The Council on Higher Education (CHE), Higher Education Quality Committee (HEQC), and JET Education Services Community Higher Education Service Partnerships (CHESP).

Gibbs, G. 1992. *Improving the Quality of Student Learning.* Bristol, UK: Technical and Education Services.

Giroux, H. A. 1997. *Pedagogy and the Politics of Hope: Theory, Culture, and Schooling.* Boulder: Westview Press.

_____. 2006. *The Giroux Reader.* Boulder: Paradigm Publishers.

Glassick, C., M. T. Huber, and G. Maeroff. 1997. *Scholarship Assessed: Evaluation of the Professoriate.* San Francisco: Jossey-Bass.

Gray, C. J., J. M. Heffernan, and M. H. Norton. 2010. *Partnerships that Work: The Stories and Lessons from Campus/Community Collaborations.* Grantham, PA: Pennsylvania Campus Compact.

Gray, M. J., N. F. Campbell, E. Heneghan Ondaatje, K. Rosenblatt, S. Geschwind, R. D. Fricker, C. A. Goldman, T. Kaganoff, A. Robyn, M. Sundt, L. Vogelgesang, and S. P. Klein. 1999. *Combining Service and Learning in Higher Education: Evaluation of the Learn and Serve America Higher Education Program.* Santa Monica, CA: Rand Corporation.

Green, J. M. 1999. *Deep Democracy: Community, Diversity and Transformation.* Oxford: Rowman & Littlefield.

Greening, T. 1998. "Scaffolding for Success in Problem-Based Learning." *Medical Education Online* 3 (4). Accessed December 2010. www.med-ed-online.org/fooooo12.htm.

Groat, L. N., and S. B. Ahrentzen. 1996. "Reconceptualizing Architectural Education for a More Diverse Future: Perceptions and Visions of Architectural Students." *Journal of Architectural Education* 49 (3): 166–83.

Gutman, J., and T. J. Reynolds. 1979. "An Investigation of the Levels of Cognitive Abstraction Utilized by Consumers in Product Differentiation." In *Attitude Research under the Sun*, edited by J. Eighmy. Chicago: American Marketing Association.

Hamdi, N. 2004. *Small Change: About the Art of Practice and the Limits of Planning in Cities.* London: Earthscan.

Hansman, B. 2009. "Enter Like a Lover." *St. Louis Currents*, no. 4: 24–29.

Haque, M. T., L. Tai, and B. V. Mey. 2000. "Horticulture; Planning and Landscape Architecture, and Sociology." In *Service Learning across the Curriculum: Case Applications in Higher Education*, edited by S. J. Madden, 23–38. New York: University Press of America.

Haraway, D. 1992. "The Promise of Monsters: A Regenerative Politics for Inappropriate/d Others." In *Cultural Studies*, edited by L. Grossberg, C. Nelson, and P. Treichler. New York: Routledge.

Harkavy, I., and L. Benson. 1998. "De-Platonizing and Democratizing Education as the Basis of Service Learning." *New Directions for Teaching and Learning*, no. 73: 11–20.

Harland, T. 1998. "Moving Towards Problem-Based Learning." *Teaching in Higher Education* 3 (2): 219–23.

Harris, D. 2004. "Race and Space." In *Towards a Bibliography of Critical Whiteness Studies*, edited by T. Engles. Urbana, IL: Center on Democracy in a Multiracial Society.

Harris, M. 1997. "Social Dynamics and Built Form: Design Studio Investigations." In *Learning by Building: Design and Construction in Architectural Education*, edited by W. J. Carpenter. New York: Van Nostrand Reinhold.

Harris Interactive. 2005. *Envisioning the Future of Central Florida: Building on the Personal Values Underlying Growth.* Orlando: myregion.org.

_____. 2007. *Utah Values and Future Growth.* Salt Lake City, UT: Coalition for Utah's Future.

Harwood, S. A., and M. Zapata. 2006. "Preparing to Plan: Collaborative Planning in Monteverde, Costa Rica." *International Planning Studies* 11 (3–4): 187–207.

Harvey, D. 1996. *Justice, Nature and the Geography of Difference*. New York: Blackwell Publishing.

_____. 2000. *Spaces of Hope*. Berkeley: The University of California Press.

Hayden, D. 1995. *Power of Place: Urban Landscapes as Public History*. Cambridge, MA: MIT Press.

Hermans, H. J. M. 2001. "The Dialogical Self: Toward a Theory of Personal and Cultural Positioning." *Culture & Psychology* 7 (3): 243–81.

Hermans, H. J. M., and H. J. G. Kempen. 1993. *The Dialogical Self: Meaning as Movement*. San Diego: Academic Press.

Hester, R. 1974. "Community Design." In *Theory in Landscape Architecture: A Reader*, edited by S. Swaffield. Philadelphia: University of Pennsylvania Press.

_____. 1975. *Neighborhood Space: User Needs and Design Responsibilities*. Stroudsburg, PA: Dowden, Hutchison & Ross.

_____. 1990. *Community Design Primer*. Mendocino, CA: Ridgetimes Press.

_____. 1999. "A Refrain with a View." *Places* 12 (2): 12–25.

_____. 2006. *Design for Ecological Democracy*. Cambridge, MA: MIT Press.

Hill, M. M. 2005. "Teaching with Culture in Mind: Cross-Cultural Learning in Landscape Architecture Education." *Landscape Journal* 24 (2): 117–24.

Holden, M. 2008. "Social Learning in Planning: Seattle's Sustainable Development Codebooks." *Progress in Planning* 69 (1), January: 1–40.

Holland, B. 2005. "Scholarship and Mission in the 21st Century University: The Role of Engagement." In *Proceedings of the Australian Universities' Quality Forum*. Melbourne: Australian Universities Quality Agency.

Hollander, E. L., J. Saltmarsh, and E. Zlotkowski. 2002. "Indicators of Engagement." In *Learning to Serve: Promoting Civil Society through Service Learning*, edited by M. E. Kenny, L. A. K. Simon, K. Kiley-Brabeck, and R. M. Lerner. Boston: Kluwer Academic Publishers.

Holston, J. 1998. "Spaces of Insurgent Citizenship." In *Making the Invisible Visible*, edited by L. Sandercock. Berkeley: University of California Press.

Honikman, B. 1976. "Construct Theory as an Approach to Architectural and Environmental Design." In *The Measurement of Interpersonal Space by Grid Technique, Vol. 2: Dimensions of Interpersonal Space*, edited by. P. Slater. London: John Wiley & Sons.

Honnet, E. P., and S. J. Poulsen. 1989. *Principles of Good Practice for Combining Service and Learning: A Wingspread Special Report*. Racine, WI: The Johnson Foundation.

Hood, W. 2003. "Beyond Nomenclature: Urban Parks for Cultural Diversity." *Places* 15 (3): 34–37.

hooks, b. 1990. *Yearning: Race, Gender and Cultural Politics*. Boston: South End Press.

_____. 1994. *Teaching to Transgress: Education as the Practice of Freedom*. New York: Routledge.

_____. 2003. *Teaching Community: A Pedagogy of Hope*. New York: Routledge.

Hou, J., and M.-J. Kang. 2006. "Differences and Dialogic Learning in a Collaborative Virtual Design Studio." Special Issue on Studio Teaching Practices: Between Traditional, Revolutionary and Virtual Models. *Open House International* 31 (3): 85–94.

Hou, J. 2007a. "Community Processes: The Catalytic Agency of Service Learning Studio." In *Design Studio Pedagogy: Horizons for the Future*, edited by A. Salama and N. Wilkinson. Gateshead, UK: Urban International Press.

_____. 2007b. "Night Market and the Reconstruction of Public Realm in Seattle's Chinatown-International District." Paper presented at the *Sixth Conference of the Pacific Rim Community Design Network*, Quanzhou, China, June 18–21.

_____, ed. 2010. *Insurgent Public Space: Guerrilla Urbanism and the Remaking of Contemporary Cities*. New York: Routledge.

Howard, J. A., and G. E. Warren. 2001. "Foreword." In *Understanding Consumer Decision Making: The Means-Ends Approach to Marketing and Advertising Strategy*, edited by T. J. Reynolds and J. C. Olson. Mahwah, NJ: Lawrence Erlbaum.

Huber, M., and P. Hutchings. 2004. *Integrative Learning: Mapping the Terrain*. Washington, DC: Association of American Colleges and Universities.

Hufford, M., and R. Miller. 2006. *Piecing Together the Fragments: An Ethnography of Leadership for Social Change in North Central Philadelphia 2004–2005*. Philadelphia: Center for Folklore and Ethnography, University of Pennsylvania. Accessed December 2010. www.sas.upenn.edu/folklore/center/fragments.pdf.

Hutchinson, J., and A. Loukaitou-Sideris. 2001. "Choosing Confrontation or Consensus in the Inner City: Lessons from a Community-University Partnership." *Planning Theory and Practice* 2 (3): 293–310.

Independent Sector. 2001. "Giving and Volunteering in the United States." Accessed December 2010. www.independentsector.org/programs/research/gv01main.html.

Innes, J. E. 1996. "Planning through Consensus Building: A New View of the Comprehensive Planning Ideal." *Journal of the American Planning Association* 4 (62): 460–72.

Irazábal, C. 2007. Urban Planning and Development, PPD227. Syllabus. Los Angeles: School of Policy, Planning, and Development, University of Southern California, Los Angeles.

Irigaray, L. 2008. *Sharing the World*. London: Continuum.

Itin, C. M. 1999. "Reasserting the Philosophy of Experiential Education as a Vehicle for Change in the 21st Century." *The Journal of Experiential Education* 22 (2): 91–98.

Jacobs, J. 1961. *The Death and Life of Great American Cities*. New York: Random House.

_____. 1998. "Staging Difference: Aestheticization and the Politics of Difference in Contemporary Cities." In *Cities of Difference*, edited by J. M. Jacobs and R. Fincher. New York: Guilford Press.

Jacoby, B. 1996. *Service-Learning in Higher Education: Concepts and Practices*. San Francisco: Jossey-Bass.

Kelley, R. D. G. 1997. *Yo Mama's Disfunktional!* Boston: Beacon Press.

Kember, D., and M. Kelly. 1993. *Improving Teaching through Action Research: HERDSA Green Guide*. HERDSA Green Guide Series, no. 14. Campbelltown, Australia: Higher Education Research and Development Society of New South Wales (HERDSA).

Kennedy, L. 2000. *Race and Urban Space in Contemporary American Culture*. Chicago: Fitzroy Publishing.

Kennedy, M. 2007. "From Advocacy Planning to Transformative Community Planning." *Progressive Planning* 171 (Spring): 24–27.

Kiesinger, C. E. 1998. "From Interview to Story: Writing Abbie's Life." *Qualitative Inquiry*, no. 4: 71–95.

King, M. L., Jr. 1957. "Facing the Challenge of a New Age." Speech given to NAACP in Atlanta. January 11.

_____. 1960. Speech in Raleigh, NC. April 15.

_____. 1967. *Where Do We Go from Here: Chaos or Community.* New York: Harper and Rowe.

King, J. T. 2004. "Service-Learning as a Site for Critical Pedagogy: A Case of Collaboration, Caring, and Defamiliarization across Borders." *Journal of Experiential Education* 26 (3): 121–37.

Kivel, P. 2002. *Uprooting Racism: How White People Can Work for Racial Justice*. 2nd ed. Gabriola Island, Canada: New Society Publishers.

Kolb, D. 1994. *Experiential Learning: Experiences as a Source of Learning and Development*. London: Prentice Hall.

Kotval, Z. 2003. "Teaching Experiential Learning in the Urban Planning Curriculum." *Journal of Geography in Higher Education* 27 (3): 297–308.

Kozol, J. 1991. *Savage Inequalities*. New York: Harper Perennial.

Krumholz, N., and J. Forester. 1990. *Making Equity Planning Work*. Philadelphia: Temple University Press.

Lauria, M., and R. Washington, eds. 1998. "Symposium on Community Outreach Partnership Centers: Forging New Relationships Between University and Community." *Journal of Planning Education and Research* 17 (4).

Lawson, L. 2005. "Dialogue through Design: The East St. Louis Neighborhood Design Workshop and South End Neighborhood Plan." *Landscape Journal* 24 (2): 157–71.

Lefebvre, H. 1974. *The Production of Space*. Translated by D. Nicholson-Smith, 1991. Oxford: Blackwell Publishing.

_____. 1996. "The Right to the City." In *Writings on Cities*, translated and edited by E. Kofman and E. Lebas. Oxford: Blackwell Publishing.

Levinas, E. 2006. *Humanism of the Other*. Translated by N. Poller. Chicago: University of Illinois Press.

Lewis, F. 2008. "Experience of a Salvatori Community Scholar: Ph.D. Candidate Ferdinand Lewis Reflects on His Year Spent Working with JEP." *The Joint Educational Project*, Spring: 9. college.usc.edu/assets/files/docs/jep/newsletter/newsletter_jep_2008_spring .pdf.

Linn, K. 2007. *Building Commons and Community*. Oakland, CA: New Village Press.

Lipsitz, G. 1998. *The Possessive Investment in Whiteness: How White People Profit from Identity Politics*. Philadelphia: Temple University Press.

Lockwood, S. 1973. "Participation: Its Influence on Planning Methodology." In *Highway Research Board Special Report No. 142*. Washington, DC: Transportation Research Board.

Locher, M. 2006. *Super Potato Design: The Complete Works of Takashi Sugimoto, Japan's Leading Interior Designer*. North Clarendon, VT: Tuttle Publishing.

Locher, M., B. Simmons, and K. Kuma. 2010. *Traditional Japanese Architecture: An Exploration of Elements and Forms*. Clarendon, VT: Tuttle Publishing.

Loukaitou-Sideris, A. 1995. "Urban Form and Social Context: Cultural Differentiation in the Uses of Urban Parks." *Journal of Planning Education and Research*, no. 14: 89–102.

Loveridge, S. 2002. "Keys to Engaging Faculty in Service: Lessons from West Virginia's Community Design Team." *Journal of Planning Education and Research* 21 (3): 331–39.

MacBeth, D. 2001. "On Reflexivity in Qualitative Research." *Qualitative Inquiry* 7 (1): 35–68.

Mandelbaum, S. J. 2003. "Narrative and Other Tools." In *Story and Sustainability: Planning, Practice, and Possibility for American Cities*, edited by B. Eckstein and J. A. Throgmorton. Cambridge, MA: MIT Press.

Markus, G. B., J. P. F. Howard, and D. C. King. 1993. "Integrating Community Service and Classroom Instruction Enhances Learning Results from an Experiment." *Educational Evaluation and Policy Analysis* 15 (4): 410–19.

Marsh, C. 2005. "The Burden of Perpetual Freedom: The Dream as Hallucination." In *The Beloved Community: How Faith Shapes Social Justice from the Civil Rights Movement to Today*, edited by C. Marsh. New York: Basic Books.

Marsick, V. J., and K. E. Watkins. 2001. "Informal and Incidental Learning." *New Directions for Adult and Continuing Education*, no. 89: 25–34.

Massey, D. 2005. *For Space*. London: SAGE Publications.

McAleavey, S. 1996. "Service-Learning: Theory and Rationale." Mesa, AZ: Campus Compact National Center for Community Colleges. Accessed December 2010. www.mc .maricopa.edu/other/engagement/pathways/rationale.html.

McConahay, J. B. 1986. "Modern Racism, Ambivalence and the Modern Racism Scale." In *Prejudice, Discrimination, and Racism*, edited by J. F. Dovidio and S. L. Gaertner. Orlando: Academic Press.

McKnight, J. L., and J. P. Kretzmann. 1988. *Mapping Community Capacity*. Evanston, IL: Center for Urban Affairs and Policy Research.

Meek, V. L., and M. Hayden. 2005. "The Governance of Public Universities in Australia: Trends and Contemporary Issues." In *Taking Public Universities Seriously*, edited by F. Iacobucci and C. Tuohy, 379–401. Toronto: University of Toronto Press.

Melchior, A., and L. N. Bailis. 2002. "Impact of Service-Learning on Civic Attitudes and Behaviors of Middle and High School Youth." In *Service-Learning: The Essence of the Pedagogy*, edited by A. Furco and S. H. Billig. Greenwich, CT: Information Age Publishing.

Miles, S., and G. Rowe. 2004. "The Laddering Technique." In *Doing Social Psychology Research*, edited by G. M. Breakwell. Malden, MA: Blackwell Publishing.

Millar, N. 1999. "Street Survival: The Plight of the Los Angeles Street Vendors." In *Everyday Urbanism*, edited by J. Chase, M. Crawford, and J. Kaliski. New York: Monacelli Press.

Miller, G. D. 1998. *Negotiating toward Truth*. Atlanta: Rodopi Press.

Molas-Gallart, J., A. Salter, P. Patel, A. Scott, and X. Duran. 2002. *Measuring Third Stream Activities: Final Report to the Russell Group of Universities*. Brighton, UK: Science and Technology Policy Research Unit, University of Sussex.

Moos, D., and G. Trechsel, eds. 2003. *Samuel Mockbee and the Rural Studio: Community Architecture*. Birmingham, AL: Birmingham Museum of Art.

Morse, S. W. 2001. *Smart Communities: How Citizens and Local Leaders Can Use Strategic Thinking to Build a Better Future*. Hoboken, NJ: John Wiley & Sons.

Mozingo, L. 1995. "Public Space in the Balance." *Landscape Architecture* 85 (2): 43–47.

Myers, D. N., M. Hill, and S. A. Harwood. 2005. "Cross-Cultural Learning and Study Abroad: Transforming Pedagogical Outcomes." *Landscape Journal* 24 (2): 172–84.

myregion.org. 2008. *How Shall We Grow?* Orlando: myregion.org. www.myregion.org/index .php?submenu=HowShallWeGrow&src=gendocs&ref=HowShallWeGrow&category =RegionalVision.

Nalencz, V. 2006. "The Owl and the Phoenix." *Temple Review*, Spring: 24–29.

National Endowment for the Arts. 2002. "University-Community Design Partnerships." New York: Princeton University Press.

Neighborhood Design Center. n.d. "About NDC." www.ndc-md.org/html/about.htm.

Neimeyer, R. A., A. Anderson, and L. Stockton. 2001. "Snakes versus Ladders: A Validation of Laddering Technique as a Measure of Hierarchical Structure." *Journal of Constructivist Psychology*, no. 14: 85–105.

Neustadt, R., and E. May. 1986. *Thinking in Time*. New York: Free Press.

Neville, H. A., R. L. Lilly, G. Duran, R. M. Lee, and L. Browne. 2000. "Construction and Initial Validation of the Color-Blind Racial Attitudes Scale (Cobras)." *Journal of Counseling Psychology*, no. 47: 59–70.

Novek, E. M. 2000. "Tourists in the Land of Service-Learning: Helping Middle-Class Students Move from Curiosity to Commitment." Paper presented at the annual meeting of the National Communication Association, Seattle, WA.

Nussbaum, M. 1990. *Love's Knowledge.* Oxford: Oxford University Press.

Oates, K. K., and L. Gaither. 2001. "Integration and Assessment of Service-Learning in Learning Communities." In *Reinventing Ourselves: Interdisciplinary Education, Collaborative Learning, and Experimentation in Higher Education,* edited by B. L. Smith and J. McCann. Bolton, MA: Anker Publishing Company.

O'Grady, C. 1998. "Moving Off Center: Engaging White Education Students in Multicultural Field Experiences." In *Speaking the Unpleasant: The Politics of (Non)Engagement in the Multicultural Education Terrain,* edited by R. Chavez and J. O'Donnell, 211–28. Albany, NY: State University of New York Press.

———, ed. 2000. *Integrating Service Learning and Multicultural Education in Colleges and Universities.* Mahwah, NJ: Lawrence Erlbaum.

O'Kane, T. 2005. *Guatemala: A Guide to the People, Politics and Culture.* Northampton, MA: Interlink Books.

Olson, J. C., and T. J. Reynolds. 2001. "The Means-End Approach to Understanding Consumer Decision Making." In *Understanding Consumer Decision Making: The Means-Ends Approach to Marketing and Advertising Strategy,* edited by T. J. Reynolds and J. C. Olson. Mahwah, NJ: Lawrence Erlbaum.

Palleroni, S. 2004. *Studio at Large: Architecture in Service of Global Communities.* Seattle: University of Washington Press.

Passel, J. S., and D. Cohn. 2008. *US Population Projections 2005–2050.* Washington, DC: Pew Research Center.

Pearson, J. 2002. *University-Community Design Partnerships.* Washington, DC: The National Endowment for the Arts.

Perry, W. G., Jr. 1999. *Forms of Ethical and Intellectual Development in the College Years: A Scheme.* San Francisco: Jossey-Bass.

Peter, J. P., and J. C. Olson. 1999. "Consumers' Product Knowledge and Involvement." In *Consumer Behavior and Marketing Strategy.* 3rd ed. Homewood, IL: R. D. Irwin.

Peterson, G., G. Cumming, and S. Carpenter. 2003. "Scenario Planning: A Tool for Conservation in an Uncertain World." *Conservation Biology* 17 (2): 358–366.

Popak, C. 2007. "Reflections on Service Leaning as Pedagogical Strategy in Composition." In *Race, Poverty and Social Justice: Multidisciplinary Perspectives Through Service Learning,* edited by J. Calderon. Sterling, VA: Stylus.

Prins, E. 2005. "Framing a Conflict in a Community-University Partnership." *Journal of Planning Education and Research* 25 (1): 57–74.

Putnam, R. 2001. *Bowling Alone: The Collapse and Revival of American Community.* New York: Simon and Schuster.

Pyatok, M. 2003. "Affordable Housing: An Option for Professional Practice?" *Oculus,* Fall. www.pyatok.com/writingsArticle1.html.

Quinlan, A., L. Corkery, and B. Roche. 2008. "Learning Enabling Design: Approaching Mutuality in an Educational Environment." In *TAKE 6: Beyond Beige: Improving Architecture for Older People and People with Disabilities,* edited by B. Garlick, D. Jones, and G. Luscombe. Canberra: Royal Australian Institute of Architects.

Ramaley, J. 2005. "Engagement and the Integration of Research and Education: A New Meaning of Quality." *Proceedings of the Australian Universities' Quality Forum,* 18–25. Melbourne: Australian Universities Quality Agency.

Reardon, K. M. 1994. "Undergraduate Research in Distressed Urban Communities: An Undervalued Form of Service Learning." *Michigan Journal of Community Service Learning*, no. 1: 44–54.

———. 1997. "Back from the Brink: The East St. Louis Story." *Gateway Heritage Winter* 1 (8): 5–15.

———. 1998. "Enhancing the Capacity of Community-Based Organizations in East St. Louis." *Journal of Planning Education and Research*, no. 17: 323–33.

———. 2000. "An Experiential Approach to Creating an Effective Community-University Partnership: The East St. Louis Action Research Project." *Cityscape: A Journal of Policy Development and Research* 5 (1): 59–74.

Reason, P., and H. Bradbury. 2001. "Introduction: Inquiry and Participation in Search of a World of Worthy of Human Aspiration." In *Handbook of Action Research: Participative Inquiry and Practice*, edited by P. Reason and H. Bradbury. London: SAGE Publications.

Reynolds, T., and J. Gutman. 1988. "Laddering Theory, Method, Analysis, and Interpretation." *Journal of Advertising Research*, February/March: 12–31.

Reynolds, T. J., and J. Norvell. 2001. "Fund-Raising Strategy: Tapping into Philanthropic Value Orientations." In *Understanding Consumer Decision Making: The Means-Ends Approach to Marketing and Advertising Strategy*, edited by T. J. Reynolds and J. C. Olson. Mahwah, NJ: Lawrence Erlbaum.

Reynolds, T. J., C. Dethloff, and S. J. Westberg. 2001. "Advancements in Laddering." In *Understanding Consumer Decision Making: The Means-Ends Approach to Marketing and Advertising Strategy*, edited by T. J. Reynolds and J. C. Olson. Mahwah, NJ: Lawrence Erlbaum.

Rice, C.. 2005. Interview with J. Byassee in *The Christian Century*, March: 88.

Rice, C., and S. Perkins. 1995. "Reconciliation." In *Restoring At-Risk Communities*, edited by J. Perkins. Grand Rapids, MI: Baker Books.

Rios, M. 2004. "Freirian Praxis in the Northern Cheyenne Youth Restoration Art Project." In *Open Space/People Space: International Conference on Inclusive Environments*. OPENspace, Edinburgh College of Art: 0013.

———. 2006. "Where Do We Go from Here? An Evaluative Framework for Community-Based Design." In *From the Studio to the Streets: Service Learning in Planning and Architecture*, edited by M. C. Hardin, 47–58. Sterling, VA: Stylus.

———. 2008. "Envisioning Citizenship: Toward a Polity Approach in Urban Design." *Journal of Urban Design* 13 (2): 213–29.

Roakes, S. L., and D. Norris-Tirrell. 2000. "Community Service Learning in Planning Education: A Framework for Course Development." *Journal of Planning Education and Research*, no. 20: 100–10.

Robinson, J. W. 2001. "The Form and Structure of Architectural Knowledge: From Practice to Discipline." In *The Discipline of Architecture*, edited by A. Piotrowski and J. W. Robinson. Minneapolis: University of Minnesota Press, 61–82.

Rose, J., A. Rose, and C. S. Norman. 2005. "A Service-Learning Course in Accounting Information Systems." *Journal of Information Systems*, no. 19: 145–72.

Rubin, V. 1998. "The Role of Universities in Community-Based Initiatives." *Journal of Planning Education and Research*, no. 17: 302–11.

———. 2000. "Evaluating University-Community Partnerships: An Examination of the Evolution of Questions and Approaches." *Cityscape: A Journal of Policy Development and Research* 5 (1): 219–30.

Rugg, G., M. Eva, A. Mahmood, N. Rehman, S. Andrews, and S. Davies. 2002. "Eliciting Information about Organizational Culture via Laddering." *Information Systems Journal*, no. 12: 215–29.

Russell, C. G., A. Busson, I. Flight, J. Bryan, J. A. Pabst, and D. N. Cox. 2003. "A Comparison of Three Laddering Techniques Applied to an Example of a Complex Food Choice." *Food Quality and Preference*, no. 15: 569–83.

Safe Passage. 2009. Accessed January 2011. www.safepassage.org/.

Sandercock, L., ed. 1998. *Making the Invisible Visible.* Berkeley: University of California Press.

_____. 2003. *Cosmopolis II: Mongrel Cities in the 21st Century.* New York: Continuum.

Sanoff, H., ed. 1990. *Participatory Design: Theory and Techniques.* Raleigh, NC: Bookmasters.

_____. 2000. *Community Participation Methods in Design and Planning.* New York: John Wiley & Sons.

_____. 2003. *Three Decades of Design and Community.* Raleigh, NC: North Carolina State University College of Design.

_____. 2007. "Editorial." Special issue on Participatory Design. *Design Studies* 28 (3): 213–15.

Satterfield, T., and S. Slovic. 2004. *What's Nature Worth? Narrative Expressions of Environmental Values.* Salt Lake City, UT: University of Utah Press.

Saunders, D., R. Hobbs, and C. Margules. 1991. "Biological Consequences of Ecosystem Fragmentation: A Review." *Conservation Biology* 5 (1): 18–32.

Savin-Baden, M., and C. H. Major. 2004. *Foundations of Problem-Based Learning.* Berkshire, UK: Open University Press and New York: Society for Research into Higher Education.

Schneekloth, L., and R. Shibley. 1995. *Placemaking: The Art and Practice of Building Communities.* New York: John Wiley & Sons.

_____. 2000. "Implacing Architecture into the Practice of Placemaking." Special Issue on Beyond Expert Culture. *Journal of Architectural Education* 53 (3), February: 130–40.

Schön, D. 1983. *The Reflective Practitioner: How Professionals Think in Action.* New York: Basic Books.

_____. 1985. *The Design Studio: An Exploration of its Traditions and Potential.* London: RIBA Publications.

_____. 1987. *Educating the Reflective Practitioner.* San Francisco: Jossey-Bass.

_____. 1990. *Educating the Reflective Practitioner: Toward a New Design for Teaching and Learning in the Professions.* San Francisco: Jossey-Bass.

Schuman, A. W. 2006. "The Pedagogy of Engagement." In *From the Studio to the Streets: Service-Learning in Planning and Architecture*, edited by M. Hardin, R. Erbes, and C. Poster, 1–15. Sterling, VA: Stylus.

Seifer, S. D., and K. Connors, eds. 2007. *Faculty Toolkit for Service-Learning in Higher Education.* Scotts Valley, CA: National Service-Learning Clearinghouse. Accessed December 2010. www.servicelearning.org/filemanager/download/HE_toolkit_with_worksheets.pdf

Sennett, R. 2008. *The Craftsman.* New Haven: Yale University Press.

Shaffer, D., and D. Marcouiller. 2006. "Rethinking Community Economic Development." *Economic Development Quarterly* 20 (1): 59–74.

Shor, I. 1992. *Empowering Education: Critical Teaching for Social Change.* Chicago: University of Chicago Press.

Sibley, D. 1995. *Geographies of Difference.* New York: Routledge.

Soja, E. 1996. *Thirdspace: Journeys to Los Angeles and Other Real-and-Imagined Places.* Oxford: Blackwell Publishing.

Sorensen, J., K. M. Reardon, and C. Clump. 2003. "Empowering Residents and Students to Rebuild Neighborhoods: A Case Study." In *Building Partnerships for Service Learning,* edited by B. Jacoby and Associates. San Francisco: Jossey-Bass.

Spanierman, L., and M. J. Heppner. 2004. "Psychosocial Costs of Racism to Whites Scale (PCRW): Construction and Initial Validation." *Journal of Counseling Psychology* 51 (2): 249–62.

Spanierman, L., and J. Sobel. 2010. "Understanding Whiteness: Previous Approaches and Possible Directions in the Study of White Racial Attitudes and Identity." In *Handbook of Multicultural Counseling,* edited by J. G. Ponterotto, J. M. Casas, L. A. Suzuki, and C. M. Alexander. 3rd ed. Thousand Oaks, CA: SAGE Publications.

Special issue. 1998. *Journal of Planning Education and Research* 17 (4).

Spence, R., S. Macmillan, and P. Kirby, eds. 2001. *Interdisciplinary Design in Practice.* London: Thomas Telfod.

Spener, D. 1992. *The Freirean Approach to Adult Literacy Education.* National Center for ESL Literacy Education. www.cal.org/caela/esl_resources/digests/FREIREQA.html.

Spinoza, B. de. 1996. *Ethics.* Translated by E. Curley. London: Penguin Books.

Stanton, T. K. 1995. "Writing about Public Service Experience: The Critical Incident Journal." In *A Guide for Change: Resources for Implementing Community Service Writing,* edited by A. Watters and M. Ford. New York: McGraw-Hill.

Stanton, T., D. E. Giles, and N. I. Cruz. 1999. "Strategy and Practice: Empowering Students to Serve Communities." In *Service-Learning: A Movement's Pioneers Reflect on its Origins, Practice, and Future,* 95–121. San Francisco: Jossey-Bass.

Steiner, S. F., H. M. Krank, P. McLaren, and R. E. Bahruth, eds. 2000. *Freirian Pedagogy, Praxis, and Possibilities: Projects for the New Millennium.* New York: Falmer Press.

Steinke, P., and S. Buresh. 2002. "Cognitive Outcomes of Service-Learning: Reviewing the Past and Glimpsing the Future." *Michigan Journal of Service Learning* 8 (2): 5–14.

Stoecker, R., and E. A. Tryon, eds. 2009. *The Unheard Voices: Community Organizations and Service Learning.* Philadelphia: Temple University Press.

Stone, D. 2002. *Policy Paradox: The Art of Policy Decision Making.* New York: W. W. Norton.

Strap, D. 2000. "Bonk! It's a Three-Wattled Bellbird." *Audubon,* May/June. magazine.audubon.org/birds/birds0005.html.

Strategic Marketing Committee, Association of Collegiate Schools of Planning. 1997. "Anchor Points for Planning's Identification." *Journal of Planning Education & Research,* no 16: 223–24.

Stringer, E. T. 1999. *Action Research.* Thousand Oaks, CA: SAGE Publications.

Subotzky, G. 1999. "Alternatives to the Entrepreneurial University: New Modes of Knowledge Production in Community Service Programs." *Journal of Higher Education,* no. 38: 401–40.

Sue, D. W., and D. Sue. 2008. *Counseling the Culturally Diverse: Theory and Practice.* 5th ed. Hoboken, NJ: John Wiley & Sons.

Susskind, L., S. McKearnan, and J. Thomas-Larmer. 1999. *The Consensus Building Handbook: A Comprehensive Guide to Reaching Agreement.* Thousand Oaks, CA: SAGE Publications.

Susskind, L., K. Emerson, and K. Hildebrand. 1977. *Using Community Settings for Professional Planning Education.* Cambridge, MA: MIT Press.

Sutton, S. E. 2001. "Reinventing Professional Privilege as Inclusivity: A Proposal for an Enriched Mission of Architecture." In *The Discipline of Architecture,* edited by A. Piotrowski and J. W. Robinson. Minneapolis: University of Minnesota Press.

Swaffield, S., ed. 2002. *Theory in Landscape Architecture: A Reader.* Philadelphia: University of Pennsylvania Press.

Swanstrom, T., P. Dreier, and J. Mollenkopf. 2004. *Place Matter: Metropolitics for the 21st Century.* Lawrence, KS: University Press of Kansas.

Symes, K., ed. 2003. *Case Studies in Community-University Partnerships: Department of Landscape Architecture, University of Washington.* Seattle: Educational Partnerships and Learning Technologies, University of Washington.

Sze, J. 2006. *Noxious New York: The Racial Politics of Urban Health and Environmental Justice.* Cambridge, MA: MIT Press.

Tai, L. M. T. Haque, G. K. McLellan, and E. J. Knight. 2006. *Designing Outdoor Environments for Children.* New York: McGraw-Hill.

Tai, L., and B. Lamba. 2003. "Building to Learn." *Landscape Architecture,* March: 50–55.

Tapia, A. 1993. "Christian Community Development Association." *National Catholic Reporter,* October 29.

Thompson, J. W. 1992. "Bad Habits, Worn Traditions." *Landscape Architecture* 82 (2): 54–56.

Thrift, N. 2008. *Non-Representational Theory: Space, Politics, Affect.* New York: Routledge.

Throgmorton, J. 1996. *Planning as Persuasive Storytelling.* Chicago: University of Chicago Press.

Titlebaum, P., G. Williamson, C. Daprano, J. Baer, and J. Brahler. 2004. *Annotated History of Service Learning, 1862–2002.* Dayton, OH: University of Ohio.

Trepagnier, B. 2006. *Silent Racism: How Well-Meaning White People Perpetuate the Racial Divide.* Boulder: Paradigm Publishers.

Tucker, P. 2006. "Teaching the Millennial Generation," *The Futurist* 40 (3), May/June: 7.

Tyler, K. 2007. "The Tethered Generation," *HR Magazine* 52 (5): 40–46

Tyson, B. T., and N. P. Low. 1987. "Experiential Learning in Planning Education." *Journal of Planning Education and Research* 7 (11): 15–27.

University of Washington Risk Management. 2009. Accessed January 2011. f2.washington.edu/treasury/riskmgmt/.

University of New South Wales. 2007. *B2B Blueprint to Beyond 2010: UNSW Strategic Intent.* Kensington, Australia: University of New South Wales.

US Census Bureau. n.d. American Community Survey 2005–2007. www.census.gov/acs/.

US Department of State. 2009. Accessed January 2011. travel.state.gov/travel/cis_pa_tw/cis/cis_1129.html.

Wagner, M., and A. Gansemer-Topf. 2005. "Learning by Teaching Others: A Qualitative Study Exploring the Benefits of Peer Teaching." *Landscape Journal* 24 (2): 198–208.

Wallerstein, N., V. Sanchez-Merki, and L. Dow. 1997. "Freirian Praxis in Health Education and Community Organizing." In *Community Organizing and Community Building for Health,* edited by M. Minkler, 195–211. New Brunswick, NJ: Rutgers University Press.

Walton, H. J., and M. B. Matthews. 1989. "Essentials of Problem-Based Learning." *Medical Education,* no. 23: 542–58.

Wansink, B. 2003. "Using Laddering to Understand and Anchor a Brand's Equity." *Quantitative Market Research: An International Journal* 6 (2): 111–18.

Waterman, A. S. 1997. "An Overview of Service-Learning and the Role of Research and Evaluation in Service-Learning Programs." In *Service-Learning: Applications from the Research,* edited by A. S. Waterman. Mahwah, NJ: Lawrence Erlbaum.

Wheaton, W. L. C., and M. F. Wheaton. 1972. "Identifying the Public Interest: Values and Goals." In *Decision-Making in Urban Planning: An Introduction to New Methodologies,* edited by I. M. Robinson. London: SAGE Publications.

William C. Velasquez Institute. n.d. "About WCVI." www.wcvi.org/about_wcvi.html.

Willis, R. 2006. "What Do We Mean by 'Community Engagement'?" Paper presented at the *Knowledge Transfer and Engagement Forum,* 15–16 June, Sydney, Australia.

Wilson, W. J. 2009. *More Than Just Race: Being Black and Poor in the Inner City.* New York: W. W. Norton.

Winter, A., J. Wiseman, and B. Muirhead. 2006. "University-Community Engagement in Australia." *Education, Citizenship and Social Justice Journal* 1 (3): 212–30.

Winterbottom, D. 2005. "The Healing Nature of Landscapes." *Northwest Public Health* 22 (1), Spring/Summer: 18–20.

____. 2007a. "Garbage to Garden: Developing a Safe, Nurturing and Therapeutic Environment for the Children of the Garbage Pickers." *Children, Youth and Environments* 18 (1): 435–55.

____. 2007b. "Working in the Margins, A Non-Traditional Approach to the Practice of Landscape Architecture." *Landscape Architecture,* December.

Wirthlin Worldwide. 1997. *Charting a Course for Utah's Future: Identifying the Underlying Values Related to Growth in Utah.* Salt Lake City, UT: Coalition for Utah's Future.

Wulz, F. 1986. "The Concept of Participation." *Design Studies* 7 (3): 153–62.

Yanow, D. 1995. "Built Space as Story: The Policy Stories that Buildings Tell." *Policy Studies Journal* 23 (3): 407–22.

Yeh, L. 2002. "Community Building through the Arts." Slought Foundation Online Content. 27 February. slought.org/content/11025/.

Yin, R. 1994. *Case Study Research: Design and Methods.* 2nd ed. Beverly Hills, CA: SAGE Publications.

Young, I. M. 1990. *Justice and the Politics of Difference.* Princeton, NJ: Princeton Press.

# Contributors

**Tom Angotti** is Professor of Urban Affairs and Planning at Hunter College and the Graduate Center, City University of New York, and Director of the Center for Community Planning and Development and coeditor of *Progressive Planning Magazine*. His recent book, *New York for Sale: Community Planning Confronts Global Real Estate* (2008), won the Paul Davidoff Award.

**Keith Bartholomew** is an Assistant Professor in the Department of City & Metropolitan Planning at the University of Utah. He received his B Mus from Northern Illinois University and his JD from the University of Oregon. He is coauthor of *Growing Cooler: The Evidence on Urban Development and Climate Change* (2008).

**Amanda M. Beer** is currently a Staff Psychologist at the University of North Carolina Wilmington Counseling Center. Dr. Beer's research interests focus on individuals' development of social justice commitments, and on student training opportunities that promote social justice and multicultural learning.

**Peter Butler** is an Assistant Professor of Landscape Architecture at West Virginia University (WVU). He integrates service projects in his studio, teaching through collaboration with communities in Appalachia as a member of the Community Design Team at WVU. His research interests focus on cultural landscapes, primarily industrial spaces and rural towns.

**Linda Corkery**, Associate Professor and Program Director of the Landscape Architecture Program, University of New South Wales, Sydney, Australia, teaches design studio and environmental sociology. She has received a Dean's Teaching Award and leads the development of service-learning and teaching opportunities in the Faculty of the Built Environment.

**Pat Crawford**, PhD, RLA, is an Associate Professor of Landscape Architecture and Senior Director of the Bailey Scholars Program at Michigan State University. Dr. Crawford's research includes the Scholarship of Teaching and Learning, public participation in design and planning, and university-community engagement. She teaches design, drawing, and site engineering.

**Lynne M. Dearborn** is an Associate Professor and Associate Director of the School of Architecture at the University of Illinois at Urbana-Champaign. She is also co-director of the university's East St. Louis Action Research Project. Her research and teaching interest focus on residential environments of marginalized populations and architectural responses to social injustice in the US and internationally.

**Cheryl Doble** is an Associate Professor in Landscape Architecture at State University of New York College of Environmental Science and Forestry and the founding director of the college's Center for Community Design Research. Her teaching and research focuses on practices of participatory design and transdisciplinary action research.

**Susan Erickson** has a BS and MLA in Landscape Architecture and is a program coordinator for Iowa State University. She works through the university's Extension to Communities and Economic Development; in this role she strives to meet community development and design needs through outreach projects that meet the academic needs of students and the research interests of faculty.

**Susan C. Harris** is the Associate Director for Research and Academic Affairs at the University of Southern California's Joint Educational Project. She is also Research Adjunct Assistant Professor of Sociology at USC. Susan is an expert in service-learning pedagogy and practice, particularly in the development of tools for reflection.

**Sally Harrison** is an Associate Professor of Architecture in the Tyler School of Art at Temple University. She teaches urban design, urban theory, and sustainable design. She is the founding director of the Urban Workshop at Temple, a university-based practice that seeks to address community design issues through participatory design process and engagement with other place-making disciplines.

**Paula Horrigan** examines and fosters the theories and practices of place-based design and acts to interlink design education, scholarship, and community needs. She is a Landscape Architecture Professor and Service-Learning Kaplan Fellow at Cornell University and is currently spearheading Rust to Green New York State, an academic-community effort to advance urban resilience in New York's rust-belt cities.

**Jeffrey Hou** is Associate Professor and Chair of the Department of Landscape Architecture at the University of Washington, Seattle. His work focuses on engaging marginalized communities in the making of urban public space. He is the editor of *Insurgent Public Space: Guerrilla Urbanism and the Remaking of Contemporary Cities* (2010).

**Clara Irazábal** is Assistant Professor of Urban Planning at Columbia University's Graduate School of Architecture, Planning and Preservation in New York City. Her research focuses on the processes and politics of planning, especially in Latin America and Latina/o US, and on their impact on community development and socio-spatial justice.

**Paul Kelsch**, PhD, ASLA, is an Associate Professor in the Landscape Architecture Program at Virginia Tech's Washington Alexandria Architecture Center. His research focuses on the cultural construction of nature and its expression in designed landscapes. These issues come to bear especially in urban forestry projects and community relationships with nature.

**Zenia Kotval**, PhD, AICP, is a Professor of Urban and Regional Planning at Michigan State University. Dr. Kotval is the author of several articles and reports on pedagogy. Her expertise is in economic impact assessments, fiscal impact analysis, quantitative methods, and economic development and planning.

**Laura Lawson** is Professor and Chair in the Department of Landscape Architecture at Rutgers, the State University of New Jersey. She has a PhD in Environmental Planning and MLA from the University of California, Berkeley. She was an active participant in the University of Illinois's East St. Louis Action Research Project from 2001 to 2010, serving as Director from 2008 to 2010.

**Mira Locher** incorporates community engagement in her courses at the University of Utah, where she is Assistant Professor of Architecture and Associate Director of the Signature Experience Project. She practices architecture in the US and Japan (www.kajikaarchitecture.com) and is the author of *Super Potato Design: The Complete Works of Takashi Sugimoto, Japan's Leading Interior Designer* (2006) and coauthor of *Traditional Japanese Architecture: An Exploration of Elements and Forms* (2010).

**Patricia Machemer** is an Associate Professor in the Urban and Regional Planning and the Landscape Architecture Programs at Michigan State University. Her research interests include participatory planning and design, active learning, and land management. She is interested in measuring the effectiveness of participatory planning and integrative learning techniques in both academia and practice.

**V. Paul Poteat** is Assistant Professor in the Department of Counseling, Developmental, and Educational Psychology at Boston College. His research examines individual and social factors that predict prejudiced attitudes and behaviors across developmental periods, with attention to mental health implications and resilience among those who experience discrimination.

**Ann Quinlan**, Senior Lecturer and Program Director of the Architecture Program at the University of New South Wales, Sydney, Australia, teaches design studio and leads curriculum innovation. She is a recipient of a Dean's Teaching Award and a Universitas 21 Fellowship, and has a research focus on learning and teaching scholarship.

**Jodi Rios** has been on the faculty of Architecture and Urban Design at Washington University in St. Louis since 1996 where she teaches community-based design studios and graduate seminars with an emphasis on transdisciplinary curricula and research. Jodi is also working toward a PhD in Architecture History from the University of California at Berkeley.

**Michael Rios** is Associate Professor in the Department of Environmental Design at the University of California, Davis. He is project director of the Sacramento Diasporas Project that focuses on the cultural and political landscapes of (im)migrant and refugee populations. Michael is also coediting a forthcoming book on placemaking in Latino communities.

**Joseph Schilling**, JD, LL.M., leads the Sustainable Communities Initiative at Virginia Tech's Metropolitan Institute that explores sustainability through the intersection of design, planning, and collaboration. His fieldwork serves as a living laboratory for research and service-learning covering topics such as sustainability planning, vacant property reclamation, urban regeneration, smart growth, and active living.

**Lynda Schneekloth** is a Professor Emeritus and Director of Landscape of the Urban Design Project at the School of Architecture and Planning, University at Buffalo/SUNY, and one of the founders of the Sustainable Futures program in Monteverde. She is author of five books and has published over fifty articles in referred journals and book chapters in architecture, landscape architecture, planning, and historic preservation.

**Scott Shannon** is the Associate Provost and Dean of the Graduate School at the State University of New York, College of Environmental Science and Forestry. Since 2003 Scott has served as a faculty member and North American coordinator for the Sustainable Futures program at the Monteverde Institute, an interdisciplinary program in sustainable design for graduate and undergraduate students.

**Lisa B. Spanierman** is Associate Professor in the Department of Educational and Counseling Psychology at McGill University. Dr. Spanierman's research focuses on the psychological investigation of whiteness, and her recent publications appear in the *Journal of Counseling Psychology, The Counseling Psychologist,* and *Cultural Diversity and Ethnic Minority Psychology.*

**Jack Sullivan**, FASLA, is a Registered Landscape Architect and an Associate Professor in the Department of Plant Science and Landscape Architecture at the University of Maryland. He is the Coordinator of the Master of Landscape Architecture Program.

**Daniel Winterbottom** is an Associate Professor in the Department of Landscape Architecture at the University of Washington and the founder of the department's design/build program. He continues to develop the design/build program working nationally and internationally. In 2009 he received the American Society of Landscape Architects Community Service Award.

# Index

newvillagePRESS

**N**ew Village Press is a nonprofit, independent publisher serving the growing field of community building. Our publications document and amplify innovative solutions to social, economic, and environmental problems as they emerge from the creativity of the grassroots. Our mission is to provide activists, educators, artists, professionals, and concerned citizens alike with new ideas for change and inspiring tools for growth.

If you enjoyed Service-Learning in Design and Planning you may be interested in other books we offer about urban planning and design:

> *Asphalt to Ecosystems: Design Ideas for Schoolyard Transformation,*
> by Sharon Gamson Danks
>
> *What We See: Advancing the Observations of Jane Jacobs,*
> edited by Stephen Goldsmith and Lynne Elizabeth
>
> *Building Commons and Community,* by Karl Linn

You may also want to check out our titles about community building and neighborhood revitalization:

> *Awakening Creativity: Dandelion School Blossoms,* by Lily Yeh
>
> *Works of Heart: Building Village through the Arts,*
> edited by Lynne Elizabeth and Suzanne Young
>
> *New Creative Community: The Art of Cultural Development,*
> by Arlene Goldbard
>
> *Arts for Change: Teaching Outside the Frame,* by Beverly Naidus

See what else we publish: www.newvillagepress.net